MW00614775

*Miracles do not happen in contradiction to nature,
but only in contradiction to that
which is known to us of nature.*

St Augustine

Great Moments
of
Modern Mediumship

VOLUME I

by

Maxine Meilleur
(ALM, Harvard)

Published by

Saturday Night Press Publications

England.

*snppbooks@gmail.com**

www.snppbooks.com

For contact with the author use email:
maxine.meilleur@post.harvard.edu.

ISBN 978-1-908421-10-4

Printed by Lightning Source

www.lightningsource.com

www.snppbooks.com

Cover design by Ann Harrison - Saturday Night Press Publications

Dedication

The great mission of Spiritualism is to make men spiritual.
William Stead

This book is dedicated to the many great mediums and
their spirit teams who have brought us all these great moments.

Thank you all and may your service never be forgotten.

Contents

(continued over page)

Introduction

Today's mediums belong to a great lineage of wonderful souls and so it is imperative that they know their heritage. This book contains accounts of some of the greatest moments in modern mediumship. It is intended to educate and hopefully inspire. The incidents detailed hereafter really happened. There were multiple witnesses to each one, and in some cases, physical evidence was produced which still stands today as a testament to what happened. These occurrences, these great moments, were not 'magic' and all of them can be explained by the phenomena of mediumship.

Mediumship, governed by natural law and the philosophy of the religion of Spiritualism, has been scientifically tested, sometimes under the most controlled circumstances, by Nobel laureates and other prominent scientists since the 19th century. These great moments are not unexplainable miracles.

Ordinary people, not holy men or saints, performed these wonders. On many occasions, they occurred in the natural settings of people's homes. Yes, ordinary people performed all these great moments in modern mediumship, but as explained hereafter, each had the help of those in the spirit world.

Mediums have often endured severe hardships during the testing of their mediumship. Nandor Fodor reports in his *Encyclopedia of Psychic Science*:

And they allowed all this in the hope of convincing the researchers and skeptics that their wonderful gift was genuine.

Prof. James found Mrs Piper's lips and tongue insensible to pain while she was in trance. Dr Hodgson later confirmed this by placing a spoonful of salt in Mrs Piper's mouth. He also applied strong ammonia to the nostrils. Drastic experiments were also tried. Prof. James made a small incision in Mrs Piper's left wrist. During trance the wound did not bleed and no notice was taken of the action. It bled freely afterwards and the medium bore the scar for life. In England Prof. Lodge pushed a needle suddenly into her hand. At another time Prof. Richet inserted a feather up her nostril. Harsh experiments in 1909 resulted in a badly blistered swollen tongue which caused the medium inconvenience for several days, while another test resulted in numbness and partial paralysis of the right arm for some time afterwards.

Many readers may be mediums at various stages of their development and passionate about working with the spirit world but few may have any knowledge of those who have come before, blazed trails through hardship and left great legacies and teachings. Although history is replete with countless moments similar to those recorded in the following pages, this book limits the events described to 1848 and later. Each great moment is mind-boggling and leaves the reader 'gob-smacked'. There are many, many more great moments and *Great Moments of Modern Mediumship: Volume II* will be published soon.

Maxine Meilleur, July 2014

What is Mediumship?

What is Mediumship?

*When Kepler found his long-cherished belief did not agree with the
most precise observation, he accepted the uncomfortable fact.*

*He preferred the hard truth to his dearest illusions;
that is the heart of science.*

*For it is far better to grasp the universe as it really is than to persist
in delusion, however satisfying and reassuring.*

Carl Sagan

Like many things, mediumship is often misunderstood and
needlessly feared. Mediumship is simply the ability to be in contact
those in the spirit world. Whether expressed in mental, physical or
healing forms, mediumship holds a sacred place in the religion of
Spiritualism as it is the communion between us, as spiritual beings,
and spirits in the spirit world. Through the love of God, or the Great
Spirit, we all exist and commune.

As well as many instances of mediumship through Trance,
Healing and Physical Phenomena there are included in this book a
few great moments in Modern Clairvoyance. Mediumship does
indeed rely on clairvoyance and other psychic abilities, but
mediumship goes beyond the psychic impressions to link with
spirit and provide evidence of spirit communication. Maurice
Barbanell in *Power of the Spirit(136)* gives the following example
of superior clairvoyant ability, but this is not mediumship as it does
not show spirit communication:

> In the Pullman coach from New York, William Button [then
> President of the American Society for Psychical Research] had
> purchased two new packs of playing cards. These were handed
> to me. I broke the seals. The two packs had the same design on
> the back of the cards. From these I selected twenty-five cards
> – aces, kings, queens, knaves, and tens. One by one, I held up
> each card, its back to Margery, seven feet away, while my wife,
> Button, Captain John W. Fife, head of Boston's naval dockyard,
> and I looked at the faces of the cards. Margery called twenty-
> one cards correctly without any hesitation. The four she missed
> were all tens. Of these, two were wrongly named, but on her

own recall, she named them rightly. ... These corrections were voluntary on her part.

The psychic sensing of a residual vibration in an object, known as psychometry, can be a form of mediumship when it brings in a spirit communicator. So there are included in this book great moments of modern mediumship involving 'billet reading' or other forms of psychometry. An example of that mediumistic psychometry is described by Nandor Fodor in his *Encyclopedia of Psychic Science:*

> Isaac Funk, the New York editor, handed a letter to medium Leonora Piper containing the word 'mother'. Mrs Piper gave the Christian name of Mr Funk's mother, told him that she was walking on only one leg and asked "Don't you remember that needle?" She hurt herself by thrusting a needle into her foot. Mrs Piper also described a grandson, Chester, of whom Funk knew nothing. On inquiry, however, he found out that a grandson of this name died twenty years previously.

Harry Edwards, the great healer, expressed these thoughts on the purpose of mediumship in his book *A guide for the development of mediumship.*

It is not necessary for a person to be a man or woman of letters or to be versed in psychic science to become a medium. In the past there have been many instances of simple folk being outstanding mediums.

Many people wish to become mediums, to see the spirit people, to hear them speak, to obtain counsel, to heal the sick, to help the bereaved, to give advice and assist those who are in need. This desire is sometimes simply that of satisfying the personal ego, to be different from other people, the wish to be looked up to, and to put on the mantle of mysticism. This is an entirely wrong approach to mediumship.

However mediumship has a purpose, and that is to demonstrate to man that he is not just a physical being, but that he is a part spirit, that this life is but an apprenticeship for the greater and fuller life that commences with the physical death.

That through this knowledge mankind will receive the impetus to adopt an enlightened code of values that in its evolvement will outlaw war, poverty and the other ignoble trends in our present way of life. Thus the true motive that inspires mediumship is a spiritual one. If this is not so, then no reason can be found for the great efforts the evolved personalities in spirit life, the teachers, philosophers, doctors and others, make to use human instruments for the progression of all souls.

Therefore aspirants to mediumship should possess that inner yearning to be used for the higher purpose, and to view their search into mediumship as a means to help others.

It should be the denial of selfishness and the giving of the self to a spiritual purpose. ... A true medium thereby becomes a participant in the divine plan for the furtherance of good.

Absent Healing

Absent Healing[1]

Absent healing is the most enlightened method of healing the sick.
Harry Edwards

Many of the great spiritual healers gave absent healing. Maurice Barbanell notes in *Parish the Healer (7)* that W. T. Parish was said to get fifteen thousand letters a year. In twenty five years of healing, Ted Fricker treated nearly a million patients, most of them through absent healing. The most astonishing though was Harry Edwards who is estimated to have helped over twelve million patients and cured almost four million of those via absent healing!

Within spiritual healing, absent healing is just as effective as contact healing. The distance between the healer and patient as well as the patient's faith [or lack thereof] does not affect the cure. Indeed, the patient needs not have any knowledge that absent healing is being sent for them! What is truly amazing about the following great moments in modern mediumship is that the whole process of absent healing is conducted through the agency of thought. In *The Healing Intelligence(104)*, Harry Edwards explains his procedure for absent healing:

> When a request for absent healing is received, it is read and answered by a healer in a condition of attunement with the spirit intelligences, and so the substance of the letter is conveyed from the minds of the healers to those in the spirit world. This often comes down to a simple thought that Mr X suffering from 'Z' complaint.

1. According to Raymond Buckland, in *The Spirit Book* (2005), absent healing is said to have originated with the Catholic priest and one-time prince, Alexander Leopold Franz Emmerich von Hohenlohe-Waldenburg-Schillingfürst. He generally cured people by laying on his hands. When the medical profession frowned on that, he would cure by simply praying for people. In 1821, he let it be known that at certain times of the day he would be offering up a special Mass for the sick. Those who wrote to him would be included in it. Apparently many were cured this way; though not actually being present. Absent healing is not to be confused with 'distant healing' which is defined as spiritual healing given to a patient who is in the same room or location as the healer, but healing is given without physical contact.

The appearance of Sambo (Ted Fricker)

Edward George (Ted) Fricker was known throughout the United Kingdom as a 'faith healer', but he was in reality a medium/spiritual healer as he consciously relied on doctors/healers from the spirit world to channel God's healing energy through him to the patient. As already quoted in the twenty five years from the 1950s to the 1970s, he treated nearly a million patients, many by absent healing. The following particular great moment in modern mediumship is chronicled in his autobiography, *God is My Witness(136)*:

Always close to Fricker, Sambo was a spiritual guide and doctor. A former African slave, he was clairvoyantly seen to be nearly seven feet tall and had black skin. His existence was not known outside the Fricker family. On one occasion, a woman rang Fricker's healing sanctuary asking for absent healing for her sister in America. Fricker instructed that she just think of Fricker by name and he would give absent healing. Two days later, an urgent telegram came from America stating to stop all absent healing. Apparently, the sister had done what was instructed when suddenly she felt the presence of someone in front of her. "I looked up", said the sister, "and there, standing in front of me, I saw a black man about seven feet tall. I got the fright of my life. Then he spoke to me and said, 'Don't worry, gel, we'll fix you up!' Then I must have fainted", went on the sister, "but in the morning when I woke up, I was completely cured!"

This great moment in absent healing also gives us an independent verification of the role of spiritual guides and doctors in absent healing.

The scent of carnations (Ted Fricker)

Healing medium Ted Fricker, again in his autobiography *God is My Witness(176)* was explaining the procedure of absent healing to a lady patient who wanted to know when she would have made contact with him. He replied that besides a feeling of calmness, she might be conscious of the scent of carnations because that was his favorite flower and he frequently had them around. She relayed that, on that very evening, she was giving a dinner party. As she finished changing into her clothes a half an hour before her husband was ready, she thought she would fill out the interval before her guests arrived by attuning to the absent healing. So, she sat down in a chair, tried to relax, and spent the next half an hour sniffing expectantly without any results. No scent of carnations rewarded her efforts. Her concentration was interrupted by the sound of the doorbell announcing the arrival of some of her dinner party guests. When she opened the door, she found four people on the doorstep, and before she had time to greet them they all exclaimed, "What a wonderful scent of carnations. You must have the house full of them!" "I haven't a carnation in the place," she said. Having shown her guests into the lounge, she went to fetch her husband, and as he descended the stairs he called to her, "I can smell the scent of carnations! Did they bring you some as a present?" The woman was healed of her affliction.

'The running child': second party absent healing (Ted Fricker)

Another excerpt from Ted Fricker's autobiography, *God is My Witness(181)*, is this great moment – an example of absent healing which is not performed through a healing medium but a second person and is termed here 'Second Party Absent Healing'. A former patient of Fricker's reported that the son of a friend of hers was desperately ill. The boy was admitted to the hospital paralyzed with fits and seizures. Mr Fricker could not treat the boy in hospital but told his father "Don't give up hope, because if you do exactly as I tell you, I will treat the child using your hands to give him healing, and this can be just as effective as though I were to treat him in person." Fricker instructed the man to visit the hospital as often as possible and to lay his hands upon the boy's head and at the same time to keep the thought of Fricker in his mind, telephoning him at intervals to report how the child was responding. The father did as instructed. Within a day or two, there was a slight improvement and treatment continued. The doctors were not encouraged and said the child would certainly be physically disabled and mentally retarded. The father persisted in the treatment and some small improvements in the left arm could be seen, despite the boy now being confirmed as deaf and blind. One morning, the father held up a small toy in front of his son's eyes which was immediately grabbed by the boy. Week by week treatment was continued by his father and steady improvement made until he could be released from hospital. With his son not being able to walk and still with partial paralysis, Fricker continued to guide the father on how and where to place his hands on the boy at home. Within another month, he was almost completely cured, and later, on 2nd January 1976, the man brought the now running boy into Fricker's consulting room to confirm that a complete cure had taken place. Fricker writes that the same procedure can be used with an adult who is too ill to think of Fricker by himself. According to Fricker, physical contact is essential where the patient is being treated by another person, and power can only be transmitted in this way. But it must be stressed that the hands must never be laid on without concentrating on the healer; otherwise, the power of the one who is trying to help will be drained away from him into the body of the sick patient.

Twelve million helped and four million cured through absent healing (Harry Edwards)

A spiritual healer for over three decades, Harry Edwards created a Healing Sanctuary in 1946 and gave public healing demonstrations even at the age of 80 before a capacity crowd of 5,500 people at Royal Albert Hall. However, this great moment in modern mediumship is the sheer volume of people positively affected by his absent healing. According to *A Guide to the Understanding and Practice of Spiritual Healing(14)*:

> The Spiritual Healing Sanctuary, Shere, Guildford, Surrey, is the world centre of Absent Healing. The numbers of people who have sought for healing by the Absent Healing method and who have been cured of afflictions are legion. Consistently, the weekly post has been between nine and eleven thousand letters; since 1948 over 14,000,000 healing letters have been received and answered. Unless there had been a high percentage of success, the inflow of letters would have waned and frittered away. Few people like writing letters, some get tired of doing so; those who get well often just stop writing without telling the healer why. So to maintain a number approaching half a

million a year is indeed an eloquent testimony to absent healing.

This is all the more significant when it is remembered that people seldom write for minor complaints, but rather when they are not responding to medical treatment, or have been declared to be 'incurable' or in cases of emergency such as severe injuries suffered in an accident.

From the records at Shere, the percentage of betterment for absent healing is around 80%, and of these a third report complete recovery. The applications for absent healing cover the whole realm of disease and affliction, therefore the figures show that no limitation can be imposed on the good that healing can do. (*A Guide to the Understanding and Practice of Spiritual Healing:55*).

Maurice Barbanell writes in *Power of the Spirit(21)* that in his sanctuary, Edwards "is a human island surrounded by a sea of letters. Ten typists handle the contents of one huge postbag and help is given by four members of the family. Every letter is read and answered by the healer. Even during his daily meals, he read and signed letters." Truly, Edwards' absent healing is a great moment in modern mediumship!

Being agnostic didn't prevent the healing (Harry Edwards)

Edwards writes in his book *The Power of Healing(14):*

My second patient was an agnostic. He was discharged from a London hospital with an 'incurable' cancer of the lung. His wife was told that the doctors could do nothing for him and that she should take him home and make him "as comfortable as possible". When she heard this tragic news she came to me to see if we could do anything through absent spiritual healing. Though they lived very near to me, I could not visit her husband personally, because he was an agnostic with very determined views, so the healing had to be sought for by the absent-healing method. The next day she came to see me again, wildly excited; her husband had got up that morning and made her a cup of tea, and there was such apparent improvement in him that his family, who had gathered to sit by his bedside, could only look at him with amazement. To my knowledge this man lived for many years and received national press publicity as a maker of hand-made violins.

Even after he was well, his wife dared not tell him of the manner of his recovery because of his antagonism to anything spiritual. Incidentally, it can be related that, when the man went back to the hospital and saw another consultant, this man questioned very strongly whether the patient ever had cancer and called for his X-ray photographs and medical history. Even these he disputed and said they must relate to another person; though the X-ray photographs bore the man's name, he said they had been wrongly labelled.

V1 bomb destroys healing records but healing continues (Harry Edwards)

When, during World War II, a V1 bomb destroyed the home and all the healing records of healer Harry Edwards, he no longer had the schedule of all the healing appointments for absent healing and all he could do was engage in intercession in an unorganized way. Much to his astonishment, good healing results continued to come, proving healing was not dependent on a schedule of healing or records kept.

The 'Miracle Girl' (George Chapman)

This great moment comes from J.Bernard Hutton's *Healing Hands(64)* and involves the healing of Dorothy James who on 12th November 1954, was hit by a speeding car and gravely injured. As soon as Mrs James arrived in the hospital in critical condition, an orderly on the hospital staff called Chapman and asked if he could perform 'distant healing' on the patient. Chapman went into trance, and his spirit doctor Dr William Lang helped stabilize her.

In an interview with Hutton ten years later, Mrs James said:

The hospital doctors were of course not aware of my being given distant healing and they couldn't understand how it was that I was alive. First they said I would never live. When I didn't die they said I would never see, or talk or walk again and if I did indeed survive, I would have to face a future in a Mental Home. You see, the specialists had diagnosed that my brain was damaged, my whole nervous system affected, and that this damage would result in mental deficiency and permanent blindness; apart from this, my right leg and ankle were crushed.

It was six weeks before George Chapman actually visited her in hospital and Dr Lang performed psychic operations on her. When Dorothy James was finally allowed to leave the hospital the staff all called her the 'Miracle Girl', because she had not only survived but had partially recovered. She was still in bad shape and faced the prospect of many more operations and a difficult road ahead, with no prospect of full recovery in sight – but that is a story for the Spiritual Healing section.

Apports

Apports[1]

On being asked an opinion of fruit and flower apports,
John Watts, Mrs Everitt's control, said in a séance on
28th February 1868, "I do not approve of bringing them,
for they are generally stolen."

Catherine Berry's 'Experiences in Spiritualism'

In modern mediumship, apports were first observed and recorded in the Spiritualist literature by Dr G. P. Billot. In *Recherchés psychologique ou correspondence sur le magnétisme vital entre un Solitaire et M. Deleuze* (1839), he describes a session on 5th March 1819, with three somnambules[2] and a blind woman, as follows:

> Towards the middle of the séance, one of the seeresses exclaimed "There is the Dove, it is white as snow, it is flying about the room with something in its beak, and it is a piece of paper which reads 'Let us pray'." A few moments later she added "See, it has let the paper drop at the feet of Madame J." Dr Billot saw a paper packet at the spot indicated. He found in it, three small pieces of bone glued on to small strips of paper, with the words 'St. Maxime, St. Sabine and Many Martyrs' written beneath the fragments.

With the same blind woman on 27th October 1820, Billot witnessed flower apports.

Apports may not have sentimental value but sometimes are shown just to prove that it can be done. Spiritualists generally believe that apport phenomenon is due to the disintegration and reintegration theory of objects. According to this theory, objects are dematerialized where they are and rematerialized in the séance room or elsewhere. One particular instance on record supports the disintegration and reintegration theory. Ernesto Bozzano writes in *Luce e Ombra* (August-October, 1927):

1. Apports (from the French 'apporter'—to bring) are defined as objects brought into the séance room by the spirit world, while an 'asport' is an object taken out of the séance room.
2. Somnambules is a French word meaning 'sleepwalker' but in the 19C was also used to mean someone in an altered state of consciousness or trance.

In March 1904, in a sitting in the house of Cavaliere Peretti, in which the medium was an intimate friend of ours, gifted with remarkable physical mediumship, and with whom apports could be obtained at command, I begged the communicating spirit to bring me a small block of pyrites which was lying on my writing table about two kilometers away. The spirit replied, via the entranced medium, that the power was almost exhausted, but he would make the attempt. Soon after spasmodic movement of the medium announced the arrival of an apport, but we didn't hear the fall of any object on the table or on the floor.

We asked for an explanation from the spirit-operator, who informed us that although he had managed to disintegrate a portion of the object desired, and had brought it into the room, there was not enough power for him to be able to re-integrate it. He told us to turn on the light. We did so, and found, to our great surprise, that the table, the clothes, and hair of the sitters, as well as the furniture and carpet of the room, were covered by the thinnest layer of brilliant impalpable pyrites.

When I returned home after the sitting I found the little block of pyrites lying on my writing table from which a large fragment, about one third of the whole piece, was missing, this having been scooped out of the block.

Tom Harrison, the son of medium Minnie Harrison, writes in the book, *Visits by Our Friends From the 'Other Side' (26)*:

We understand from our Spirit helpers that they usually de-materialize the article, bring it 'through' the structure of the room and then rematerialize it in the room. Occasionally they would de-materialize the wall or woodwork and bring in the article as it was. Such apported articles remained in the room after the sitting finished and should not be confused with ectoplasmic materializations which were in the room only during the period of sitting whilst the ectoplasm was emanating from the medium.

In the first six months of sitting, over sixty apports were reported in the home circle of Minnie Harrison, mainly flowers but also coins and various other items.

Concerning the origin of apports, Maurice Barbanell writes in *Power of the Spirit(67)*:

> Naturally, we all wanted to know where these stones had come from. "Well", answered White Hawk with a smile, "there is a man in Holland who has a large collection, but it is gradually getting smaller." We roared with laughter. "But how is he repaid?" we asked. "Surely you don't steal them." "No", he said laughingly, "I send him good customers in exchange."
>
> He became serious for a moment and said "The truth is that these stones have been lost and never reclaimed.".

Barbanell also asked White Hawk how apports were brought:

> "I can explain it only by telling you that I speed up the atomic vibrations until the stones are disintegrated. Then they are brought here, and I slow down the vibration until they become solid again."
>
> White Hawk added that he enlists the aid of elementals, or nature spirits. Once they have the stones [or other apports] in their possession, they do not want to release them. He has to cajole them, or catch them off their guard. Hence the sudden grabbings in space. I have heard him say, for example, that there is an apport in the room, but he will have to wait until the attention of the elemental is distracted before he can get it. …Sometimes White Hawk will tell sitters that their gifts are presents from relatives or friends in the spirit world and name them.

And Red cloud had a similar answer:

> …When I asked Red Cloud where these presents came from, he was as jocular as White Hawk, and replied with a laugh "The Land of Anywhere." He, too, affirmed that nature spirits helped to bring the apports and that they were reluctant to release them once they were in their possession and had to be coaxed.

A single red rose from a husband in spirit (Estelle Roberts)

At an Estelle Roberts séance, her spirit guide Red Cloud spoke through direct voice and complimented Lady Segrave on her courage. Red Cloud was followed by Lady Segrave's husband, who, after a long conversation with her, said he had brought a small tribute. Out of the darkness something fell lightly into her lap and touching it, she knew it was a flower. When the sitting was over and the lights were switched on, we saw it was a single red rose, almost as fresh as when first cut. Yet it had arrived at the end of a séance lasting an hour and a half, with doors and windows tightly closed, and the room oppressively warm and airless. If the rose been in the room for the whole of the time it must have shown signs of drooping. As soon as she saw it lying in Lady Segrave's lap, Iris went downstairs to the sitting room where, a few minutes before the circle began, she had arranged a dozen beautiful red roses. Counting them, she found only eleven and the lower half of the stalk of the twelfth.

A budgerigar as requested by a sitter (Estelle Roberts)

As the séances of Estelle Roberts were often accompanied by apports, Estelle wondered whether, by their production, it might be thought this was through somebody else's loss. However, her guide Red Cloud made it quite clear that there can be no question of their having been stolen from their rightful owner; that, he said, just does not happen and assured her that they were all items previously lost or abandoned, with a number of them being drawn up from the sea.

One of the more remarkable incidents of this type was when a sitter asked that a budgerigar from the bottom of the garden be brought to the séance. Estelle recorded that Red Cloud declared that it would be done, and as he finished speaking, one of the two luminous plaques on the floor took flight and darted quickly about the room. Then it returned...its glowing phosphorus background showing the clear-cut silhouette of a budgerigar. Each of the sitters came up to the bird and touched it, having been assured by Red Cloud that the bird had been entranced and was wholly unaware of the events taking place. *(from www.zerdinisworld.com)*

Apport from Egypt as requested (Estelle Roberts)

In Estelle Roberts' book *Fifty Years a Medium(96)* we read:

Red Cloud has several times made gifts of this nature to those who sit with me, usually warning us in advance of his kindlyintention. Not unnaturally we look forward to such occasions with keen anticipation. I remember the discussion of a promised distribution of apports between my daughter Iris, her husband Kenneth, and Charles Tilson-Chowne, whom I later married. A good deal of light-hearted banter went on between them as they speculated on what each of them might receive. "It's all very well for you people", Kenneth said, "you've all had apports before. I haven't, and I think that entitles me to something especially nice." "What would you consider to be 'especially nice'?" Iris asked. "Oh, I don't know. Something interesting ... something unusual. Could I have something from Egypt, do you think?" "You'd better be careful," I warned him with a smile. "If it comes from Egypt, it will be probably be a beetle. I'm sure it's all you deserve." "A beetle will be fine," Kenneth said with great satisfaction. Iris, knowing that it would probably be her task to hand out the apports as they came from the trumpet, added "I hope it is a dead one. I hate beetles."

There were fifty sitters when we met to receive Red Cloud's gifts and there was a strong atmosphere of expectancy as I took my chair in the centre of the darkened room. Red Cloud entranced me and then addressed the company through the trumpet. He was in high good humour as he welcomed us to his 'party' and hoped we would enjoy our evening. Then the trumpet took flight and darted around the room like a glistening firefly. A moment later, when there came a loud rattling inside, it paused in its gyrations and delivered its apport into Iris'cupped hands[3]. As it did so Red Cloud's voice pronounced the name of the recipient. One after another the gifts came rattling down inside the trumpet, sometimes delivered into Iris's hands, sometimes directly into the hands of the sitters for whom they were intended. The demonstration ended with an avalanche of a dozen or more apports gushing from the trumpet like water from a tap. They included exquisite little stone

3. Several other references exist to apports being delivered inside the cupped hands of sitters. Among them is Henry Sausse, in his *Des Preuves? En Voila*, observing many instances of his medium forming her hand into a cup, in trance and in full light, in the cavity of which a small cloud was seen to form, transforming itself instantly into a small spray of roses, with flowers, buds and leaves complete.

figures, likenesses of Buddha, precious and semi-precious stones. Many of the gifts were much too large to pass through the narrow neck of the trumpet – as was clearly demonstrated at the end of the séance – yet pass through they did, and without any outside help. After about thirty gifts had been distributed, Iris was called by Red Cloud to receive Kenneth's gift. As the apport came rattling through the trumpet, Red Cloud said "Take care. It is frail and easily broken. You are fortunate my son, in this granting of your wish. To you is given a sacred beetle of Egypt."

"Where in Egypt does it come from?" Maurice Barbanell asked. "Abydos," came the instant reply, spelled out letter by letter. So it was that Kenneth received his beetle from Egypt, and a very beautiful specimen it was - brilliant green, edged with gold. Though it was no more than a hollow shell and extremely fragile, it was perfect in every detail. Kenneth was fascinated by it. Determined to find out more about it he took it to the British Museum where it was pronounced genuine. Abydos, he was told, was quite likely its source.

A ring apported inside a sitter's cupped hands (Kathleen Barkel)

Kathleen Barkel was a medium of high repute in the mid-20th century, and was known for apports. Maurice Barbanell, in *This is Spiritualism(86)* writes that the only physical indication that Mrs Barkel had that an apport séance would shortly take place was the curious fact that for days beforehand her figure began to swell and at the end of the séance her body resumed its normal size. Barbanell's theory was that her body somehow stored the ectoplasm required to re-materialize the objects after they had been brought through the atmosphere. Maurice Barbanell, goes on to tell us that White Hawk, the spirit guide to medium Kathleen Barkel, frequently had apport 'parties', as he called them. White Hawk thought they were a lot of fun, and the sitters usually agreed with him. At one of Barkel's séances, a ring materialized between the cupped hands of Barbanell. When he examined it, he found it to be a plain nine-carat gold ring with the words *Per ardua ad astra—B* engraved on the inside. Barbanell was told that the ring came from the late author,

Dennis Bradley. He immediately recognized that *Per ardua ad astra* – meaning "Through difficulties towards the stars" – was the motto of the Royal Air Force, in which Bradley had served. Also, Bradley's first book about Spiritualism had been titled *Towards the Stars*. The letter B was appropriate both for Bradley and for Barbanell.

For some apports, White Hawk would place Mrs Barkel's hand over those of the sitters, where the stone would grow in between them. Again in *This is Spiritualism(87)* we have this from Maurice Barbanell:

> The production of the apports was a fascinating experience. The entranced Kathleen Barkel was made to stand up by White Hawk, and walk around the room with her right hand outstretched. Then he usually called one or two people to 'help' him. I did so several times. I was asked to place one hand on the medium's wrist and another on her arm. In this fashion we walked round the room while White Hawk made quick grabs in space with the hand that was free. Suddenly, he would exclaim delightedly, "Got! Got!"
>
> Then he put the medium's hands between my two hands, asking three or four people to come forward. Each had to put one hand above mine, and the other below it. This, said White Hawk, enabled the object to be restored to its original form. I was then asked to remove my hands but to keep them clasped. Presently, he asked me whether I had received my gift. "I cannot feel anything," I replied.
>
> A few seconds later, there was a sensation of heat between the palms of my hands. Then, slowly, I felt an object becoming solid. "Hold on to it," he said. "Don't unclasp your hands." I resumed my seat, maintaining my clasped hands, noticing that the object gradually became cooler. Every few minutes, as they received their gifts, other members of the séance resumed their seats, clasping their hands. When the séance was over, we were free to examine the apports. Mine, on this occasion, was an amethyst.

Kathleen Barkel's mediumship was of further significance to Barbanell. For many years she worked at the British College of

Psychic Science where she was frequently put under test conditions. White Hawk was instrumental in convincing Maurice Barbanell that spirit guides collaborated with one another to bring evidence through. White Hawk confirmed powerful evidence which Barbanell had received through another well-known guide who then also confirmed that he knew Barbanell had been to see his 'friend'.

Bird's nest (Charles Bailey)

The Australian medium Charles Bailey, through his guide Abdul, apported such items as live fish, crabs and turtles, live birds sitting on eggs in their nests, rare antiques and coins, a stone from beneath the sea still dripping with salt water, a human skull, and ancient clay cylinders with Babylonian inscriptions. Once an eighteen-inches-long shark, and at another time a thirty-inch snake appeared mysteriously in the séance room. The apport of jungle sparrows passed the test of a committee of investigation in Milan. Other apports included an Indian blanket containing a tomahawk, a block of lead said to be found in Roman strata at Rome and bearing the name of Augustus, a quantity of gravel alleged to have come from Central America and quite unlike anything seen in Australia, two perfect clay tablets covered with cuneiform inscriptions and several thousands of years old, said to have been brought direct from the mounds at Babylon. Bailey produced apports for over forty years; the manufacture of which would have cost him a fortune and would necessitate a large factory with skilled hands. In *The History of Spiritualism(vol ii,214)*, Sir Arthur Conan Doyle writes:

We placed Mr Bailey in the corner of the room, lowered the lights and waited. Almost at once he breathed very heavily, as one in a trance, and soon said something in a foreign tongue... the voice then said that he was a Hindu control who was used to bring apports for the medium, and that he would, he hoped, be able to bring one for us. "Here it is," he said, a moment later, and the medium's hand was extended with something in it. The light was turned full on and we found it was a very perfect bird's nest, beautifully constructed of some very fine fibre mixed with moss. It stood about two inches high and had no sign of any flattening which would have come with concealment. The size would benearly three inches across. In it lay a small egg, white, with tiny brown speckles. The guide went on to explain that it came from India and that the accompanying bird was the Jungle Sparrow.

Arthur Conan Doyle additionally reports this, in *The Wanderings of a Spiritualist(103),* on the apport of the bird's nest:

The medium, or rather the Hindoo control acting through the medium, placed the egg on his palm and broke it, some fine albumen squirting out. There was no trace of yolk. "We are not allowed to interfere with life," said he. "If it had been fertilized we could not have taken it." These words were said before he broke it, so that he was aware of the condition of the egg, which certainly seems remarkable. The nest remained in my possession and I spent a morning with Mr Chubb, of the local museum, to ascertain if it was really the nest of such a bird. It seemed too small for an Indian Sparrow, and yet we could not match either nest or egg among the Australian types. Some of Mr Bailey's other nests and eggs have been actually identified. Surely it is a fair argument that while it is conceivable that such birds might be imported and purchased here, it is really an insult to one's reason to suppose that nests with fresh eggs in them could also be in the market. Therefore, I can only support the far more extended experience and elaborate tests of Dr MacCarthy of Sydney, and affirm that I believe Mr Charles Bailey to be upon occasion a true medium, with a very remarkable gift for apports. It is only right to state that when I returned to London I took one of Bailey's Assyrian tablets to the British Museum and that it was pronounced to be a forgery. Upon further inquiry it proved that these forgeries are made by certain Jews in a suburb of Bagdad – and, so far as is known, only there. Therefore the matter is not much farther advanced. To the transporting agency it is at least possible that the forgery, steeped in recent human magnetism, is more capable of being handled than the original taken from a mound. Bailey has produced at least a hundred of these things, and no Custom House officer has deposed how they could have entered the country. On the other hand, Bailey told me clearly that the tablets had been passed by the British Museum, so that I fear I cannot acquit him of tampering with truth – and just there lies the great difficulty of deciding upon his case. But one has always to remember that physical mediumship has no connection one way or the other with personal character, any more than the gift of poetry.

A cup of tea (Mrs Paton)

Mrs Paton was a little known medium from Australia who was mentioned only a few times in Spiritualist literature. Her phenomena were mostly recorded between 1872 and 1878. The first reporting of Mrs Paton was in W. C. D. Denovan's *The Evidences of Spiritualism: lectures, addresses and record of the spiritual phenomena* published in Melbourne by W. H. Terry in 1882. She was known as a 'non-professional' (meaning she accepted no fees for her séances) apport medium of Melbourne, Australia who flourished in the 1870s. Paton was not always entranced, but was often markedly convulsed during her apport phenomena, It often happened that things were apported from her own house over a distance of two miles from the séance location. Occasionally, the objects were very heavy or difficult to handle like a glass of wine or a burning hot flat iron. A stone apported from the seashore was found to weigh 14 pounds and came with a mass of seaweed with shrimp-like creatures on it. One of the most notable apported household objects was a soup plate with twenty eggs on it.

One of the most astonishing apports occurred at the house of a Miss Finlason, a resident of Castlemaine. During the séance, Paton mentioned to one of the sitters that before leaving her home, two miles away, she had made a cup of tea, but had forgotten to drink it. The cup of tea and saucer appeared as an apport on the table. At another séance on 6th April 1874, an iron wheel weighing sixteen and a half pounds fell with a crash on the table, brought from the yard outside.

The fact that the items apported had no known personal significance to the sitters raises the question of why the spirit world would apport them. However, it is reported that Mrs Paton always worked under strict test conditions. She was searched before every séance and completely enveloped in a large mosquito net bag, which was tied and sealed. Further, the apports arrived on a table in the dark, but on some occasions, arrived even in bright light. Finally, as she was unpaid for her séances, it is unlikely financial gain could have motivated any possible fraud. *(from www.encyclopedia.com)*

A sunflower complete with clods of earth (Agnes Nichol Guppy Volckman)

In the séances of Agnes Guppy-Volckman[4], requests from the sitters for specific apports were often honoured. When a friend of psychical researcher Dr Alfred Russel Wallace asked for a sunflower, a six-foot high specimen with a mass of earth around the roots immediately fell upon the table. When the Princess Marguerite at Naples desired specimens of a prickly cactus, more than twenty dropped on the table and had to be removed with tongs. The Duchess d'Arpino wished for sea sand. It soon splashed down with sea water and live star fishes. The sea was about a hundred yards from the house. Later the apports arrived in light, provided that a dark space was available to deposit them. *(www.survivalafterdeath.info)*

Asported gifts for needy children (Minnie Harrison)

In his book *Life After Death: Living Proof(185)*, Tom Harrison writes:

> As a family with five young children we naturally had a Christmas tree each year which we re-decorated especially for these sittings with small inexpensive toys like rattles, cars, aeroplanes, dolls, ships, strings of beads, baubles etc. and always told the Spirit children they could remove them from the tree, play with them in the room and take away as many as they wanted – if they could manage it.

---

4. The complete absence of financial motives by Agnes Guppy greatly puzzled Frank Podmore, author of many books including *Modern Spiritualism*. He considered every medium a fraud, out for financial gain. He writes, "But Mrs Guppy, even during the few months in which, as Miss Nichol, she practiced as a professional Mesmerist, can scarcely have found her main incentive in the hope of gain. On the assumption of fraud, the mere cost of the flowers lavished on her sitters must have swallowed up any probable profit from her increased mesmeric clientele. And even such a motive would have ceased with her marriage ." (After Mr Guppy's death in 1875 she then married Volckman.)

Needless to say that every year they took us at our word and when the light went on at the end of each sitting, we saw that some of the toys had been removed from the tree and were not in the room. Aunt Agg told us that the children used to remove them from the tree, play with them on the floor and then de-materialize them to take them out of the house. We never knew the exact destination of each toy but were told the Spirit children took them to the areas where very poor, deprived children lived and simply re-materialized them alongside such a child, who was overjoyed to find a new plaything – thus sharing joy and happiness in both worlds!

Apported candy from parties in London (Minnie Harrison)

In *Visits by our friends from the 'Other Side'(24),* describing events at another Christmas Party Tom Harrison writes:

Conversely we often received small gifts like wrapped toffees which were apported into the room and dropped on our knees in the darkness during the sitting. Most interestingly, on one of these occasions Sydney examined the wrappers and was intrigued to note that, from his knowledge of the confectionery trade, these particular sweets were a brand not available in the Middlesbrough area! We were told at a later sitting that they had been apported from a large party in London and the few we had would not have been missed from the dozens of dishes around the room.

Asported bread and apported letter of thanks (Isa Northage)

From *A Path Prepared: The Story of Isa Northage* by Allan MacDonald *(209),* we read:

August 6, 1941 – We were requested during a séance by General Victor De Cazale, Frenchman (in Spirit), to help his old comrades of his regiment, who had been taken prisoner when the Germans had entered France in 1941. On asking how we might help, he replied in French "Put out five loaves in the centre of the séance room," adding that he and friends in Spirit would dematerialize the bread and apport it to these men in a prison camp (who had no food during the previous five days). The men were wounded, hungry and dirty. One of the sitters (a lady) left the séance room to purchase bread. The rest of the sitters (twelve in all) remained to continue the sitting. When the bread arrived it was placed as requested in the centre of the room, within three minutes it had all disappeared. (dematerialized)

The note of thanks apported from prison camp was written with pencil on paper and read, "Sanctuaire. Dieu, et Mon Droit (God and my Right). H. Chaunterell. On the back of the paper was written "Des Amis du Sanctuaire" (From the Friends of the Sanctuary.)

Birthday present in the kitchen pantry (Minnie Harrison)

In *Visits by Our Friends From the 'Other Side'(34)*, Tom Harrison tells us of another unusual apport:

One of the most unusual and certainly the largest apport received through my mother's mediumship occurred not in a Home Circle sitting, but in my mother's home on her 53rd birthday – 17th March 1948. Mam and Dad had a kitchen with a small 'walk-in' type of pantry with no window, only a zinc-gauze vent. I lived about ten-minute drive from them and about four o'clock our telephone rang. It was Mam asking me if I could go straight there as there was something unusual she wanted me to see.

When I arrived Mam and Dad were sitting in the kitchen having a cup of tea. Mam usually had a smile on her face, but on this occasion it seemed rather enigmatic. She realized I was keen to see what she had telephoned about and immediately said "Just open the pantry door, son, but be very careful." Naturally I was very curious and not a little apprehensive – but did exactly as I was asked. I opened it very slowly but because of the lack of light saw nothing unusual for a moment or two. Then as I opened it wider to step inside I was halted in my tracks!

There at my feet on the floor of the pantry was a mass of lilac blossom – filling the whole floor space and as high as the first shelf – about three feet high! I turned and looked at Mam who, with an even bigger grin, said "I thought you'd be surprised," an understatement if ever there was. But the explanation was even more surprising. Mam had made the customary pot of tea in the afternoon, got the milk jug out of the pantry, closed the door behind her and sat on her chair adjacent to the door. She then realized that she had forgotten the sugar, turned on her chair and opened the door again – to be confronted by this amazing sight on the pantry floor. One moment earlier, when she got the milk, the floor had been absolutely clear. Now it was packed with lilac blossom. Naturally they were both dumbfounded and Mam's first thought was to ring me. I was as amazed as they were. Instinctively I knew it was not a practical joke. Mam and Dad didn't do those things, and Mam wouldn't bring me back to the shop 'on a fool's errand'.

It had certainly happened as Mam said. There was no doubt about that. A few other instances of individual flower apports had occurred outside the circle room, but usually during the time we were actually sitting. This mass of lilac blossom however was quite exceptional and Mam was clearly non-plussed but very excited. Needless to say we immediately removed it, made it up into a number of bunches and I took them round to many of our delighted friends where they lasted two or three weeks – as normal.

Come the following Saturday evening circle, Aunt Agg again pre-empted our question by asking us to tell our Min, as she always called my mother, that they had been delighted to be able to bring her such a special birthday gift from her many spirit friends who were so close to her! The darkness of the pantry had afforded the ideal conditions and it was another example of Mam's remarkable mediumship. But for a change, this time she had been the first to witness it!

Arthur Findlay's match-box apported from the cloak room (John Sloan)

Arthur Findlay, in *Where Two Worlds Meet(16),* notes this case of apportation in which an item known to be outside the séance room was apported into it. He writes:

41

On one occasion I left a gold match-box, having my initials on it, in my overcoat ticket-pocket. I said nothing about this to anyone, hung up my coat in the entrance passage, entered the séance room, locked the door, put the key in my pocket, put a mat up against the bottom of the door and took my seat with the others sitting around in a circle for the séance about to begin Two trumpets were in the middle of the circle for the voices to speak through, and it was not long after the light was put out when a trumpet came in front of my face and a metallic object was rattled inside it. A voice said "Please put out your hand," when something was heard to slide down the inside of the trumpet into my hand. It was the same gold match-box that I had put into the ticket pocket of my overcoat. When the séance was over I found the window still tightly shuttered, the mat was at the door as I had placed it, and the door was still locked. That is what is called an apport.

Hundreds of apports in a single séance (Keith Rhinehart)

In a séance in 1958 in Japan, hundreds of apports were manifested. Just before the end of the séance, Mrs Asana reports:

... the guide requested that a basin be put near the medium, ready for him for when he was taken from the trance state. As soon as this was done the medium tore off the adhesive plaster that bound his mouth spat out hundreds of polished agates in rapid succession. After this more agates came from the trumpet that was poked through the cabinet curtain. There were a total of 720 pieces of agate which were later examined by Kenichi Ikeda, a jeweller who valued them at more than five hundred yen apiece.

The following account of his own experiences with Rhinehart is relayed by George Cranley on his website 'Zerdini's World'

Cranley begins by telling us that apports are said to come from sunken ships, old ruins, large factories with such vast quantities of small, inexpensive objects that a few would never be missed, or somewhere of like nature. The alleged spirits seem to be very careful to do nothing really dishonest in the securing of apports.

He then continues:

Although there was no evidential value in the apport sitting I attended in Seattle two dozen white carnations dropped neatly into my arms where I was sitting in the third row, and red rosebuds were handed to me inside a trumpet.

The next apport séance that was scheduled was therefore planned to give me the maximum of assurance. Keith himself suggested that the lights be left on. This is not often done because it is said to be extremely hard on this medium to produce ectoplasm in the light – even though he is inside of his cabinet at the time. After the séance he was reported to be ill for several days.

However, as I said, the suggestion that this session be held in the light was made by Rhinehart himself, and I cannot but give him credit for it. Before the meeting I was given the opportunity to examine the entire room, particularly the stage area, to make sure that no objects were hidden there. There was no basement under that part of the building, as I knew from personal inspection. The floor was covered with wall-to-wall carpeting, which was fastened tight to the stripping along the wall, and the chair in which the medium sat would have to be moved in order to pull it back. The walls were of plaster, with no recesses or indentations where anything could be hidden. I almost took the medium's chair apart, but found no trick arms that would come loose, no false bottom of any kind, no hollow legs or arms.

The medium's cabinet was in the outside corner of the room, which was at the outside corner of the building, almost against the street. Keith's cabinet was composed of two purple velvet curtains that were pulled out on a rack from the wall to make a square in the corner of the room. The top is about two feet down from the ceiling.

After my examination of the room, I asked two men from the audience to come up and search Keith. One was Clyde Beck, who has been a member of the American Society for Psychical Research for some years. The other was a man who had never attended a séance before and did not believe any mediums were genuine. They stripped him of all his clothing and examined him carefully. (Of course, there was no way to give him an internal examination to make sure that he had nothing hidden within his body, but the nature of the apports themselves would seem to preclude that.)

Keith then resumed his shorts and shirt, and I entered the cabinet and tied him securely to his chair with a heavy cord that frayed if one were to attempt to loosen it. His wrists and bare feet were tied so tightly that afterward there were deep red grooves in them. Now, in order that his audience will not think that he is practising ventriloquism when the voices are heard, Rhinehart always has his mouth filled with water and then taped shut before going into trance. After the séance is over he spits out the water to indicate that he has held it in his mouth all the time. On this occasion I gave him milk instead of water, which he still retained when the session was over. I placed a wide strip of adhesive tape across his mouth and made marks on it extending out onto his skin so that if the tape were removed it would be evident. This is also part of his usual procedure.

I have learned from experimenting, however, that it is possible to loosen the centre of the tape and talk without disturbing the correlation of the markings; I also know that one can do a little talking with water or milk in his mouth, and that it is possible for some persons to swallow a fluid which they later can regurgitate. I am not sure whether it would be possible under these conditions for a variety of voices to be produced, ranging from very deep, sonorous tones, to children's prattle, to a beautiful tenor voice singing, when the medium's natural voice is a mediocre baritone. I don't know either whether conversation can be sustained for hours on end under these conditions, as I have heard it at the Seattle séances.

The room itself on this afternoon was illuminated by several ceiling lights and visibility was excellent. I sat in the second row of the audience, the front row of seats being vacant, and watched everything that occurred. What did occur, in the light, with the medium bound and gagged, were apports. Susan, the cabinet guide – the little spirit entity who acts as master of ceremonies – called out the name of each person in the audience in turn. Then she passed each person's apport under

44

the cabinet curtain for him, talking as she did so about where it had come from, what it was, or why it was particularly appropriate for that individual. I observed each object land outside of the cabinet before it was picked up.

On that Sunday afternoon, in the light, with the medium gagged and tied up, some fifty apports were dropped out of the cabinet, varying in size from tiny plastic disks and inexpensive items of jewelry and scarabs, to a Mayan or Aztec relic of stone about two inches high, a plain oval rock almost two inches long, a jagged-edged arrowhead three inches long, and several smaller arrowheads. My particular present was a bronze Roman coin from about the second century AD.

My own testimony about Keith Rhinehart's apports is enhanced; it seems to me, by a colour movie taken in the brightly lighted church one Sunday before I arrived in Seattle. In it the medium is seen spewing from his mouth quantities of small objects as he did in the Japanese séance. The most curious thing about this film, however, is that apports are seen in his ears. I have talked to men, whose powers of observation seem perfectly reliable, who were standing right beside the medium at the time. They saw that he was not by any kind of sleight of hand sticking those black stones in his ears, but that the stones seemed to arrive as bulges in his neck, which then inwardly popped up into his ears one by one and were removed as they appeared.

Apports by the thousands (Mrs Maggs)

According to Nandor Fodor, in his *Encyclopedia of Psychic Science*, there could hardly be anything to surpass in wonder the accounts of the apports experienced by General 'Lorrison' (Major General A.W. Drayson) at Portsmouth. The medium was Mrs Maggs, the wife of a local editor and a writer herself. In a strictly private circle, apports arrived by the thousands. The household in the south of England was supplied with eggs straight from a spirit circle in Brooklyn in the United States and gifts were exchanged through similar means with circles in countries as distant as Spain, Australia, India and China.

It is claimed that once a letter was apported, was read, a corner torn off for identification and then re-apported. Ten days later it was returned, addressed to General Drayson. The torn off piece fitted in and the contents were identical. According to the Portsmouth Temple of Spiritualism, Portsmouth came into prominence in psychical matters in 1880, through the experiments of Major General A. W. Drayson and Archdeacon Colley, who conducted a number of psychical experiments in physical phenomena and apports, with the mediumship of Mrs Maggs.

Flower apports (Madame d'Esperance – Elizabeth Hope)[5]

It was a favourite feat of Yolande, the control of Elizabeth d'Esperance, to put a glass of water into the hand of one of her particular friends and tell him to watch it. She would then hold her slender tapered fingers over the glass and while her eyes were closely scrutinizing the water within it a flower would form itself upon it and fill the glass.

Matching fern leaves and roses of any colour on demand (Madame d'Esperance – Elizabeth Hope)[5]

Sitters frequently brought fern leaves and asked Yolande to match them. The request was always complied with. Roses were produced from nothing and freely given away. They were frequently produced in the water pitcher carried on Yolande's shoulder. If a special colour was required it was obtained. Once, a black rose was requested. Yolande dipped her fingers into the pitcher and instantly brought out a dark object, dripping with moisture. It was a rose of distinctly blue-black colour which none of those assembled had seen.

The Ixora Crocata (Madame d'Esperance – Elizabeth Hope)[5]

During a séance on 4th August 1880, in the presence of William Oxley of Manchester, Yolande directed a Mr Reimers to pour sand into a water carafe, which he did until it was about half full. Then he was instructed to pour in water. Yolande took it, placed it on the floor, covering it lightly with the drapery she took from her shoulders. The circle was directed to sing. While singing they observed the drapery to be rising from the rim of the carafe. Yolande several times came out of the cabinet to examine the thing growing under the drapery. Finally she raised the drapery altogether and disclosed a perfect plant, its roots firmly grown and packed in the sand. She presented it to Oxley. Through raps, instructions were given not to discuss the matter but sing something and be quiet. They obeyed. More raps came and told them to examine the plant again. To their great surprise they observed a large circular head of bloom, forming a flower fully five inches in diameter that had opened while the plant stood on the floor at Oxley's feet. The plant was 22 inches [56cms] in height, with a thick woody stem that filled the neck of the water carafe. It had twenty-nine leaves, each smooth and glossy. It was impossible to remove the plant from the water bottle, the neck being too small to allow the roots to pass; indeed the comparatively slender stem entirely filled the orifice.

The plant was a native of India, an *Ixora Crocata*. It had some years of growth. Marks could be seen where other leaves had grown and fallen off, and wound-marks which seemed to have healed and grown over long ago. But there was every evidence to show that the plant had grown in the sand in the bottle as the roots were naturally wound around the inner surface of the glass, all the fibres perfect and unbroken as though they had germinated on the spot and had apparently never been disturbed. The plant was photographed. It lived for three months under the care of Mr Oxley's gardener and then shrivelled up.

Ixora Crocata
produced for Mr William Oxley
of Manchester at a séance held
4th August 1880.

5. These 3 extracts about Mme d'Esperance are from Fodor's *Encyclopedia of Psychic Science* on www.spiritwritings.com

The Golden Lily (Madame d'Esperance – Elizabeth Hope)

The last and greatest apport work of Yolande was achieved on 28th June 1890, when she apported a seven-foot high Golden Lily. It bore eleven large blooms, and the flowers were perfect, five fully blown. The feat was witnessed by Professors Boutlerof, Fiedler, Aksakof and others. The power was not sufficient for its de-materialization (Yolande insisted that the plant was borrowed and she had to return it) and, on instructions to keep it in darkness the flower remained in the house for eight days and then vanished in an instant, filling the room with an overpowering perfume.

On the evening of the 28th June 1890, conditions for a séance seemed poor. Mme D'Esperance had accidently scorched her arm and had been suffering from a slight but irritating toothache all day. Together with a violent windstorm which shook the house to its foundations, it did not promise much for the success of our séance. They were about to give up when a strong scent of flowers was noticed. Yolande with the assistance of Mr Aksakof had mixed sand and loam in the flower pot and she had covered it with her veil, as she had done in the case of the water bottle in England when the Ixora Crocata was grown. The white drapery was seen to rise slowly but steadily, widening out as it grew higher and higher. Yolande stood by and manipulated the gossamer-like covering till it reached a height far above her head, when she carefully removed it, disclosing a tall plant bowed with a mass of heavy blooms, which emitted the strong sweet scent I had complained of. The flowers were completely perfect, measuring eight inches in diameter; five were fully blown, three were just opening, and three in bud, all without spot or blemish, and damp with dew.

Everyone was told to remain perfectly quiescent to enable Yolande to dematerialize the plant. They tried to comply with the request, but after sitting till midnight Yolande despairingly told them that she could not take the plant away. Another control, Walter, communicated "Yolande only got the plant on condition she brought it back. She finds the medium is exhausted and cannot stand any more. You must let the plant remain in darkness till she can come again and take it." Mr Fidler and Mr Boutlerof then carried the plant to a dark closet in an adjoining room, where it was locked up, till the rest of the sitters should receive instructions how to act in respect of it. But on July 5th, the plant vanished as mysteriously as it came. At 9:23 pm it stood in the midst of the company, and at 9:30 pm it was gone. Not a vestige remained except the photographs and a couple of flowers, which had fallen off. The soil was emptied out of the pot where it had stood for eight days, but no sign of it was left.

Another curious circumstance in respect of the lily was that Yolande, not being able to tell where she got the plant, said she would let them know in another way. On the night of its disappearance, before it vanished, a piece of grey cloth which contained 2584 threads to the square inch was found to be on the stem of it; the stem was in fact through a hole in the centre of the cloth. How it came there was a mystery like all the rest. It was not there when the plant was photographed in daylight. Yet to

The Golden Lily, produced at a séance, 28th June 1890.

all appearances it had grown there, and could not be removed. Yolande, however instructed Mr Aksakof to draw it from the stem, which he did; there was no rent in it, nothing but the round hole through which the stem had passed. She told the sitters that she got the piece of cloth from the same country as that where the flower had grown. On examination the piece of grey cloth was found to be a scrap of mummy cloth, still aromatic with the perfumes used in embalming. This led the sitters to conclude that the plant had been brought from Egypt. (*Shadow Land: Or, Light from the Other Side*, E. d'Esperance, 1897: adapt.)

Jewels appear then vanish (William Eglinton)

Abdullah, the one-armed control of medium William Eglinton, appeared bedecked with diamonds, emeralds and rubies. The materialization of precious stones is thus described by Mrs Nichols in the *Spiritualist* for 26th October 1877[6]:

> For some time he moved his hands as if gathering something from the atmosphere, just as when he makes muslin. After some minutes he dropped on the table a massive diamond ring. He said "Now you may all take the ring, and you may put it on, and hold it while you count twelve." Miss M. took it and held it under the gaslight. It was a heavy gold ring with a diamond that appeared much like one worn by a friend of mine worth £1,000. Joey said the value of this was 900 guineas. Mr W. examined it as we had done.
>
> He [Abdullah] now made, as it seemed, and as he said, from the atmosphere two diamonds, very clear and beautiful, about the size of half a large pea. He gave them into our hands on a piece of paper. We examined them as we had the others. He laid the ring and the diamonds on the table before him, and there next appeared a wonderful cluster of rubies, set with a large ruby about half an inch in diameter in the centre. These we all handled as we had the others. Last there came a cross, about four inches in length, having twenty magnificent diamonds set in it; this we held in our hands, and examined as closely as we liked. He told us that the market value of the gems was £25,000. He remarked "I could make Willie the richest man in the world, but it would not be the best thing, and might be the worst." He now took the jewels in front of him and seemed to dissipate them, as one might melt hailstones in heat until they entirely disappeared."

Forty butterflies (Agnes Nichol Guppy Volckman)

Miss Houghton, in her *Evenings at Home in Spiritual Séance,* writes of a farewell séance held by Mr and Mrs Guppy before their departure from England. There were a good many flowers brought. She writes:

"By and by, Mrs Guppy exclaimed that there were creeping creatures about, and begged to be allowed to light the candle. Upon

---

6. From www.encyclopedia.com/doc - free material

her request being granted, there was a quantity of butterflies travelling about among us and the flowers, some of which were caught and put away in a box; altogether we reckoned that there were about forty of them."

Sir Arthur Conan Doyle apports the key to his study (Mrs Caird Miller)

According to Maurice Barbanell in *This is Spiritualism(91)* we read:

About a month after Conan Doyle's death, she heard a voice declare in clear tones, "I am Arthur Conan Doyle. I want you to get into touch with my wife and send her a message."
This surprised Mrs Miller who had never met the great writer. She did not know his wife or any member of his family. Her reserve was a barrier to approaching Lady Doyle unless she was absolutely sure of her ground. "Give me some proof of your identity," she demanded. The voice replied by giving the initials of every member of his family. When she made inquiries, she found that they were all accurate. Still hesitant, she said to the Doyle voice when it next repeated the request, "Where shall I find your wife?" The reply came quite clearly. The voice gave her a telephone number, told her she would not find it in the telephone book, but said it was the unlisted number of the Doyle cottage in the New Forest. This was a test.
Still curious, Mrs Miller decided that before approaching Lady Doyle, she would try to ascertain whether the number was correct. She inquired of the telephone exchange, but was met with the reply that they were not allowed to divulge such information. Here was a deadlock. Mrs Caird Miller hesitated for a few moments and then asked the operator to call the number the voice had given her. The number was accurate, for soon she was talking to Lady Doyle. At that time the Doyle family was being flooded with alleged spirit messages from all over the world. Lady Doyle and her two sons rightly insisted that they would not accept spirit communications claiming to emanate from Sir Arthur unless they were accompanied by irrefutable evidence to prove their authenticity. This was indeed a rebuff.

Mrs Miller had carried out the instructions of the voice, and had met with failure. She determined to have nothing more to do with it. But Sir Arthur was undismayed. A few days later she heard his voice again. He knew about the rebuff, he said, but was determined to prove himself through this new medium. "Will you go and have a séance with Mrs Deane", he asked, "and I will appear on a photograph?" This sitting with Mrs Deane, a medium for spirit photography, was arranged anonymously, and no hint was given of its purpose.

When the plate was developed and the print made, in addition to Mrs Caird Miller's photograph there was a striking 'extra' of Conan Doyle above her head. The spirit 'extra' was shown to Lady Doyle, who admitted that it was a remarkable one that bore an unquestionable resemblance to her husband. Even then, however she demanded still more proof. That, thought Mrs Miller, was the last straw. But the persistent Conan Doyle provided the required proof. It came a few days later, when Mrs Miller was in her London flat. She had not long awakened and gone into another room.

When she returned to her bedroom, she found a key lying on her pillow. She looked at the key in amazement. It did not belong to any door in her flat. How it got there was a mystery. As she stood there, wondering, she heard the now familiar Conan Doyle voice say "That is my key. It comes from the door of my study, which is always kept closed, at Crowborough. Send for my son, Denis."

Here was a test – if the statement were true. Mrs Miller telephoned Denis Conan Doyle at Crowborough, Sussex, and told him what had happened. In a few minutes he had jumped into a motor car and was on his way to London. He arrived at Mrs Miller's flat, and took the key back to Crowborough.

Later he telephoned to say that it was certainly the key of his father's study. Sir Arthur had transported it a distance of forty miles. That convinced Lady Doyle. Thereafter, Mrs Caird Miller became the medium through whom spirit messages were regularly transmitted from Sir Arthur to his wife and family.

Automatic Writing

Automatic Writing

The pen writes itself.
It seemed as though what I wrote was blown through my mind
as with the rushing of a mighty wind.

Geraldine Cummins

Harriet Beecher Stowe on writing 'Uncle Tom's Cabin':
I have been surprised at the observations made by some of my
characters. It seems as if an occult power was moving the pen. The
personage does or says something, and I ask:
'How did he come to think of that?'

W. M. Thackeray

Automatic writing, also known as 'psychography'[1], is a form of automatism in which the medium is able to go into an altered state of conscious and allow their hand to be taken over or influenced by a spirit person. Writing can sometimes be at a supernormal speed, in languages unknown to the medium, in reversed order or about subjects totally outside their knowledge. Sometimes the writing is exceptionally small and sometimes it is reversed and can only be read in a mirror but usually it is written without the need for editing. The term Automatic writing introduced by William T. Stead, (himself an automatic writer) is misleading. Stead uses it to avoid saying 'spirit writing', the very idea he believes in and wishes to convey. 'Automatic' writing implies writing that is fully independent of the medium's mind but it can occur with the medium aware. In some Spiritualist literature, an automatic writer is called an 'automatist'.

Although many great works[2] have been received via automatic writing, some of what is thought of as automatic writing actually may have come from the subconscious mind of the writer[3] as it

1. Term may have been coined by Medium/Automatist William Stainton Moses but is also used by Kardec in *The Mediums' Book* 1876.
2. In the preface of his famous poem *Jerusalem*, Blake says that it was dictated to him, "The grandest poem that this world contains; I may praise it, since I dare not pretend to be other than the Secretary; the authors are in eternity. I have written this poem from immediate dictation, twelve or sometimes twenty or thirty lines at a time without premeditation and even against my will." Parts of the Old Testament were received through automatic writing. "And there came a writing to him from Elijah the prophet saying . ." (2 Chronicles XXI. 12).
3. These cases might be evidence of a past life.

provides no actual evidence of mediumship. Mrs Harriet Beecher Stowe, the author of *Uncle Tom's Cabin* said that she did not write it – 'it was given to her, it passed before her'. However, there are many cases of automatic writing which are mediumistic because they provide evidence of spirit communication. Certainly the speed at which automatic writing occurs refutes the theory that automatic writing stems from the writer's subconscious. Mediums who use an Ouija[4] board, especially blindfolded, are performing another type of this automatism.

The After-life explained via automatic writing (William Stead)

William Stead was a gifted automatic writer who had given the world important messages from the world of spirit. *After Death or Letters from Julia* was a slim volume of observations from the other side written through Stead by his friend Julia who had passed to spirit in 1891. The messages provide Julia's interpretations of what happens upon death of the physical body and awakening in the realm of spirit. After being available for more than 100 years, the letters are still captivating reading and nowadays can be downloaded from the Internet. Some mediums, like Stead, were fully conscious and aware during delivery and others automatists were deeper in a trance state. Stead in his *Letters from Julia* explains:

Automatic writing is writing that is written by the hand of a person which is not under control of his conscious mind. The hand apparently writes of itself, the person to whom the hand belongs having no knowledge of what it is about to write. It is a very familiar and simple form of mediumship, which in no way impairs the writer's faculties or places his personality under the control of any other intelligence. This writing may proceed from his sub-conscious mind, or it may be due to the direct action of independent, invisible intelligences. What is certain is that it does not emanate from the conscious mind of the writer, who often receives messages containing information as to past events of which he has never heard, and sometimes perfectly accurate predictions as to events which have not yet

---

4. The term 'Ouija' comes from the French and the German words for 'yes' - 'oui' and 'ja' respectively. 'Ouija' is now a registered trademark of the game publishers Parker Brothers.

happened. It was in this way that I began to receive the communications, some few of which are collected in this little volume. All the Letters from Julia were received by me in the same manner. Sitting alone with a tranquil mind, I consciously placed my right hand, with the pen held in the ordinary way, at the disposal of Julia, and watched with keen and skeptical interest to see what it would write.

A word written every few seconds for more than an hour (Geraldine Cummins)

One of the most accomplished automatic writers of the 20th century was Geraldine Cummins of Ireland. She authored fifteen books received by automatic writing, – which she preferred to call 'directed' writing. Several are now considered classics in the field, including *The Scripts of Cleophas*[5]*; Beyond Human Personality; The Road to Immortality*[6] , *Mind in Life and Death,* and *Swan on a Black Sea.*

Psychic investigator Edith Beatrice Gibbes described Cummins' condition during the automatic writing as a "semi-trance or light

5. *The Scripts of Cleophas* was communicated by Cleophas, a Christian convert of the first century, through seven scribes collectively called the 'messengers'. As these messengers explained it on page xii of its introduction, Cleophas, was too elevated to communicate directly, and so "plucks from the tree of memory all these matters that had been within his knowledge, gives them to the Scribe, who gives them to the 'messenger, who enters into the thought of the writer'. *The Scripts of Cleophas* supplements the *Acts of the Apostles* and the *Epistles of St. Paul*. It is a historic narrative of the early church and the work of the apostles from immediately after the death of Jesus to St. Paul's departure from Berea for Athens. In her second volume, *Paul in Athens,* the narrative is taken up and continued. The third volume, *The Great Days of Ephesus,* follows the same line of thought. The production of these automatic scripts was witnessed by eminent theologians and other authorities. Recognized scholars who edited her books endorsed their intrinsic merit. They give new meaning to several obscure passages in the *Acts of the Apostles*, they show close acquaintanceship with the apostolic circle and that age. They contain much which militates against subliminal origin. To take a single instance, only a very profound student could have given the head of the Jewish community in Antioch the title of Archon as the usual title was Ethnarch not long before the time referred to in the chronicle of Cleophas.

6. *Beyond Human Personality* and *The Road to Immortality* were communicated by Frederic W. H. Myers, the pioneering psychical researcher who died in 1901. They contain much about the nature of the afterlife. Sir Oliver Lodge, another pioneering psychical researcher and a good friend of Myers, reviewed the scripts and found them to be very characteristic of the Myers he knew.

dream-state or sometimes in a deeper condition of trance. Her hand is assumed to be controlled by some outside entity or influence, quite separate from her own personality." According to Cummins' book, *They Survive*, the method adopted by her is as follows: she would sit at a table, cover her eyes with her left hand, her right hand resting on a block of foolscap paper and concentrating on 'stillness'.

In her introduction to *The Road to Immortality* Cummins said of her writing state:

> Soon I am in a condition of half-sleep, a kind of dream-state that yet, in its peculiar way, has more illumination than one's waking state. I have at times distinctly the sensation of a dreamer who has no conscious creative control over the ideas that are being formulated in words. I am a mere listener, and through my stillness and passivity I lend my aid to the stranger who is speaking. It is hard to put such a psychological condition into words. I have the consciousness that my brain is being used by a stranger all the time. It is just as if an endless telegram is being tapped out on it.

Her hand would then begin to write. Usually, her 'control', Astor, would make some introductory remarks and announce that another entity was waiting to speak. The handwriting almost always resembled that of the communicating entity when alive.

Because of her semi-trance condition and also because of the speed at which the writing would come, an assistant would sit beside her and remove each sheet of paper as it was filled. Cummins' hand was quickly lifted by the assistant to the top of the new page, and the writing would continue without a break. In such a state, she consistently wrote at approximately 2,000 words an hour or 24.5 words per minute which works out to a word every few seconds! In one sitting, Cummins wrote at this rate for more than one hour, whereas her normal compositions were four times slower—perhaps 800 words in seven or eight hours.

Maurice Barbanell in *Power of the Spirit(144)* describes watching Geraldine Cummins doing her writing:

> I was fascinated to watch Geraldine Cummins at work. She sits at a table, with numbered sheets of ruled paper in front of

57

her. Her eyes are shaded with her left hand, while the elbow rests on a small table. In her right hand she holds a fountain pen poised above the paper. Then, in a few seconds, it becomes galvanized. On her right sits Miss E. B. Gibbes, her great friend, whose presence appears to act as a stimulant to Miss Cumin's mediumship. While the writing is being done, Miss Gibbes steadies the sheets of paper with both hands. The only time she guides the pen is when each page is completed. For over an hour, the three of us, Miss Gibbes, the medium and I, sat in silence, broken occasionally by a whispered 'Yes' or 'No' from Miss Gibbes.

I witnessed the production of writing from one of the medium's guides and from Frederick W. H. Myers, the distinguished classical scholar who espoused Spiritualism in his earthly life. After making some comments that were appropriate to my presence, he continued an essay started at a previous séance. It covered nine pages of foolscap paper and was written in beautiful prose, all as if it were one word. With great rapidity, the pen moved to the edge of the paper, never slipping, although the medium could not see.

During the séance, Geraldine Cummins appears to be in a light trance. When the writing ceased, she dropped her pen and gave a few shudders as the communicator made his departure. I made a rapid calculation and discovered that in just over an hour she had written nearly fourteen hundred words.

When Geraldine Cummins is writing normally, she produces six or seven hundred words in a couple of days and confesses that it is rather laborious. She has to make many corrections. When, however, she is the medium for automatic writing, the matter flows from her pen without a pause or a correction. Although no t's are crossed or i's are dotted, the script is always legible and intelligible. Frequently, at séances lasting an hour and a half, she has produced over 2200 words.

The Willett Scripts (Geraldine Cummins)

After her death in 1956 at the age of 81, Mrs Winifred Margaret Coombe Tennant, a well-known English medium, who was also an automatist, began to communicate through medium, Geraldine Cummins. As in life, she used the psuedonym 'Mrs Willett' and wrote a long and detailed book of personal memories which was published under the title *Swan on a Black Sea*. The book contains a numerous details about Mrs Coombe Tennant's personal life and about her relationships with her children; but Geraldine Cummins had never met Mrs Coombe Tennant or her children. The object of communicating through Cummins, by automatic writing; was to let her family know she was still very much alive in the spirit world. The forty scripts which were given between 1957 and 1960 are essentially an afterlife memoir of Mrs Coombe Tennant and they provide a fascinating insight into her world beyond death. Many researchers, including Colin Wilson in *After Life: Survival of the Soul*, consider this communication to be convincing proof of the reality of life after death

Reading one book while writing another   (William Stainton Moses)

William Stainton Moses wrote a number of books through automatic writing under the pen name 'M. A. Oxon' [a reference to his degree from Oxford], between 1872/3 and1883, although his pace slowed in the latter five years (1877 to 1883). Among the best known is *Spirit Teachings*, but there is also *Spirit Identity, Psychography*, and *Higher Aspects of Spiritualism*.

Initially, the writing was very small and irregular, and it was necessary for Stainton Moses to write slowly and cautiously. However, the writing quickly became more regular and more legible. Most of the early messages came from a spirit called 'Doctor', but after a time others started using Moses' hand. The writing of each was distinguished by a different handwriting as well as peculiarities of style and expression. When some spirits found that they could not influence Moses' hand, they called upon a spirit called 'Rector' for assistance. 'Rector' even acted as an amanuensis, writing for a spirit called 'Imperator' who was the spirit influence during the period that the *Spirit Teachings* were given. In the Introduction to that book Moses described the procedure of automatic writing as follows:

At first the writing was slow and it was necessary for me to follow it with my eye, but even then the thoughts were not my thoughts. Very soon all the messages assumed a character of which I had no doubt whatever that the thought opposed my own. But I cultivated the power of occupying my mind with other things during the time that the writing was going on, and was able to read an abstruse book and follow out a line of close reasoning, while the message was written with unbroken regularity. Messages so written extended over many pages and in their course there is no correction, no fault in composition, and often a sustained vigour and beauty of style.

Automatic writing proves survival after medium dies (William Stainton Moses)

As outlined in *Life is forever: Evidence for survival after death (149)* by Suzy Smith, it was only after Stainton Moses' death that a series of chances led researcher Frederic Myers to discover the magnitude of this great moment in modern mediumship. During Moses' lifetime, one Sunday night a spirit (to whom Myers later gave the pseudonym of Blanche Abercromby, to protect her privacy) began to write through his hand. She had died on that Sunday afternoon   at a country home some two hundred miles from London. Of her illness and death, Moses knew absolutely nothing, but she wrote that she 'had just quitted her body'.

A few days later, his hand was again controlled and a few lines were given purporting to come from Blanche Abercromby. She asserted that her script was in her very own handwriting, as a proof of her identity. There is no reason to suppose that Moses had ever seen her handwriting, for he had only met her once casually at a séance. Since the facts she gave were private, he mentioned the correspondence to no one, and gummed down the pages of writing in his notebook, marking them 'private matter'.

When after the death of Reverend Stainton Moses his documents were examined, Myers obtained permission from the executors to open these sealed pages. To his astonishment, he found the communication said to be from Blanche Abercromby, a woman he had known. When he compared the handwriting of the script with letters from her while on earth, he found the resemblance to be incontestable.

Myers submitted the communication to the lady's son and also to a handwriting expert, and both affirmed that the writing by the spirit and that by the lady while living were from the same person. Numerous peculiarities were found common to the two, and the contents of the automatic script were also characteristic of the deceased. The ordinary handwriting of Moses was quite different from that which usually came in his automatic script, and both were totally unlike the calligraphy of Mrs Abercromby.

According to some views of mediumship, there are three distinct phases of writing – inspirational, automatic, and independent[7].

Inspirational writing is a mental phase of mediumship and in the *Encyclopedia of Psychic Science* Nandor Fodor writes that, inspiration is a psychic state in which one becomes susceptible to creative spiritual influence to a varying degree, and unwittingly lends oneself as an instrument for through-flowing ideas; adding –

Schiller – wondered where his thoughts came from; they frequently flowed through him independent of the action of his own mind.

Mozart said "When all goes well with me, when I am in a carriage, or walking, or when I cannot sleep at night, the thoughts come streaming in upon me most fluently; whence or how is more than I can tell."

Beethoven stated "Inspiration is for me that mysterious state in which the entire world seems to form a vast harmony, when every sentiment, every thought re-echoes within me, when all the forces of nature become instruments for me, when my whole body shivers and my hair stands on end."

In automatic writing, the message comes from the mind of the spirit entity and is not filtered through the consciousness of the medium; the medium's hand is controlled or used, with their

7. Automatic writing is not to be confused with Independent writing (also known as 'direct writing') which is a form of physical mediumship usually occurring in a séance wherein a materialized hand or ectoplasmic rod is used to produce the writing and moves a pen 'independently' usually in a darkened séance room. (see: Harrison, *Life After Death:Living Proof* (2008:61-63).

consent, by the spirit. The medium may be reading a book or carrying on a conversation with another person while the message is being written. Communications obtained through the planchette, Ouija board or table tipping are modifications of automatic writing and continued communications may be obtained by interchanging these methods. Note that the line between inspirational writing and automatic writing can be very subtle indeed.

Liszt composes again (Rosemary Brown)

Although Rosemary Brown had taken some piano lessons, she had no real talent and was unacquainted with the technicalities of writing notes. Her chief communicator was Franz Liszt, but she wrote many other pieces from composers including Chopin, Schubert, Debussy, Rachmaninov, Beethoven, Mozart, and Bach. Her obituary in *The Guardian* in December 2001 states; 'the 1969 composition called *Gruebelei* (meditation), partly dictated under the watchful gaze of BBC reporter Peter Dorling and a television studio crew, is undoubtedly a most spectacular and unusual piece. It has strong harmonies, cross-rhythms and occasional instructions in French – a point conferring authenticity' – and almost impossible to fake.

At first, she became aware of her hands being 'taken over' while she was playing the piano. Afterward, it could be a laborious process getting it onto paper note for note, but she gradually became more adept at 'taking dictation' from dead composers. Rosemary also produced three volumes of her own writing to include an autobiography and philosophical observations titled: *Unfinished Symphonies, Immortals at my Elbow* and *Look beyond Today*.

"Pray for Hugh Lane" (Hester Dowden)

In *Power of the Spirit(149)* is this record of an early written communication through Hester Dowden:

> One of the first remarkable proofs to come through Mrs Dowden was when Lennox Robinson, the author, who is the medium's son-in-law, was present. One message came: "Pray for Hugh Lane."
>
> When they asked who was speaking, through Mrs Dowden's

hand was written: "I am Hugh Lane; all is dark." Later thecommunication continued "It is Sir Hugh Lane, drowned. Was on board the Lusitania." While these words were being received, boys were selling the evening papers in the streets. Lennox Robinson ran out to buy a copy. When he returned, he pointed to the name of Sir Hugh Lane, which was given in the account of the Lusitania disaster. Sir Hugh Lane described, through Mrs Dowden, the scene on the Lusitania before it was told in the newspapers: "Panic. Boats lowered. Women went first. Lost in a crowded boat, fell over. Lost all memory until I saw a light at the sitting."

It so happened that Mrs Dowden knew Sir Hugh Lane and had heard that he went to America a fortnight before the sinking of the Lusitania [May 1915]. On her way home on the day of the séance, she saw the newspaper posters with the words, 'Lusitania reported sinking', but she says she had no personal interest in the news as she did not know anyone on board.

"Oscar Wilde is not dead" (Hester Dowden Smith)

In *This is Spiritualism(58)* we read of another example from Hester Dowden:

Wilde's spirit signature, through Hester Dowden Smith, was an exact replica of his earthy one. The handwriting disclosed his peculiarities. Events from his childhood days were mentioned and inquiry proved them to be accurate. The literary style, which was the acid test, was highly characteristic. It all began at a séance one night with the words "Lily, my little Lily. No, the lily is mine – crystal thread – a silver reed that made music in the morning."

"Who are you?" they asked. Immediately, the writing began again "Pity Oscar Wilde – one who in the world was a king of life. Bound to Ixion's wheel of thought, I must complete for ever the circle of my experience. Long ago I wrote that there was twilight in my heart, but this is the (last?) twilight of the soul.

"In eternal twilight, I move, but I know that in the world there is day and night, seed time and harvest, and red sunset must follow apple-green dawn. Every year, spring throws her green

63

veil over the world and anon the red autumn glory comes to mock the yellow moon. Already the may is creeping like a white mist over lane and hedgerow, and year after year the hawthorne bears blood-red fruit after the white death of its may."

Asked "Why have you come here?" he replied "To let the world know that Oscar Wilde is not dead."

She also received a play by automatic writing from Oscar Wilde. Without disclosing the spirit authorship, she showed it to some theatrical managers. They all rejected it, one giving the reason that it was too much like Oscar Wilde!

Pearl tie-pin Case (Hester Dowden and Geraldine Cummins)

In December 1915, an Ouija board session was held with mediums Hester Dowden and Geraldine Cummins. The note-taker was the Reverend Savill Hicks, a Presbyterian minister of some renown. Also present, as an observer, was the prominent psychic investigator, Sir William Barrett[8] who recorded this event in his book *On the Threshold.* During the session, the name of a cousin of Cummins was unexpectedly given. Cummins knew he had been killed in battle a month before. When asked if he had any message, the reply was "Tell my mother to give my pearl tie-pin to the girl I was going to marry. I think she ought to have it."

When asked for the name and address of his fiancé, the communicator spelled out a full name (withheld for privacy purposes, but we are told it was an uncommon last name) and an address in London. And then the soldier said good-bye. No one at the session knew of an engagement or recognized the woman's name that was given. Communications with the deceased officer's family revealed that they knew nothing of any pearl tie-pin nor of any marriage plans and had never heard of such a woman. When the post office returned a letter written to the address given, the group assumed that the message was a subconscious fiction or dream and let the matter drop. But that, of course, is not the end of the story.

---

8. Sir William Barrett, a Professor of Physics at the Royal College of Science for Dublin, was a key founder of the Society for Psychical Research.

Six months later, in a chance conversation, it emerged that the officer had been engaged, shortly before he left for the front, to the lady whose name was given. This was verified when the War Office sent over the deceased officer's effects. Then it was discovered that the soldier had put the woman's name in his will, both first and last names being precisely the same as given through the board, and among the young man's meagre possessions was found a pearl tie-pin. (retold in Conan Doyle's *History of Spiritualism, vol ii 240*)

Housewife writes in an archaic Anglo-Saxon language (Pearl Leonore Curran)

Pearl Curran was a St Louis housewife who was persuaded by a friend, Emily Hutchinson, to use an Ouija board. On 8th July 1913, the board started spelling out a message which began "Many moons ago I lived. Again I come; Patience Worth my name." Patience identified herself as a seventeenth century Englishwoman and, through the mediumship of Pearl Curran, progressed from the Ouija board to automatic writing, eventually producing seven books, some short stories, several plays, 2,500 poems, and countless epigrams and aphorisms – in short more than four million words. Patience Worth would be acclaimed a literary genius. Her works were compared with Shakespeare, Chaucer, and Spenser. In a compilation of America's best poetry of 1917 five of Patience Worth's creations appeared alongside fewer compositions each by other acclaimed poets such as Amy Lowell, Vachel Lindsay and Edgar Lee Masters.

In the beginning, Pearl spelled out every letter with the Ouija board, but as time passed, the mere touch of her hand on the pointer loosed a flood of spoken words. The pointer would fly around the board and Pearl would call out words at the rate of 1,500 or so an hour. When she abandoned the board entirely, a feeling of slight pressure in her head would announce Patience's arrival and Pearl would begin writing.

As she did, she behaved normally, with her eyes open and her senses alert to the faces and noises around her. A visitor recalled "Sometimes, she looks over to a guest while writing and asks some question entirely foreign to what she is spelling out; again answers the telephone or inquires what the message was; exchanges a few words of greeting to late visitors as they enter and goes on with the work without a moment's hesitation." Occasionally, she'd even smoke a cigarette.

In the section titled 'Songs of Patience Worth' on the Patience Worth website it says: "Those who believe that Pearl Curran wrote from her subconscious mind, need to remember that all the writing of Patience Worth was given sometimes letter by letter or word by word as fast as it could be written down by the stenographer. There was no hesitation, no fumbling for the perfect word, no writing and rewriting, no re-arranging lines as is often done by poets as their subconscious mind provides them with thoughts to write down. It is as if the poem had already been composed and Patience Worth (via Pearl Curran) was just reciting it for her listeners."

Michael Tymn in his article, *"The Medium behind Patience Worth"* writes:

> Curran's limited education and travel were totally inconsistent with theories of conscious fraud or subconscious memories. English scholars struggled with some of the archaic Anglo-Saxon language. In one of her novels, Patience dictated "I wot he fetcheth in daub-smeared smock." Even in the early 1900s, the word 'fetch' was rarely used, but when used it meant to 'go and get' someone or something. Patience used it as synonymous with 'came' or 'cometh', which philologists confirmed as the word's original meaning.
>
> W. T. Allison, Professor of English Literature, observed that Patience Worth dictated words found only in ancient times and some of them had no meaning until researched in dialectic dictionaries and old books. Allison, who closely observed Curran, reported that in one evening fifteen poems were produced in seventy-five minutes, an average of five minutes for each poem. "All were poured out with a speed that Tennyson or Browning could never have hoped to equal, and some of the fifteen lyrics are so good that either of those great poets might be proud to have written them," Allison offered. He went on to say that Patience Worth 'must be regarded as the outstanding phenomenon of our age, and I cannot help thinking of all time'.

Patience's most celebrated work, *The Sorry Tale,* a 644-page, 325,000 word novel about the last days of Jesus, was released in 1917. As journalist Casper Yost, who was present when much of the book was dictated, explained, the story was begun without any previous knowledge on the part of Pearl Curran of the time and conditions of Palestine beyond what is revealed in the New Testament. Yet, the story goes far beyond what might be gleaned from the New Testament. "In one evening, 5,000 words were dictated, covering the account of the crucifixion," Yost reported.

In its review of the book, *The National* wondered how the mysterious story-teller became familiar with the scent and sound and colour and innumerable properties of Oriental market places and wildernesses, of Roman palaces and halls of justice. *The New York Globe* stated that it exceeded *Ben Hur* and *Quo Vadis* as 'a quaint, realistic narrative'. The *Columbus (Ohio) Dispatch* opined that no other book gives one so clear a view of customs, manners, and character of the peoples of the time and place.

None of this information was known to Pearl Curran.

Automatist aids in archaeological excavations (John Allan Bartlett)

Dave Howard in his article *Automatic Writing Champions* on the spiritcommunion website believes that one of the most novel uses of automatic writing was during excavation of the buildings at Glastonbury Abbey in the south-west of England. An architect, Frederick Bligh Bond, was hired by the Church of England in 1908 to supervise archaeological investigations of the ancient abbey and he remained in that capacity until 1921. Throughout the project, Bond consulted an automatic writing medium, Captain John Allan Bartlett, who wrote down detailed instructions and maps allegedly dictated by deceased Glastonbury monks. Bond even recorded that he usually read out loud unrelated literature to Bartlett while the automatic writing was in process in order to make certain that the medium's conscious mind was occupied with things other than what was being written by his hand. Messages, written in Middle English,

Low Latin and modern English, often had to be deciphered or translated but they were always on target which resulted in amazing finds at the site.

Bond recorded the experience in his book, *The Gate of Remembrance* (available on the Internet). Another Bond book which reveals even more about Glastonbury and automatic writing predictions of World War I is *The Hill of Vision* (also online).

Automatic writing with simultaneous trance speaking (Leonora Piper)

Leonora Piper was among the most tested and studied mediums in history. Most of her mediumship consisted of trance sittings which were recorded and studied. Autonmatic writing developed as a facet of her trance sittings. She developed the ability to have two, and sometimes three, different spirits communicating through her at the same time. Dr Richard Hodgson of the Society for Psychical Research (SPR), stated in a report that he had many times witnessed a spirit communicator speaking through Mrs Piper (in a state of trance) while at the same time her hand was writing a message about a totally different subject to himself. Nandor Fodor writes that Hodgson also tells of a sitting, when a lady sitter was engaged in a very personal conversation with Phinuit concerning her relations:

> ... the hand [of Mrs Piper] was seized very quietly and, as it were, surreptitiously, and wrote a very personal communication to myself purporting to come from a deceased friend of mine and having no relation whatsoever to the sitter; precisely as if a caller should enter a room where two strangers to him were conversing, but a friend of his is also present and whispers a special message into the ear of the friend without disturbing the conversation.

On one occasion, both of Piper's hands were writing and a voice was speaking through her – apparently three spirits communicating at the same time. This occurred on 18th March 1895, in a sitting with Miss Edmunds. Dr Hodgson's deceased sister wrote with one hand and George Pelham with the other, while Phinuit was talking, all simultaneously on different subjects.

John Lamond, D.D. testified that he personally witnessed Leonora Piper writing upwards of 1714 words in seventy minutes which in itself he regarded as supernormal. This is a rate of twenty-four words per minute or a word every few seconds for more than one hour!

Fodor records: "In the respect of multiple communications Mrs Piper's case is not unique. Dr Underhill, in his story of the mediumship of Abby Warner, quotes affidavits and his own experience that Abby Warner often gave at her circles three separate communications at once, one with her right, another with her left hand and a third one through rapping. Robert Dale Owen testifies to the same versatility of Kate Fox.

Sir William Crookes confirms this in the following statement: "I have been with Miss Fox", he writes, "when she has been writing a message automatically to one person present, whilst a message to another person on another subject was being given alphabetically by means of raps and the whole time she was conversing freely with a third person on a subject totally different from either."[9]

Writing 4600 lines in 72 hours (Achsa W. Sprague)

Although better known for her trance addresses (see section on "Inspirational Trance Speaking"), for which she earned the nickname 'The Preaching Woman', American Achsa Sprague was also an automatic writer and could even paint blindfolded. She wrote 4,600 lines of her work, *The Poet and Other Poems*, in seventy-two hours and while lying on her back. She always thought herself under the control of divine and mystic energies.

On the Vermont History website we read that only a very small part of what she produced has been published in her books, *I Still Live:a Poem for the Times* and *The Poet and Other Poems*. Among her unpublished writings, which include essays, journals, and a play, is an autobiographical poem of 162 pages, which she composed in six days in such a nervous state that 'spinning-wheel, latches, and

9. Interesting experiments were initiated by Miss E. B. Gibbes (*Psychic Science,* July, 1931) concerning the simultaneous communication from the same spirit communicator through two different mediums. An entity who claimed to be the discarnate Myers, successfully sent messages through Miss Cummins and Mrs Dowden, and Miss Cummins and Mrs Leonard.

roosters were muffled for her peace of mind'. Via automatic writing, she also wrote a poetic play of seventy-five pages dealing with the Biblical story from Eden to Calvary. According to the December 1941 edition of the *Proceedings* of the Vermont Historical Society, her long *I Still Live, a Poem for the Times* is:

> ... a cry for freedom, a treatment of the contemporary scene, dedicated to hearts offering their lives at the shrine of liberty. It is a moving didactic piece in pentameter couplets. Written before the American Civil War, it extols the names of Washington, Adams, Jefferson, and Webster; it refers to civil war, to a house divided against itself, to the Union; it is an intense exhortation in behalf of emancipation in America, a vigorous denunciation of slavery and oppression.

Her versatility in subject matter and technique is shown in her collected poems, *The Poet and Other Poems*. The chief themes are nature, patriotism, and religion. Among the outstanding compositions, certain of a permanent place in our poetic literature, are *The Soldier's Shroud, The American Eagle, Wendell Phillips, Mountain, Emancipation in the District of Columbia, The Stoic Soul's Defiance* and *Shame on the Coward Souls*.

Many of her unpublished manuscripts are considered to be more superior works.

Writing in 28 Languages (Carlos Mirabelli)

On his website under *Evidence for the Afterlife* Victor Zammit writes that Carlos Mirabelli submitted himself to the *Academia de Estudos Psychicos "Cesar Lombroso"* for research experiments in trance speaking, automatic writing and physical phenomena. The report on his mediumship was published in 1926 and confirmed that his automatic writing included writing in twenty-eight languages, among them three dead languages, namely Latin, Chaldaic and Hieroglyphics. Many of the spirit controls who were writing through Mirabelli were well known international figures. Johan Huss impressed Mirabelli to write a treatise of nine pages on the independence of Czechoslovakia in twenty minutes, Camille

Flammarion inspired him to write about the inhabited planets, fourteen pages in 19 minutes in French; Muri Ka Ksi delivered five pages in twelve minutes on the Russo-Japanese war in Japanese; Moses wrote in Hebrew on slandering; Harun el Raschid made him write fifteen pages in Syrian, and an untranslatable writing of three pages came in hieroglyphics in thirty-two minutes.

458 published books with more than 50 million copies sold (Francisco de Paula Cândido 'Chico' Xavier)

Dave Howard writes on an internet blog;

> The all-time champion of automatic writing will have to be given to a man who never wrote a word of English and who is largely unknown in North America or Europe. Chico Xavier was a humble, slightly educated Brazilian who holds the record as being the second most prolific author in the Portuguese language and every word of it, he claimed, was dictated by spirit guides. His output was over 458 published books which have sold more than 50 million copies. Regrettably, few of Chico's works have been translated into English. Chico's books cover a wide range of literary fields from historical novels, poems, and religious teachings to philosophy and medicine. He took no payment for any of the books, donating all proceeds to charity which, in part, earned him a nomination in 1982 for the Nobel Peace Prize.

> "When I am writing automatically", he said, "I can see, hear and I have often registered the presence of the communicator without knowing anything about the subject matter on which he is writing." Indeed, most of what came through Xavier's pen was beyond his capability and understanding.

> Chico Xavier was a Spiritist, the philosophy and religion very similar to Spiritualism that emanates from the teachings of Frenchman Allan Kardec.

It is from Kardec's descriptions that we get the word *psicografia* or psychography. More is to be found about Xavier in Guy Leon Playfair's book *Chico Xavier, Medium of the Century.*

Book Tests

Book Tests

*The most exciting phrase to hear in science, the one that heralds
new discoveries, is not 'Eureka!' but 'That's funny ...'*

Isaac Asimov

According to Ray Buckland in his book, *The Spirit Book*, the idea
of book tests was started by Sir William Crookes, when he tried to
devise a way of ensuring that a medium working with a planchette
was not picking up any information through extrasensory perception.
Crookes asked the spirit if it could see the contents of the room and,
on getting an affirmative answer, he reached back to the table behind
him and picked up a copy of *The Times* that was lying there. Without
looking, he placed a finger haphazardly on the open page. He then
asked the spirit to give the word that was covered by his finger. In
this instance the spirit spelled out 'however'. Crookes found it to be
the correct word. This result was published in the *Quarterly Journal
of Science* for January 1874.

In some book tests, the spirit communicates through the medium
to give correct quotes from a book placed in a locked box, a book
selected haphazardly by a bookseller and wrapped with others, and
from a book sealed and given to a third party. Usually the book
selected is one that the spirit knew and enjoyed when alive. The spirit
is asked to give the passage from a particular randomly selected page
and paragraph of the book, found on a particular shelf of a bookcase
in the home of the sitter at the séance. Mediums through whom the
spirits were particularly accurate included William Stainton Moses
and William Eglinton.

The first plain book tests were said to have been recorded by
Stainton Moses. Under the direction of his control, 'Rector', in
automatic writing he wrote "Go to the book case and take the last
book but one on the second shelf, look at the last paragraph on page
94, and you will find this sentence..." The sentence was found as
indicated. The experiment was repeated a number of times.

William Eglinton worked differently and was particularly
successful in 'direct'-writing book-tests. Many of these cases are
described in John S. Farmer's *Twixt Two Worlds*. The page and line

were selected by tossing coins and reading the last numbers of the dates.

In *The Mediumship of Mrs Leonard(115)*, Suzy Smith states that book tests came to be used extensively by Feda and Mrs Leonard's other communicators who were in fact said to have originated it [this is in contradiction to Ray Buckland's previously shown account]. Regardless, Henry Sidgwick, in 'An examination of book tests obtained in sittings with Mrs Leonard', published in *Proceedings of the Society for Psychical Research* Spring Volume XXXI April 1921 wrote that a good book test would exclude ordinary telepathy from the sitter as an explanation and would make it extremely difficult to suppose that Feda [Mrs Leonard's main control] derives her information from any living human being.

Book tests combined with xenoglossis are described in Judge Ludwig Dahl's *We Are Here*, published in 1931. The Norwegian judge writes of the mediumship of his daughter, Ingeborg, and describes how her two (deceased) brothers 'were represented as going into another room and reading aloud passages from a book still on the shelves, the number of which was selected by one of the sitters – the medium successfully repeating or transmitting what they read in a foreign language and far beyond her comprehension'.

Related to book tests were 'newspaper tests' in which the communicator described an item which he said would appear in a subsequently published newspaper. According to Raymond Buckland, in *The Spirit Book*:

> Newspaper tests were experiments set up initially for testing the medium Gladys Osborne Leonard. They were recorded by the Reverend C. Drayton Thomas in his book, *Some Recent Evidence for Survival*. The purpose was to rule out telepathy as the explanation for apparent spirit communications. Many other psychic researchers have subsequently used similar tests. The method required the medium to ascertain, from spirit communication, the details of certain columns that would be published in *The Times* on the following day. The messages were received at a time of day before the newspaper had assembled its pages, therefore no one would know what words, or even which column, would appear on specific pages. The predictions

were given to the Society for Psychical Research by 6 pm on the same day the messages were received. In tests conducted on 13th February 1920, at 3:00 pm, of the twelve items that were given, only two were completely incorrect.

Enquiries at *The Times* revealed that at the time of the séance, in some cases the particular columns and wording referred to might have been set in type but the position in the paper, with regard to page and column placement had not been decided. In other cases, the type had not even been set.

'Bim', the beetle and the book test (Gladys Osbourne Leonard)

An excellent example of a simple Leonard book test is described in *The Earthen Vessel* by Pamela Glenconner. Edward Wyndham Tennant, known as 'Bim', a son of Lord and Lady Glenconner who fell in the Battle of the Somme, is the purporting communicator. At a Leonard sitting on 17th December 1917, Bim's brother, David Tennant, and his father were the sitters.

In the years before the war, Lord Glenconner's chief interest was forestry. Often in the course of family walks through the woods, he would gloomily say that the trees were being ruined by the beetle. Young Bim sometimes whispered to his mother at the start of a family walk "See if we can get through the wood without hearing about the beetle." Feda, MrsLeonard's control, gave a book test which she said was from Bim. "This book is particularly for his father," she said. "Underline that", he says. "It is the ninth book on the third shelf counting from left to right in the bookcase to the right of the door in the drawing room. Take the title, and turn to page 37."

When the father and son returned home and went to their bookshelf, they found that the ninth book on the third shelf was *Trees* by T. H. Kelman. On page 36, it read, quite at the bottom and running over to page 37 "Sometimes you will see curious marks in the wood; these are caused by a tunneling beetle, very injurious to trees." Needless to say, Mrs Leonard had never been in the Glenconner drawing room.

Colonel Beadon tells his wife about his grave (Gladys Osborne Leonard)

Suzy Smith, in *She talks to the dead: The Life of Gladys Osborne Leonard(81)* reports this complicated book test:

> On 29th September 1917, Mrs S. E. Beadon was the sitter and the communicator was her deceased husband, Colonel Beadon. Feda started off by announcing that in a square room there was a row of books running between the window and to the corner. "Counting from the right to left, remove the fifth book," she said. "On page 71, second paragraph or about in the middle of the page, will be found a message from him to you, not as beautiful as he would like to make it, but you will understand he wants to make the test as good as he can."

Feda then said that the message would bring out the following points for Mrs Beadon:

> It refers to a past condition.
> It also has an application to the present.
> It is an answer to a thought which was much in mind at one time but is not now – especially since you have known Feda.
> On the opposite page is a reference to fire.
> On the opposite page is a reference to light.
> On the opposite page is a reference to olden times.
> On the same page or opposite page or perhaps over the leaf is a very important word beginning with S.

"These last four", said Feda, "have nothing to do with the message but are just tests that you have the right page." The room referred to was found to be the dining room of Mrs Beadon's mother's house where she was then staying. Mrs Leonard had never been inside that house. The fifth book from the right was a volume of poems by Oliver Wendell Holmes, whose poetry Mrs Beadon had never read. The second paragraph on page 71 was T*he Pilgrim's Vision*. It is about early settlers in America – the 'past condition' of Item 1. It also had an application to the present, as suggested by Item 2, – for it applied to the communicator's own situation. The poem read as follows:

The weary pilgrim slumbers,
His resting place unknown,
His hands were crossed, his lids were closed,
The dust was o'er him strown.
The drifting soil, the mouldering leaf
Along the sod were blown,
His mound has melted into Earth
His memory lives alone.

Mrs Beadon's husband had been killed in action in Mesopotamia and was buried by the chaplain and officers that same night, near where he fell. He received reverent burial but his resting place was unknown. The officer in charge wrote to Mrs Beadon that all traces of the grave had been carefully obliterated to avoid desecration. After she received the news, Mrs Beadon was quite worried for a time because her husband was in an unmarked grave. She wondered constantly whether it would be possible later to identify the spot with the help of the officers who had been present at his burial, so that when the war was over his grave could be marked with a cross. This was obviously a reference to Item 3. Since she began to receive communication from her husband through Gladys, however, she had thought about that idea very little and had not felt as concerned as she did at first that his grave was unmarked and unknown. On the opposite page were Items 4, 5, and 6, the references to fire, light, and olden times, in the following verse:

Still shall the fiery pillar's ray
Along the pathway shine,
To light the chosen tribe that sought
This Western Palestine.

On the following page, there was the title of a poem, *The Steamboat*, fulfilling Item 7 – an important word beginning with S.

Spirit success 36%: Random physical choice 4.7% (Gladys Osbourne Leonard)

Nora Sidgwick, widow of the first President of the SPR, evaluated 532 items from Feda's book tests, with the aim of finding out how many hit the mark. She discovered that 92 could be classed as successful; 100 approximately successful; 204 complete failures; 40 nearly complete failures; 96 dubious. Putting the first two groups together, Mrs Sidgwick concluded that 36% of the tests were approximately successful.

Mrs Sidgwick also made a study of the element of chance in book tests: Was it possible that the apt phrases Feda and the communicators directed sitters to could be found by chance in any book? She chose at random page numbers and lines and then looked up these references in randomly selected books, seeking messages which might be considered applicable to her. She found that very few seemed suitable in any sense. I have found the same thing to be true. It is actually difficult to find any randomly selected phrase or sentence in a book that will make any sense at all in its application to you personally. Nora Sidgwick's experiments were too limited to base definite conclusions on, but as far as they went, they tended to show that chance is not a likely explanation of success in even simple book messages.

Taking Mrs Sidgwick's pioneer work as a model, the SPR conducted a group of similar tests on a larger scale. Under controlled conditions a number of people were asked to turn to specified locations in given books and to try to find messages which might apply to them personally. The results of the tests were then analyzed by Colonel C. E. Baddeley, whose report was published by the SPR. From 1,800 items, complete success was found in 34, partial or slight success in 85, complete, partial, and slight success in 138. All the rest were negative. The percentage of complete and partial success was 4.7%. Thus Mrs Sidgwick's analysis of the 532 items in the book tests conducted by Feda showed a percentage of complete or partial success very much greater than that obtained by the SPR random experiments – 36% versus 4.7%.

The maidservant shifted the books (Gladys Osbourne Leonard)

According to Nandor Fodor's *Encyclopedia of Psychic Science*, in the preface to *Some New Evidence for Human Survival* by the Rev. Drayton Thomas, Sir William Barrett writes the following communication from Frederic Myers to him through the mediumship of Mrs Leonard:

There were some books on the right-hand side of a room upstairs in your house in Devonshire Place. On the second shelf, four feet from the ground, in the fourth book counting from the left, at the top of page 78, are some words which you should take as direct answer from him (Myers) to so much of the work you have been doing since he passed over.

Asked if the name of the book could be given, the reply was, "No", but that whilst feeling the cover of the book he got a sense of 'progression'. "Two or three books from this test book are one or two books on matters in which Sir William used to be very interested, but not of late years. It is connected with studies of his youth."

Barrett remarked that Mrs Osbourne Leonard never visited his house. He had no idea what books were referred to, but on returning home found that in the exact position indicated, the test book was George Eliot's *Middlemarch*. On the first line at the top of page 78 were the words, "Ay, ay. I remember – you'll see I've remembered 'em all." which quotation was singularly appropriate, as much of his work since Mr Myers passed over has been concerned with the question of survival after death and whether the memories of friends on earth continued with the discarnate. But the most remarkable part of the test was yet to be discovered. In dusting the bookshelves the maidservant, unknown to Barrett, had replaced two of George Eliot's novels by two volumes of Dr Tyndall's books, viz., his *Heat* and *Sound*, which were found exactly in the position indicated. In his youth William Barrett was, for some years, assistant to Prof. Tyndall, and these books were written whilst he was with him.

His name, his wife's name and age in tomorrow's newspaper (Gladys Osbourne Leonard)

One of the simplest examples of a newspaper test was given on 19th December 1919. It was written down just after it was received at 3:10 pm and was verified in the *London Times* of the following day. The Rev. Drayton Thomas said "Having been directed to the first page and rather more than one-third down column three, I was asked to look to the left where, almost in a line with that spot, would appear my name and a little above it that of my wife. And within an inch of those names I was to see my wife's age." On examining that part of the *Times* the next day, Thomas saw his first name, Charles, and his wife's name, Clara, within one inch of one another. Just one and five-eighths inches above their names was the number fifty-one, Clara's age until her birthday a week before.

Cross-correspondence Tests

Cross-correspondence Tests

*The existence of a spiritual world will have to be recognized not
as a matter of faith, but as a branch of the organized system
of knowledge that we call science.*

Sir Oliver Lodge

Cross-correspondence, also known as 'concordant automatism',
was first used in 1876 by Alice Johnson, Research Officer of the
Society for Psychical Research (SPR). According to Nandor Fodor
in his *Encyclopedia of Psychic Science*:

> Miss Alice Johnson is said to have first discovered it through
> the messages received through various mediums about the
> same time, in places as far apart as India, New York, and
> London. In the scripts of mediums Mrs Rosina Thompson,
> Mrs Forbes, Mrs Margaret Verrall, Mrs Winifred Willett
> (pseudonym of Winifred Coombe-Tennant), Mrs Leonora
> Piper, Mrs Holland (pseudonym of Alice Fleming) and others,
> she found fragmentary utterances which had no particular point
> or meaning but were found to be supplementing each other
> when selected and put together, giving, in each instance, a
> coherent idea. "Thus, in one case", writes Miss Johnson, "Mrs
> Forbes' script, purporting to come from her son, Talbot, stated
> that he must now leave her, since he was looking for a sensitive
> who wrote automatically, in order that he might obtain
> corroboration of her own writing. Mrs Verrall, on the same
> day, wrote of a fir-tree planted in a garden, and the script was
> signed with a sword and a suspended bugle. The latter was part
> of the badge of the regiment to which Talbot Forbes had
> belonged, and Mrs Forbes had in her garden some fir-trees,
> grown from seed sent to her by her son. These facts were
> unknown to Mrs Verrall."

Miss Johnson's conclusions were "We have reason to believe that
the idea of making a statement in one script complementary to a
statement in another had not occurred to Mr Frederic W. H. Myers
in his lifetime – for there is no reference to it in any of his written

utterances on the subject that I have been able to discover. Neither did those who have been investigating automatic script since his death invent this plan, if plan it be. It was not the automatists themselves that detected it, but a student of their scripts; it has every appearance of being an element imported from outside; it suggests an independent invention, an active intelligence constantly at work in the present, not a mere echo or remnant of individualities of the past."

The spirit of then-deceased Frederic W. H. Myers suggested that cross-correspondence was originated by spirit to demonstrate that there was no human telepathy at play. Hundreds of pages of the SPR Proceedings were devoted to the subject and aroused great controversy. Cross-correspondence groups were formed as far apart as New York, London, and Bombay. Paul Beard, President of the SPR for sixteen years, wrote in *Living On: A study of altering consciousness after death* that cross-correspondence tests form the best sustained and carefully recorded evidence we have of survival and continuing purpose after death.

Ray Buckland writes in *The Spirit Book*:

A cross-correspondence occurs when spirit communication received through one medium is connected to communication received through another, different, medium or mediums. The two or more mediums are usually located at some considerable distance apart and frequently unaware of the connecting message(s).

Buckland continues by stating that discovering a connecting message can involve a great deal of research on the part of a co-ordinator who has to sift through all of the received information and has to be able to recognize the connections between the messages. For example, two separate mediums or groups of mediums ('A' and 'B') might be used with an unbiased coordinator. Each group starts by advising its particular spirit contact of what they wish to do. This may be done in the following fashion:

Spokesperson "We want to do a cross-correspondence with our other group. They are meeting at 115 Main Street, tomorrow night at 9:00 pm. During our sitting here tonight please start a message that you will continue with them." Somewhere within the material that each group receives will be part of a message, though it may not be obvious. On the face of it there will be nothing unusual; the particular message may blend in with whatever else is received. Each group sends the records of its sitting to the coordinator who should be an intelligent, fairly learned person. The coordinator's job is to search through both sets of material and find a total message.

Here is an example of such a cross-correspondence. Among the many pages of Group A's material might be:

"What sort of place are you in now?"

IT IS VERY PLEASANT, AS THOUGH THE WINTER IS PAST, THE RAIN IS OVER AND GONE, AND EVERYTHING IS NICE AND FRESH AGAIN. ALMOST A REBIRTH.

Group B's material might include:

"Was there anything you knew on this level that you miss?"

NO.

"Can everything be experienced where you are, then?"

YES.

"The different seasons?"

YES. EVEN WHEN THE FLOWERS APPEAR ON THE EARTH, THE TIME OF THE SINGING OF BIRDS, GAMBOLING OF LAMBS—EVERYTHING REALLY.

The coordinator may then recognize the whole phrase as a quotation from *The Bible, The Song of Solomon* (ii. 11-12) "For lo, the winter is past, the rain is over and gone; the flowers appear on the earth; the time of the singing of birds is come, and the voice of the turtle is heard in our land."

The first part was received by Group A and the second part by Group B. Such a cross-correspondence could be continued for a number of sessions. The main point is that neither group/medium would see the other's notes and neither know what quotation to expect.

In actual practice though, according to Troy Taylor (see www.prairieghosts.com,) there are three types of cross-correspondences: simple, complex and ideal. In simple correspondences, two or more mediums produced the same word, words, phrases or similar phrases that were connected or related. In complex cross-correspondences, messages are indirect and must be deciphered. Ideal correspondences involved messages that were incomplete and which had to be put together like a puzzle. The mediums can be organized to be engaged in sittings at the same time, but in separate locations from one another.

Dog Watch (Mina 'Margery' Crandon and Sary Litzelman)

Hannen Swaffer writes in *My Greatest Story(211)* :

> Then, next night, for another test, Wendell Murray arranged that at nine o'clock he should sit at Revere Beach, his country home, that Sary Litzelman should sit at Cambridge and that a small Margery group should sit at the Crandon's home. Murray was to choose a phrase which was to be transmitted by Walter to Sary and also to Margery. Well, on the afternoon of the second sitting, Margery, Button, Mrs Mabel Kellerby and I drove over to Cambridge, where live Sary Litzelman and her husband, who is in the book business. Sary developed, nine or ten years before, the power of mirror writing. She sits and talks to you and, while she sits, writes very rapidly backwards.
>
> "Let's ask Walter about Murray's test tonight," said somebody. Immediately Sary began to write, her hand moving from right to left. She covered several sheets. Then, when we held it up to a mirror, this is what we read "In regard to the sitting tonight, he says that it will be a very good thing to try Wendell's test, making it as uncomplicated as possible. He suggests that you choose your own committee. We will do the best possible. I would like to tell Mabel that she should develop the gift which has been given to her. Let her try writing. There is much power there."
>
> Soon after, I called up Wendell Murray and suggested he should sit with a small committee in his home, which is miles from the Crandons, and choose something definite. "General ideas", I said, "are hard to get. Choose some definite words." Well, soon after we started sitting at the Crandons, Walter, speaking in the direct voice, said with a laugh "I am going to be different. I am going to say, 'Here am I'." When, downstairs, Margery, as she often did after sitting, did automatic writing. She wrote "Mr Murray will say 'I am here.' I say 'Here am I.'

God only knows what Sary will write. You may call her."

We called up Sary, who said the message she had got from Charles, her guide was 'I am here.' When we called up Wendell Murray, he told us his test had been "I'll be here." Now, if Walter had given the words, "I'll be here." as no doubt, Murray expected, someone might have said, "Margery merely read Murray's mind." By twisting it into a joke, he gave evidence of a mind working behind the test.

Tests of this kind, trivial as they may seem, are the ones demanded by sitters. On one occasion, for instance, naval officers at the Boston Naval yard took part in a similar test. Sary, at home, could not understand, but all she could do was to go to a drawer in which there were half-a-dozen wrist watches. "All I get is watch." she said. At the Crandons', where they had been washing a dog, Margery merely said, "dog, dog, dog." and then adding, "Give me your pen." wrote down the word 'dog'. "It's a washout," said Button, who was there. But, the next day, the Navy Yard called up to say that their test had been 'dog watch'.

Water Melon ('Margery' Crandon and Sary Litzelman)

In *Power of the Spirit(134),* Maurice Barbanell writes:

When I was in the USA and staying with the Crandons, Walter suggested at an impromptu séance that we should have a test of cross-correspondence. He asked a sitter, Captain John W. Fife, head of Boston's naval dockyard, to select six people who were to choose a word or object the next night at 7 pm. Walter would then try to give this word to Margery and Sary Litzelman, another Boston medium who obtained her results via automatic writing which was reversed so that it had to be held to a mirror before it could be read. Fife was starting the next morning on an automobile trip with his children. He knew he would be motoring through New Hampshire, but he did not know where he would be at 7 pm. But he promised to find a group to select the word and to sign a statement telling what they had done. Then Fife was to telephone French's Store at Royalston, about seventy miles from Boston, and give the word to them. The next morning, Margery, my wife, and William HButton, then president of the American Society for Psychical research, left for Margery's country place, a collection of cabins in the forest, about a mile from Royalston. Sary Litzelman and her husband were staying there. There was no telephone at this forest home. For that reason, French's Store was chosen, it being the nearest place with a telephone. I called and saw the manager, a man named Wilcox, and told him to take down any message he received soon after 7 pm and I would collect it.

At 7:10 pm, Margery sat in one cabin and Sary in another. In the presence of Button, her Japanese servant and myself, Margery wrote, 'Water Melon'. Sary, in the presence of my wife, wrote the same words! While she was writing, the Japanese servant was playing with Margery's dog, making him growl. The medium told him to stop, but the distraction made no apparent difference to her writing. I went by car to French's Store and collected from Wilcox the message he had received a few minutes earlier. He handed me a sealed envelope. Inside it I found the words 'Water Melon' on a slip of paper. All those who participated gave their signed testimony.

'No one stops to kick a dead horse' ('Margery' Crandon, George Valiantine, Dr Hardwicke, and Sarah Litzelmann)

According to Nandor Fodor in his *Encyclopedia of Psychic Science*,

> The most recent and most baffling cases of cross-correspondences were recorded in the history of Margery Crandon's mediumship. They were instigated by her control, Walter, and they have been given simultaneously through Margery in Boston, George Valiantine in New York, Dr Hardwicke at Niagara Falls and Mrs Sarah Litzelmann of Maine, about 60 miles from Boston. Drawings, geometrical figures, sentences were given in part through each medium, in some cases in Chinese characters. Their reception was immediately verified by telephone or telegraph and the message deciphered by setting the piecemeal communications into a whole. The ingenuity of these cross-correspondences is

best illustrated by the following instance:

A cardboard box was brought into the séance room. It contained slips of paper with certain symbols, and a calendar, the sheets of which could be torn off a sheet at a time, and thus indicate a desired number. Walter declared that he had torn off a sheet and added "Margery will make up a problem and Valiantine and Hardwicke will each make half the answer." He then closed the box.

The sitter in whose charge it was given after the séance did not open it. Margery and the company descended to the library. There Margery passed into a light trance and wrote automatically "11 x 2 – to kick a dead." The box was now opened: they found in it, at the left the calendar, the top sheet of which showed the date of 11th, next to it an X from the enclosed symbols and lastly the torn off sheet which bore the number 2. The arrangement of the contents of the box, therefore, completely agreed with the part of the cross-correspondence Margery wrote.

New York was rung by telephone. Judge Cannon who was in charge of the Valiantine circle reported that they received from Walter the following message "2–no one stops." Next morning a telegram from Hardwicke from Niagara Falls, announced this fragment "2 horse."

The fragments put together show that the problem Walter worked out was this: "11 x 2 = 22. No one stops to kick a dead horse."

The case of Raymond (Gladys Osborne Leonard and Alfred Vout Peters)

The case of Raymond is an excellent example of cross-correspondence because different information came from separate mediums who had no interaction between them. Amongst the evidence was description of a photograph of Raymond and descriptions of Raymond's activities and nicknames. Most of the evidence was not in the memory of the sitters and none of it was known to the mediums. A complete account is under "Trance Sittings".

The Palm Sunday Case (Margaret Verrall, Alice Fleming, Helen Verrall, Winifred (Coombe-Tennant) Willett, and Leonora Piper)

This case spanned more than 30 years and takes its name from the death of the communicator, Mary Lyttleton. She fell in love with Arthur Balfour, but became ill and died on 21st March 1875 (Palm Sunday) before they could marry. At first, Margaret Verrall began receiving communications. They were veiled in symbolic references and laced with Latin and Greek terms and classical material. All of the communications were fragmentary and filled with obscure and classical references. None of the mediums knew the story of the Balfour-Lyttleton romance that had been cut short by death. All of the messages that came through though seemed to be directed at Arthur Balfour. Many of the symbolic references had personal meaning only to him and concerned Lyttleton and the circumstances surrounding her death.

It became clear that the purpose behind all of the communications were her efforts to reach Balfour and to tell him how much she loved him. Balfour at first refused to believe it. By the time he was sixty-four years-old and thirty-seven years had passed since Mary had died, he finally agreed to sit with Mrs Willett while she tried to receive messages. The information that came was cryptic but started to make more sense. Then trance sessions became the focus of the case although Helen Verrall and Margaret Verrall continued to receive messages via automatic writing until Margaret's death in 1916. As the years passed, Balfour eventually accepted the idea that Mary was still communicating with him. During one sitting in 1926, the apparition of a young woman appeared to him. She communicated to Balfour that he was never alone, that her spirit was always with him and that she was 'absolutely alive, and herself and unchanged' on the other side.

In October 1929, six months before Balfour died, Mary communicated that she was finished with trying to provide evidence of after-death survival and was now only interested in the companionship of Balfour. In all, Mary had devoted thirty years to takencommunicating with Balfour. *(from Troy Taylor's article on www.prairieghosts.com)*

Cross-correspondence in Chinese ('Margery' Crandon and Dr Henry Hardwicke)

Fodor (1934) reports that during a séance on 22nd March 1928 with medium Margery Crandon, two columns of Chinese were written in total darkness, on specially marked paper. Walter, Margery's control, announced that he would try a Chinese-English cross-correspondence with Dr Henry Hardwicke, of Niagara Falls, a distance of 450 miles from Boston. He asked a witness, Malcolm Bird, to pick out a sentence which should be given through Hardwicke in Chinese. Malcolm Bird chose, 'A rolling stone gathers no moss.' The response from Niagara Falls was Dr Henry Hardwicke's script. It showed a Maltese cross within the circle, a rectangle enclosing the name Kung-fu-tze, the symbols for Bird and Hill, and the Chinese sentence, the general meaning of which is, 'A travelling agitator gathers no gold.' Johnson's analysis revealed a further important element. On the left hand column the words are found "I am not dead, Confucius." An exact of this was in the right hand column of an earlier Margery script.

Besides Dr Hardwicke, cross-correspondences were given in Chinese through Mrs Sarah Litzelmann, who knows no Chinese either and sat at Ogunquit, Maine, a distance of eighty miles from Boston and the mediums. Drawings, geometrical figures, and sentences were given in part through each medium, in some cases they were also given in Chinese characters. Their reception was immediately verified by telephone or telegraph and the message deciphered by joining the pieces into a whole.

Direct Voice

Direct Voice

I have been boxed up, tied up, sealed up, gagged, bound and held, and still the voices have come to speak their message of life eternal.

Leslie Flint

Direct voice communication is perhaps the most convincing evidence of survival after death but it is a rare occurrence in physical mediumship. However, it is one of the most widely tested forms of communication as, Nandor Fodor reports in his *Encyclopedia of Psychic Science*:

> The medium was often asked to hold water in her mouth to see whether the voices are independent. With Mrs Emily French, of Buffalo, the voices were tested in exacting conditions, by Prof. Hyslop, Dr Isaac Funk and others for a full week. Findlay records how often he had his [toy] car at [medium John] Sloan's mouth when one or more voices were speaking and no sound came from it. In other experiments a special solution was used which, under the effect of the saliva, changes colour in proportion to the time during which it is held in the mouth. If one of the sitters also takes an amount into his mouth and ejects it at the same time the colour should be identical. It was by this test that Dr Abraham Wallace contended to have established the good faith of Susannah Harris.

In his book *No, Not Dead; They Live* Dr Wilson G. Bailey gave this testimony,

> I filled her mouth with water and then with salt, and still the voice came through without interruption or impediment and I also punctured her arm when in trance and although I drew blood she did not feel any pain.

Some direct voice mediums require no trance or darkness at all. It is reported that during an operation on Eileen Garrett in 1931, whilst she was unconscious and gagged, the doctors in attendance heard voices in her proximity. One voice spoke fluently in a tongue which none of the doctors understood.

Voices speak through a voice-box constructed of ectoplasm, a substance taken from the medium's body or through a megaphone known as a trumpet[1]. The trumpets when used for this type of communication are mainly a tin or aluminum conical shaped object open at both ends. The trumpet is usually placed in the centre of the circle of people present, when the atmosphere is right for spirit they will sometimes make the trumpet float in the air and make it fly around the room stopping at a person they may want to speak to.

The voices heard in a direct voice séance can come from any part of the room and may be human whether man, woman, child, old, young, in any language or accent or even of the animal kingdom. In a London séance, with Etta Wriedt, Lieut. Col. E. R. Johnson heard the barking of three dogs. Dennis H. Bradley in *The Wisdom of the Gods* speaks of a direct voice séance in which very loud and distinct barks were heard and then there came back an answering bark of his Alsatian wolfhound in an outhouse some distance away from the room in which the séance was being held.

Maurice Barbanell reports in *Spiritualism Today(29)* that he heard the sound of a kiss through the trumpet as a spirit communicator expressed their affection to a sitter.

If a trumpet is not used, voices can be heard by a replica of a larynx which must be constructed. Red Cloud described it thus – the larynx is formed of ectoplasm (drawn partly from the sitters but largely from the medium) acting on psychic rods of power, the whole delicately pitched to the mental vibrations of the medium. It is said the larynx when constructed is surrounded by walls of light.

In Estelle Roberts' book we also learn that a successful demonstration of direct voice is as much dependent on the spirit communicator as on the medium. He must know precisely the message he wants to convey. Estelle Roberts' guide, Red Cloud, said it was not unusual to rehearse the hesitant ones to be able to transmit their messages with clarity. The communicator must be allowed to deliver his message without interruption. Here the circle members play an important part. They must be sympathetic and receptive. Any attempt by one of the sitters to project his own ideas at such a moment will defeat the object of the séance because strong thoughts

1. According to Nandor Fodor, in his *Encyclopedia of Psychic Science,* it was spirit John King to whom we owe the invention of the trumpet.

impose barriers which the communicator cannot break down. It is easy to harass and confuse a communicator by posing a question for which he has not come prepared with the answer.

Yossel/Yosha (Mrs E. Roberts Johnson)

In *Power of the Spirit(62)*, Barbanell writes:

I was invited to bring a party of friends and selected a group of young Jews, who had their doubts about Spiritualism. It was suggested, in the early part of the séance, that if Hebrew hymns were sung, these might create favorable conditions to attract Jews who have passed on. My friends hummed three Jewish airs. Two of them were often sung in synagogues. The third is regarded as the Jewish national anthem. My friends did not know, except for a few fragments, the words of these compositions. Yet through the trumpet there were heard voices which accompanied them, and in each case they sang every word! It sounded as if a fully-trained choir was present, one which was accustomed to singing these age-old tunes.

The luminous trumpet moved over to a friend seated near me and a spirit voice addressed him. My friend answered and a lengthy communication followed. While this happened, I engaged Mrs Johnson, who was in the chair next to me, in conversation. Several times, I heard her voice and the spirit speaking through the trumpet simultaneously.

The spirit communicator, claiming to be the uncle of my friend, gave his name in Yiddish as Yossel – the equivalent of Joseph. There were several outstanding facts in this communication. The spirit reproduced his earthly voice. Its distinguishing characteristics were easily recognised by my friend. His uncle had been a cantor in a synagogue and the intonation was typical of his profession.

The communicator displayed an intimate knowledge of his nephew's domestic surroundings. He referred to the fact that my friend's mother, the uncle's sister, was at that time in hospital and the doctors had broached the subject of an operation. They wanted the family to give their consent. The suggested operation was a most difficult one, for they were told its chances of success were one in a thousand. Yet, if the woman were not operated on, she could not be expected to live for long.

The dead uncle advised his sister to have the operation, which he said, would be successful. On the strength of the spirit assurance, my friend told his mother the next morning what was said at the séance. He broached the subject gingerly, for she was not favorably disposed towards Spiritualism. She, in turn, related her previous night's dream, in which this same brother had appeared to her and advised in favour of the operation.

The family was called in for consultation, and after hearing the story of the séance and the dream, gave their sanction. Arrangements were made for the delicate operation to take place. The family eagerly awaited the result. There was a long crisis, but eventually the mother pulled through – 'as if by a miracle', the hospital authorities said. The spirit forecast was correct.

Here, you would say, was a water-tight case for survival and for spirit prophesy. But there was one flaw. Though the communicator's name was Yossel, the family always called him by his nickname of Yosha. This would be the equivalent to a man named Joseph being called Joe.

"It seems strange to me", said the nephew, "that my uncle should not have given his name by which the family always knew him."

"Perhaps, in his eagerness to get the message through", I replied, "it escaped his memory." "That may be so", I was told, "but it is the only flaw in an otherwise perfect case."

A few days later, there was a dramatic sequel. Once again, I took a party of friends to another Mrs Robert Johnson séance. The nephew was included. About half-way through the sitting, the trumpet moved close to him. The same voice of his uncle spoke once more. On this occasion, however, there was no greeting, and there was no sustained conversation. Instead, the spirit merely said five times "Yosha-Yosha-Yosha-Yosha-Yosha." The trumpet then moved away. The communicator had returned to correct his mistake.

Séance of the Century (William Cartheuser)

According to the records of the American Society for Psychical Research, the books *The Margery Mediumship, The Invisible World,* and *The Traits of Truth,* a direct voice séance held on April 23, 1933 was termed the 'Séance of the Century'. The medium was William Cartheuser who was known to have a severe speech defect because of a harelip and cleft palate. Although he was difficult to understand during normal conversation, the spirit voices which spoke at his séances were free of impediments. This séance was held in a recording studio at the World Broadcasting Company (WBC) (later Decca Records) in New York. Sound engineers recorded nine long playing records of this séance with many examples of direct voice phenomena in this two-and-a-quarter hour séance.

This account of the séance has been posted by George Cranley on his website Zerdini's World:

J. Gay Stevens, a member of the American Society for Psychical Research's(ASPR) investigative team, together with his colleagues, Dr Hereward Carrington, a lifelong psychic researcher, Helen T. Bigelow, the society's secretary, Chester Grady, Louis Anspacher and the organizer, Dr Frank Black, met at the studios situated at 50 West 57th Street, New York. The séance was instigated by Dr Black, a leading musical show producer and part owner of the WBC. He suggested to the ASPR that it should supervise the recording of a voice séance in his studios and the resultant recordings would be donated to the society for reference and study.

The sound engineers, who were extremely skeptical, took care of the test conditions intent on unmasking the voice makers. To a man they were certain there was no such thing as a spirit voice and regarded this as a heaven-sent opportunity to prove it in their own studio under their own recording conditions.

At this time the Western Electric Company was, installing some of the latest sound equipment into the World studios. Hearing of the séance project they joined their World colleagues, making probably 'the most formidable array of sound engineering talent ever organized to debunk a spirit voice'.

The studio itself was a large 40-foot long, windowless room. It was soundproof and two storeys high. Seats for the sitters were arranged around the stand microphone – 'mike one'. Two additional microphones, (mikes two and three), hung close to the ceiling in diagonally opposite corners. All voices spoken in the circle would be recorded on mike one. The ceiling equipment had such a short range of sensitivity that it would not record voices from the studio floor. Pointing to the control room, curtained off to keep out the light, a technician indicated a recessed loudspeaker through which the engineers could communicate with those in the studio.

A man was stationed at the only exit door to see that no one entered or left during the séance. Stevens comments "We had no way of knowing that the engineers, after a week or so of conferring, had hit on a very simple plan that covered all possibilities.They concluded that, no matter what tricks the 'voice-maker' used, he had to work on the floor. If the sounds were authentic spirit voices then they need have no such limitation in space."

The ceiling mikes were 20 feet from the sitters and 20 feet in the air. All extra furniture had been moved out of the studio to prevent anyone standing on it in an attempt to speak into the mikes. In order for either mikes two or three to pick up a voice the speaker had to be within twelve inches. Both were highly directional – they had to be spoken into head-on and not from an angle. To make things more difficult, the engineers had turned the microphones at right angles to the circle of sitters. Each mike had its own line of communication with the control room. The technicians knew which mike was bringing in each voice by listening to the three independent loudspeakers and watching the dial connected to each line. The sitters were unaware what the engineers had planned and proceeded with a normal direct voice séance.

Eventually a trumpet, ringed with luminous paint, lifted into the air. It circled the sitters and tapped each one lightly on the head in greeting. Soon voices built up through the trumpet. Communicators identified themselves – and were recognized – as the sitters' 'dead' relatives and friends. Occasionally they asked the spirit voices to speak into mike one, but says Stevens, it never occurred to them to suggest they talk into the other microphones. The séance was interrupted by a voice over the control room loudspeaker. "Are these what you call spirit voices?" asked a cynical engineer. The trumpet fell to the floor. Several minutes of oppressive silence followed.

Suddenly a man's resonant voice "seemed to pop out of space in front of us, directly above mike one," writes Stevens. They could still see the phosphorescent ring of the trumpet on the floor. This was independent voice. In a brisk business-like manner, the spirit communicator expressed interest in the experiment. The sitters asked what he meant. He said he was referring to the engineers' conditions. "We think they have worked out a very interesting testing procedure for us on their equipment." A voice from the control room asked who was speaking. The communicator moved in close to mike one and said he was an engineer in the spirit world. Together with a couple of colleagues, he told the earthly technicians he would like to collaborate in making the important recording.

He added "We have a definite plan in mind for your tests. We are perfectly willing to meet any conditions you set up, or make any demonstration you have in mind ... if it is within our power. Just let us know what you would like to have me do." The control room voice asked "Do you think you could speak to us over one of those microphones located up at the ceiling?" Immediately, the engineer heard the communicator say "How's this?" It came from mike two on the ceiling! The spirit engineer added "Does it any difference to you which microphone I use up here?" The shocked control room operators listened in amazed silence. "Is this all right?" asked the eager communicator once more. "Yes ... yes, that's fine," the engineer replied. "Would you mind lowering your voice a little? We have no volume control on that line." The spirit voice apologized at a normal level. The control room asked if he could now speak from mike three on the other side of the room. Before the request was even completed, the communicator's voice came over on the other ceiling microphone.

As before, it was answering from within inches of the mike. It had travelled across the room in a matter of a second. The puzzled sitters listened to this in silence. Then a voice asked the engineers if they were ready with their experiment. "It's all over as far as we're concerned," came the control room reply. They began to talk among themselves, but the spirit voice interrupted them. It was speaking at mike one, on the floor. The communicator politely suggested to the technicians that if they had finished their tests, "We have a demonstration or two we would like to show you." Without waiting for an answer the voice explained he would make a complete circuit of the three microphones while speaking a short, simple sentence.

An engineer yelled "Go!" Speaking at normal conversational pace the voice said "I am now making a complete circuit of all three microphones and am now back at number one." The technicians followed the voice as it progressed around the loudspeakers. "As revealed later", says Stevens, "that voice had moved at such incredible speed between mikes it sounded as if it had been recorded on one mike." The communicator then introduced a colleague, a 'one-time research engineer in the science of sound'.

This new spirit speaker said evidence had been given that the communicators were not earthly but that they were 'surviving personalities speaking to you from another dimension'. He continued with an offer to show that spirit voices could give a sound performance beyond earthly scope. He explained that he was talking at the normal level for a male human being, around 300 cycles.

Then he asked the engineers to listen as he moved his voice slowly up the scale of sound frequencies in an unbroken flow. Stevens likened the achievement to the 'glissando of a musical instrument, from a resonant baritone to a bright tenor, to a soprano'. Through it all the spirit voice never stopped speaking. The communicator announced that his voice was now at the 1,100 cycle level, which was about the highest point the human voice can articulate. He then increased the cycle frequency until it was beyond the range of earthly hearing. As the pitch soared he gave the levels 3,000 and 5,000, with relevant remarks, until the only audible sound was similar to the twittering of a bird, though the words could still be understood.

Eventually his commentary became a thread of sound like 'an ncredibly distant radio signal'. The control room loudspeaker interrupted the silence. "We know that none of you could have done that," said an engineer. Repeating the test the communicator descended through the frequency cycles. His voice deepened to 'a bass-profundo and on down to the lowest reaches of an orchestral string bass'. He paused to explain that he was 100 cycles below where the human vocal chords can enunciate recognizable words. Continuing to speak clearly his voice slid further down the scale until it sounded like a 'giant mumbling at the bottom of a well'. It faded into a swishing sound, 'like the lowest note on the longest pipe in a giant organ'. Then it vanished. The silence was interrupted by the original spirit engineer's voice. He thanked the medium, sitters and recording staff for collaborating in the experiment and offered to co-operate in future tests.

The historic séance was over. A few days later Dr Frank Black delivered the records to the ASPR as promised. But Stevens ends with this comment "This séance and its records made little impression in official circles. Only the engineers in the control room were in a position to testify to the reality of the discarnate voices. But they, like so many others, were not about to go on record officially. So one of the technically best test cases for the reality of spirit voice phenomena went officially unconfirmed."

The return of Bessy Manning (Estelle Roberts)

During a séance with Estelle Roberts, the details of which were given by Maurice Barbanell in his book, *This is Spiritualism(54)*. Barbanell related how, halfway through the séance, Red Cloud, the guide of Estelle Roberts, advised him there was a girl who wished to communicate with regard to her mother. Barbanell asked whether he knew her, and Red Cloud simply replied "No, but you can help her."

The trumpet then moved towards Barbanell and he could hear a young girl speaking; aware that encouragement often assisted communicators, he asked her to talk to him. Whereupon she 'very slowly, but distinctly' said that her name was Bessy Manning, and she had died during the previous Easter from tuberculosis. She then added that Tommy, her brother, was with her; he had been killed in a road accident. She went on to explain that her mother, having read some of the accounts written by Barbanell, was praying that Red Cloud would bring her daughter to one of Estelle's séances.

Bessy then told Barbanell "Tell mother that I still have my two long plaits. I am twenty-two, and I have got blue eyes. Tell her I want her to come here. Could you bring her?" adding "She is poor." Barbanell assured Bessy that he would do his best and she thanked him and stressed how important it was, as her mother was very distressed having lost two of her children. Barbanell asked for the address where the mother could be contacted, and Bessy advised him this would be at '14 Canterbury Street, Blackburn'. He then discussed the matter with Red Cloud and it was clear that the mother was to be contacted and invited to the next séance.

Without delay or hesitation, in view of his absolute confidence in Red Cloud, Barbanell sent a telegram to a Mrs Manning at the address given saying 'Your daughter, Bessy, spoke to us at Red Cloud's circle last night'. There was, however, no reply to the telegram, and Barbanell therefore dispatched a further one. A few days later, Barbanell received two letters from Mrs Manning; the first expressing her absolute joy on having received the first telegram saying "I laughed and cried all at once," and that the telegram, telling her of Bessy's communication, was worth "more to me than untold gold." In the second letter, she apologized that Barbanell had needed to send a second telegram but she explained that she lacked the funds to reply by anything other than letter (in fact she had other children and her husband was unemployed). Once again, she expressed her joy and said the telegrams were beyond value. She further explained that Bessy had died the previous Easter and her son had been killed nine years earlier, and if she had not been helped by a Spiritualist family, "I would have gone raving mad." At this stage, Barbanell viewed Bessy's séance communication 'as flawless evidence for the after-life. No theories of telepathy or the subconscious mind can explain it away...Mrs Manning had never met Estelle Roberts, or corresponded with her or any member of her family'.

Barbanell arranged for Mrs Manning to travel to London and took her to where the séance was to be held. It was not long before Bessy was speaking with her mother, with the trumpet on one occasion falling to the ground with the excitement. After Bessy had told her mother that Tommy was with her, Mrs Manning asked whether she ever returned home. Bessy replied that she did and commented on how she saw her mother pick up her photograph and she would speak to, and kiss it. Barbanell reported that Mrs Manning later told him this was absolutely correct. Bessy continued by telling her mother that she had seen her talking with her father that same morning and referred to the subject of their conversation; this was followed by yet further evidence, all of which was correct.

Before Mrs Manning returned to Blackburn, Estelle Roberts gave her another sitting, when, once again, Bessy 'continued to prove her identity with detail after detail, none of which the medium could have known'. Only a matter of days later, Mrs Manning wrote to Barbanell thanking him for his involvement and supplying him with a statement that he could use: in this she detailed all that had occurred and confirmed that, "I heard my own daughter speak in me, in the same old loving way, and with the self-same peculiarities of speech. She spoke of incidents that I know for a positive fact no other person could know."

Barbanell added a note that after some years had elapsed, he attended another séance with Estelle Roberts and after Red Cloud announced that he had a visitor, Barbanell heard someone attempting to speak through the trumpet. After some encouragement, he heard "You helped me very much by enabling me to talk to my daughter." Barbanell recognized the communicator as Mrs Manning who continued by saying "I have got Bessy and Tommy here. Can you tell my family?" Barbanell wrote to the old Blackburn address but the letter was returned. However, he then received a letter from Mrs Smith, one of Mrs Manning's married daughters who had been told by someone about an article written by Barbanell regarding Mrs Manning's return. The daughter confirmed that her mother had suffered a seizure while alone, and by the time her children reached her, she was unable to speak before she died. The daughter said that her mother's passing was 'a cruel blow' but went on to express her joy on receiving news about her survival and successful communication.

Mystery of the buried crosses (Sophia Williams)

According to Michael Tymn, author of *The Articulate Dead*, an amateur American direct voice medium, Sophia Williams was involved in the famous 'Mystery of the buried crosses' case as reported by researcher Hamlin Garland in his 1939 book of that name. Garland reported that in 1934 he was given some 1,500 crosses and other artifacts allegedly unearthed by Gregory and Violet Parent between 1914 and 1924. He was told that Mrs Parent began communicating with 'dead souls' in 1914, just after she recovered from a serious illness. The communicating spirits directed her to buried treasures and artifacts all over southern and central California. They were said to be buried by North American Indians during the missionary period of California. He was informed that there were more crosses and artifacts to be found. Sometime around July 1937, Garland selected Williams, who did not charge for her services, to help him in his search. Unlike most direct-voice mediums, Williams did not require darkness and did not go into a trance. She would place the larger end of a megaphone against her breast while Garland would listen for voices at the smaller end and relay them to a stenographer. In his very first 'sitting' with Williams, Garland was greeted by one of his oldest friends, Henry B. Fuller, who had helped him research cases of mediumship when he was alive. Always on the lookout for fraud, Garland wondered if Williams had read of Fuller in one of his books. A few minutes later, another voice was heard. The spirit identified himself as Lorado, his wife's brother, who had died the prior year. Garland noted that Fuller called him by his last name, while Lorado addressed him by his first name, exactly as they had done when they were alive. He further noted that the voices, which were high in vibration, sometimes seemed to be coming from the megaphone and at other times from the air above the medium's head.

The most convincing evidence came when a voice addressed the stenographer, Gaylord Beaman. A voice was heard to say "Gay, this is Harry." When asked for a last name, 'Friedlander' was given. The astonished Beaman explained to Garland that Harry Friedlander was a friend who died in a plane crash in San Francisco Bay. The spirit then gave some details concerning the crash. Garland was certain that Williams knew nothing of Beaman and could not have researched this information beforehand. Two days later, the second sitting took place. Garland first heard a voice say "This is Turck, Dr Turck." Turck went on to tell Garland that he (Turck) was an 'old fool' for having called Garland's psychical research so much 'humbuggery' when he was alive. Here again, Garland concluded that the medium could have known nothing about Turck's attitude. When the voice changed, Garland asked the speaker to identify himself. "Doyle," the voice replied. It was Sir Arthur Conan Doyle, another psychical researcher known to Garland when he was alive. Doyle said that Sir William Crookes and Dr Gustave Geley, two more famous psychical researchers who had died, were there with him. They all spoke and said they were there to help Garland communicate with their side of the veil. Geley began speaking in French until Garland told him that he was not fluent in French. Geley then switched to English. Professor William James also spoke, but Garland was unable to understand what James was saying.

More spirits came, including one who identified himself as Harry Carr, another of Beaman's friends. Carr asked Beaman to contact his friend Lee Shippey to see if his manuscript might now be published. Here again, this was highly evidential as the names and information were well beyond the scope of research. At the direction of spirits who spoke through the medium's megaphone, Garland and Williams travelled hundreds of miles through southern and central California and Mexico searching for more artifacts. They discovered sixteen artifacts similar to those found by Gregory and Violet Parent. The spirits would tell them where to drive, where to walk, and then where to dig. Twelve of the sixteen artifacts are now on display at the West Salem Historical Society Museum in Wisconsin.

The séance in the garden (Mollie Perriman)

This outdoor séance in a garden in close proximity to a London road comes from *Broadcasting from Beyond(120)* written by the medium's husband:

> One of the more spectacular demonstrations of Mollie Perriman's mediumship was undoubtedly the occasion when a séance was conducted in a garden. As successful communications had taken place in both red and white light (sometimes as strong as 100 watts), a séance in a garden environment at dusk, seemed to be the next logical, and surely the most pleasant step for those seeking communication with their loved ones. In this instance, Mr Perriman together with three friends sat in the garden of one of the friends and he records how, 'we noticed that his wife, Mollie Perriman [the medium] appeared to be covered with some luminous substance...The voices spoke apparently from the air'. After the main control, Belle, had spoken, 'then came the father of one sitter. He gave very good evidence, mentioning family names

and telling of 'incidents which were at once recognised'. After other communicators made themselves known to those present, the conclusion of the sitters was that, 'the séance was remarkable, having regard to the close proximity of the garden to a main London road with its continual stream of motor traffic. During the séance, psychic lights flitted around our feet.'

The séance that saved a life (Mollie Perriman)

Sometimes sitters at séances are so bereaved they are contemplating suicide. Their loved ones in the spirit world know this and offer evidence and loving communication of encouragement, hope and love. From *Broadcasting from Beyond* (128) we read:

Illustrating that mediumship is not limited to only providing evidence of survival, medium Mollie Perriman was also able to prevent suicides by those who were grieving the passing of their loved ones. In one case a woman had a sitting with Mollie, with nothing being known about her beforehand. After the séance began, a boy began speaking to the sitter saying that his father was also present. He referred to her grieving and told her that she should not carry out the action she had been contemplating as 'you won't join us, as you think you will'.

After the séance ended, the sitter explained that after her husband and only son had died, she had often thought of committing suicide and had even attempted it on more than more occasions. However, after hearing the words of wisdom from her son, Mr Perriman notes, 'it was a very different person who left our house that evening.'

Violin asked for and played (Isa Northage)

In *A Path Prepared: the story of Isa Northage(55)* are many reports which had been sent into the *Two Worlds* magazine. The author obtained permission to reprint them in his book and permission has again been granted to use them in the new edition.

From *Two Worlds* February 14th, 1941 we read: "Mrs Northage paid a very successful visit to Ashington, Northern Counties, where her fine mediumship was much appreciated. Two séances were held and brought conviction to many. My brother came and spoke to us through the trumpet. I suggested that it was a pity we had not a violin with us, as he was a skilled violinist. He said 'Bring one tomorrow night and I will play it for you.' We borrowed one, and on the following evening he picked up the violin from outside the cabinet and asked us to sing Auld Lang Syne while he played for us."

Premature child speaks to father and asks for a name   (Isa Northage)

Allan MacDonald writes in *A Path Prepared: The Story of Isa Northage(92)* of a testimonial by a Mr W. Molson, 26th January 1959 on this emotional reunion and revelation via the direct voice mediumship of Isa Northage. We read:

It is difficult to single out one visit from someone in the world of spirit as being more impressive than another. Yet one incident stands out in my mind as truly impressive. Here I should indicate that I had been married previously and that the wife of my first marriage had once had a child prematurely born to her. While we were sitting marvelling at the clarity of the communications which had been received, and the breadth of the knowledge which they had concerning each one of us personally, the trumpet slowly rose, in a nervous, halting fashion, and came towards me. I encouraged the unseen one endeavouring to communicate by bidding whoever it might be welcome to our gathering, while Mrs Isa Northage, who had remained fully conscious, did likewise.

After a few moments of such encouragement, a child's voice spoke quite clearly to the medium, saying "I want my daddy." This perplexed her for a moment for there were only two males present, but the trumpet turned slowly to me and said "Daddy, Grandma Molson has brought me."

The child then went on to explain that she was the child of first marriage and asked to be given a name. The reader will realize that, faced with such a revelation, it is not easy to answer such a request immediately, but I thought quickly and suggested that she might like the name Alice, which was the second name of my mother. This appeared to please her, and she seemed satisfied, although I have noticed on subsequent sittings that this is not the name she commonly uses, announcing herself as 'Fragrance', the name doubtless given to her by those in the spirit world.

Following that brief conversation with the child, my mother spoke firmly to me, saying that if only I could see the child standing there I should feel none of the bitterness in my heart which I had allowed to gain hold when my marriage was broken, not through death, but through circumstances beyond my control.

That was the first visit of the child, speaking with all the tenderness which a child of but a few years of age displays when speaking to her father or mother. I have been able to speak to her on several occasions through the mediumship of Mrs Northage during succeeding years, and have witnessed her development and growth to the stage where she is now a young person, showing many of the characteristics which one attributes to one in adolescence.

The knowledge that young children, or children who have known no earth life, continue their lives after passing and grow in age and understanding, but maintain close connections with their parents and grandparents, who have often joined them, should be a source of comfort to many.

George Cranley knew Mona van der Watt well and gives us these two outstanding moments from her mediumship.

Direct voice in daylight with the medium's pulse stopping (Mona van der Watt)

Mona van der Watt was an outstanding medium but not well known because she lived mainly in South Africa. When demonstrating her mediumship in public or in private, everyone could hear the spirit voices talking to her. This took place in the light. It reportedly took more than eight years for the voices to manifest. Mona was given a choice by her guides: she could sit in complete darkness and develop direct voice, which would be limited to a small number of people or reach a larger audience, but the voice would be weaker. She chose the latter. On one occasion she was tested by six doctors. As the *Psychic News* reported "They examined the medium with a stethoscope. Wherever they put it, they heard the voice speaking. Yet it was impossible for them to trace the source." The guide who was entrancing her said that he would stop her pulse and asked the doctors to verify it. When he stopped her pulse, the doctors agreed that by their standards she would be classed as dead. Her guide then said he would put 'power' back into one finger which he did – and then placed the medium's finger on the forehead of one of the doctors who immediately collapsed on the floor as though struck by lightning. The guide restored her pulse and Mona returned to normal."

Direct voice 1000 miles away from the medium (Mona van der Watt)

Mona's spirit guides repeatedly demonstrated their ability to produce the spirit voice even when she was more than 1000 miles away. In transit to the 1960 and 1963 International Spiritualist Federation's congresses, Mona's guide made a promise. While the medium was on the ship they would link with her in Cape Town during the Sunday service and try to make the spirit voice audible. On both occasions, it was clearly heard by the whole congregation at some point during the demonstration of clairvoyance.

Direct voice in broad daylight during a tea party (unknown medium as related by Sylvia Barbanell)

In *Some Discern Spirits(138)*, Sylvia Barbanell writes that in broad daylight, in a crowded room where a tea party was in progress, she sat chatting with a medium whose name she did not now remember. "While we balanced our teacups in their hands, I was suddenly addressed in a direct voice. The voice came from the vicinity of the medium's solar plexus." Sylvia's name was called affectionately, endearingly. She responded and asked who was speaking to her. "I am your grandmother," came the clear reply. "You were named after me." They talked together for some time and Sylvia was given a message for her mother. Then Sylvia's brother spoke in the same manner. Sylvia Barbanell was only two when her grandmother died but she was told that she was taken into the grandmother's room as an infant for some time every morning.

Return of Sir Henry Segrave (Estelle Roberts)

Hannen Swaffer, in his book *My Greatest Story,* mentioned the case of Sir Henry Segrave as one that particularly touched him. Segrave was a famous British sportsman who had set a number of land and water speed records, and was the first person to exceed 200 mph on land. He was killed in an attempt to set a new water speed record on 13th June 1930.

Swaffer, who had been a friend of Segrave's, asked his fellow journalist, Maurice Barbanell, if he could arrange a sitting with Estelle Roberts for Segrave's widow. Barbanell had planned to accompany two other friends to a sitting with Mrs Roberts on 22nd January 1932, but when one of them came down with the 'flu the friends were forced to cancel. Barbanell then contacted Lady Segrave to see if she could make it, but she already had another engagement and so he went by himself as a proxy. As was routine, nothing was said to Roberts of the intended sitters.

After Roberts entered the trance state, Red Cloud gave his usual introductory remarks, after which Barbanell heard a voice addressing him. Barbanell asked who was speaking. "Segrave", was the response to which he added, "Thank you for trying to bring my wife." Barbanell asked him for a message for his wife, which he readily gave. Two weeks later, Lady Segrave sat with Estelle Roberts and thus began a series of sittings in which she conversed with her husband. Much of it was personal information unknown to Roberts or anyone else. Lady Segrave, as reported by Barbanell in *Across the Gulf(31),* said. "The whole of his conversation was very characteristic, full of intimate details, so that I knew beyond doubt it was my husband."

Lady Segrave brought a former friend of her husband's to one séance. He was the Earl of Cottenham. Speaking through the trumpet, Segrave addressed him by his first name, Mark, and carried on a personal conversation with him. "I have publicly affirmed, and here I do so again, that I have no reasonable doubt of the genuineness of these psychic communications," the Earl of Cottenham wrote in Barbanell's book, *The Trumpet Shall Sound(66)*. "After patient and searching investigation, such common sense and logic as I possess can find no other explanation that that I have actually conversed with friends and relatives whose physical bodies I know to be dead."

Public direct voice séances for up to 500 people at a time (Estelle Roberts)

Maurice Barbanell in *Power of the Spirit(54)*, tells us:

> To give larger numbers a chance of hearing the direct voice, Estelle has held some of these séances in public, at the Aeolian Hall, with audiences of about five hundred people. The hall lighting made it impossible for the medium to sit in full view of the audience. A 'cabinet' was improvised by arranging a curtain in front of Estelle's chair and the trumpet was placed in that recess. These public demonstrations were highly successful, but the medium found that they caused a strain and left her temporarily exhausted.

Leslie Flint also gave public demonstrations of direct voice for audiences up to a thousand people as described in G. Trevor's *Death's Door Opens(106)* and also in Flint's autobiography *Voices in the Dark*.

The first ever public Direct Voice séance in full light was given at the Kingsway Hall in London in 1946 in front of a thousand people. Flint sat on an ordinary chair within the small space of the lightproof cabinet which was also virtually sound proof; a microphone was placed about 18 inches in front of it and very quickly the voices came loud and clear with Mickey opening the proceedings with his chirpy "Proper crowd 'ere tonight, ain't there?" After many joyful and tearful reunions the evening closed with the actress Ellen Terry's cultured, precise tones exhorting the audience to have faith, sit in sincerity of spirit and use your gifts to serve mankind.

This was the first of many more demonstrations to be given by Flint throughout the country.

The following sections on Leslie Flint and Emily French are taken with permission from Victor Zammit's book *A Lawyer Presents the Case for the Afterlife* (2005) available on line.

Boxed up, tied up, sealed up, gagged, bound and held, and still the voices came (Leslie Flint)

Flint describes, in his autobiography *Voices in the Dark(169)*, how he was 'boxed up, tied up, sealed up, gagged, bound and held, and still the voices have come to speak of life eternal'.

In a 1972 test sitting, he allowed scientists to gag him and bind him to his chair without any effect on his mediumship. Flint describes how he gave sittings *extempore* in hotel rooms, in houses of strangers, in foreign countries, in halls, theatres and churches. In 1948, Flint submitted to a series of experiments conducted by scientists from the Society for Psychical Research. The *Psychic News* of 14th February 1948 reports in detail one experiment where he conducted a séance with bandages over his lips and his hands and legs tied to a chair. The observers concluded that in spite of the above restrictions the voices were soon speaking with their usual clarity, even shouting. Some twelve persons in the room all heard more than enough to convince the most obdurate skeptic that the sealing of Mr Flint's lips in no way prevented the unseen speakers from saying anything they wished. At the conclusion of the experiment, they found the plaster and the cords intact and undisturbed.

Flint goes on to tell us that even with his mouth taped shut or full of water literally thousands of different voices of discarnate persons have, over a period of forty years, been tape-recorded for posterity, speaking in different dialects, in foreign languages unknown to him and even in languages no longer spoken on this earth. In one séance, a sitter was too late to be admitted to the séance room so she sat outside the séance room door but she was still able to hear the voice of her deceased son speaking from just inside the door.

Flint rebuts the skeptics (Leslie Flint)

In his autobiography *Voices in the Dark(167)*, Flint gives some examples of the ludicrous theories put forward by some psychic researchers. One was that the voices were not real but produced by a combination of hypnotic power on his part coupled with mass auditory hallucinations on the part of the sitters. This was disproved when the voices were recorded. Another theory was that Flint was a ventriloquist. This was disproved when a throat microphone was attached to his throat so that the slightest sound made through his larynx would be magnified enormously while observers watched him through an infrared telescope. When they could come up with no further explanations, one of the psychic researchers put forward the idea that Flint could talk through his stomach. Those who, being unable to think of any other explanation, alleged fraud against Flint, believing that a two-way voice channel to another room existed where accomplices could mimic the voices of the departed or that he might have concealed tape-recorders which play prepared messages from the dead. There is no end to the ingenious theories which have been thought up by those determined not to believe.

Flint could also ask these stubborn cynics how these supposed accomplices, however skilled, could produce the recognizable voice of a wife or a husband or other dead relative of a sitter who is, as likely as not, newly arrived from Australia, India or Timbuktu. One expert who did investigate Leslie Flint and thoroughly vouched for his authenticity was Professor William R. Bennett, Professor of Electrical Engineering at Columbia University in New York City. Modern investigation techniques, not available at the time of earlier tests, corroborate previous conclusions by indicating that the voices are not his.

Lawyer identifies judge's voice (Leslie Flint)

Dr Aubrey Rose, OBE, CBE, one of the most brilliant lawyers in England, attended many sittings with Leslie Flint and claims that through Flint he received the most detailed evidence of survival of the individual beyond this life. In his recent autobiography *The Rainbow Never Ends* he states that his investigation into the afterlife began when he heard a tape recording of a voice he recognized as that of deceased Judge, Lord Birkett, speaking through Leslie Flint. Rose became a close friend of Leslie Flint and went on to become a spiritual healer himself.

112

Direct voice every week for 14 years (Emily French)

Another American direct voice medium who was thoroughly investigated over many years was Emily French of Buffalo New York. For fourteen years, this frail elderly woman sat in a séance every week at the home with a leading lawyer from Buffalo, New York, Edward C. Randall, his wife and his close associates. For five of those years they were joined by a prominent judge, Dean Shuart of Rochester, 'a learned jurist and man of such impeccable character that he had been repeatedly elected to the responsible office of Surrogate Judge'.

Every person who attended the circle was initially skeptical and sure that the voices were fraudulent. And each person was allowed to conduct however many exacting experiments they needed to be convinced that they were genuine. It is inconceivable that these people would waste their time in this manner if they had any hint that the phenomena were not 100% genuine.

Mrs French was from a well-known family, had a reputation in her close community for over sixty years, as a person of unimpeachable integrity and never took a cent for her involvement. In 1905 Edward C Randall wrote to Isaac K. Funk D.D. LL.D, a prominent psychic researcher and co-owner of the publishing house Funk and Wagnalls New York/London asking him to arrange for Mrs French to be scientifically investigated. Dr Funk agreed on condition that Mrs French would come to New York City and conduct sittings every day for two weeks in the homes of people she did not know surrounded by highly experienced and skeptical observers. Then seventy-two years old, extremely feeble and frail with a dangerous heart condition and almost totally deaf, Mrs French sat with Dr Funk with barely any time to rest after a long journey from Buffalo. She was surrounded by people who were skeptical of her. And night after night she produced magnificent direct voice evidence of the afterlife. The full results of these detailed tests were published by Dr Funk in his book, *Psychic Riddle*, and are reprinted in Chapter 11 of N. Riley Heagerty's book *The French Revelation*.

Arthur Findlay becomes convinced after hearing his father's voice (John Sloan)

Through the direct voice mediumship of John Sloan, Arthur Findlay became convinced of the reality of Spiritualism. For many years, Sloan gave sittings without charge to small groups of friends. One of his long-term sitters was Arthur Findlay who, until he met Sloan, was an agnostic. From *Looking Back: Autobiography of a Spiritualist(175)*, we read:

> So it was arranged that the following night I would meet him at seven o'clock at the corner of North Frederick Street andGeorge Street and he would take me to a séance which was held every Monday evening in a house nearby. When I returned and told my wife where I was about to go, she wondered if it were a wise thing to do. To go with a strange man to a strange house seemed to her taking an unjustifiable risk, but she raised no objection and I kept the appointment next day as arranged.
>
> Consequently on the following day Monday 20th September 1918, we met at the place arranged and walked along a quiet street to a house, the entrance to which was by a passage. He told me we were going to the house of John Sloan, who was a medium. We entered the passage, and my unknown guide knocked at the door on the right-hand side. It was opened and we were ushered into a small room in which were ten people, all sitting on chairs in a circle. The light was on and talking was general. A man was playing a hymn on a harmonium.
>
> We were both given seats in the circle and no introductions were made. All that was said by my guide was a remark to the man at the harmonium that he had brought someone with him. That was all. My guide did not know my name, I did not know his, and the rest of the people were all complete strangers to me. I put them down as belonging to what is called the working class, nice, kindly decent people who gave me a very friendly welcome.
>
> The man at the harmonium then said it was time to start, and he switched off the light. A hymn was played and sung and then another, but before it ended the organist turned round and took his place in the circle. Shortly after this a man's loud voice spoke right in front of my right-hand neighbour I heard

everything said and the name it gave, the conversation being an intimate one between my female neighbour and this voice.

She had evidently spoken to the voice before, and took it all quietly and naturally. The voice seemed to know everything of importance she had done since the last conversation, and ended with love and the promise to be back again at the next séance.

When the voice had finished speaking, she calmly announced to everyone that she had been speaking to her husband, whom I took to be dead. This went on for three hours, dozens of voices speaking to different people, men's voices, women's voices,children's voices, all of which I was told came from people called dead. A woman's voice spoke to a man sitting on my   left. It gave a name and referred to happenings at his home. It specially referred to Tom, who was giving his father trouble, and then came advice as to how he should be dealt with. Intimate family matters were discussed between my neighbour and this female voice, and finally with love it said "Good-bye." "That was my wife," he whispered to me. "I never come here but she comes back to me. She always knows everything that goes on at home."

I was now beginning to feel that I was the only one to be omitted from this strange medley of conversation which seemed to go on and on without stopping. Everything said was claimed to be correct, and I wondered how it was possible for any human being to be so intimate with all the dead friends, and the private doings of the sitters, as to be able to impersonate their deceased relations in the way that was taking place. Not only did the imagined impersonator know intimately about their dead friends and relations but every voice was different, the mannerisms were different, in fact each voice had a different personality. What a wonderful actor there must be amongst us to be able to carry on like that for hours on end, and to remember in the dark where everyone was sitting, as the right person was directly addressed every time with never a mistake.

Such were my thoughts, when suddenly right in front of my face a strong voice spoke to me. "Yes, who are you?" I enquired, to receive the answer "Your father, Robert Downie Findlay." The voice continued speaking, and referred to something that only my father and I, and one other man, ever knew about on earth, and that other man, like my father " was dead. I was therefore the only living person on earth with any knowledge of what the voice was talking about. It was a private matter that neither I, nor my father nor the other man when on earth, ever spoke about to any other person.

All this was extraordinary enough, but imagine my surprise when my father concluded by saying "David Kidston is standing beside me and would also like to talk to you about this matter."

Now David Kidston was the name of the other man who knew about this private affair. He was my father's partner and he was my partner after my father's death. Only the three of us knew about this private affair and here I was in a Glasgow artisan's house, a complete stranger to everyone, being told by two different voices about something known only to me and two dead men. Moreover the voices which spoke claimed to be the voices of these two men, and Kidston continued the conversation quite naturally which my father had started.

What my father said after giving his name was this "I am very sorry I did not take you into my business. I would have liked to do so but Kidston opposed it. If you had been with me it would have greatly eased my life, as I found business a great strain on me. David Kidston is standing beside me and would also like to talk to you about this matter."

Then a voice claiming to be that of David Kidston spoke, saying "I am David Kidston. I was wrong opposing your coming into our office. I am sorry I did but now you need have no regrets. I am glad to get that off my chest at last."

That was all true, but only my father myself and Kidston knew about it and the incident referred to happened when my grandfather died in 1904, fourteen years previously. When he passed on, I said to my father that I would like to enter Findlay Kidston & Goff's office, as now my prospects of becoming a partner in Patrick Henderson & Co. were not so bright. My grandfather's influence had gone and I might have to wait years before I became a partner. My father agreed and said he would speak to Kidston about it as I would be a great help to him. My disappointment was great when he told me that

Kidston would not agree, because the business earned enough for only three partners. He evidently foresaw the day when my father would want me to become a partner and that would mean less to go round.

Kidston was so short-sighted that he could not foresee me bringing in enough new business to the firm to justify my being made a partner but he was a very difficult man to work with and my father had some unpleasant times with him. He was rough in his manner and domineering, so much so that my father rather feared him. So I knew that what Kidston had saidwas final and I never raised the matter again, but, as neither he nor Goff had sons, I saw something good slipping away from me. So my request and its refusal remained known only to us three. Nevertheless, here was I listening to what had happened fourteen years previously in a strange house, and in the company of people I had never seen before in my life.

That indeed was a problem. No spy system, however thorough it was, no fraud or impersonation by the medium or anyone else could be responsible for what I had experienced. I was up against something quite inexplicable. That then, was my first introduction to Spiritualism, and, when the séance was over I was introduced to the medium John Campbell Sloan, the man who was at the harmonium when I entered. I thanked him for his hospitality and asked him if I could come back again, as I was anxious to know more about this subject.

The return of Eric Saunders (John Sloan)

In his book *On the Edge of the Etheric*, Arthur Findlay tells of an experience involving his brother whom he took with him to a séance shortly after he was demobilized from the army in 1919. The brother knew no one present and was not introduced. No one, except Arthur, knew that he had been in the army, or where he had been stationed. His health had not permitted him to go abroad, and so he spent part of the time near Lowestoft at a small fishing village called Kessingland, and part of the time at Lowestoft, training gunners.

After various voices had come for others, the trumpet tapped Arthur's brother on the right knee, and a voice directly in front of

117

him said "Eric Saunders." The brother didn't recall anyone of that name and said so. Since the voice was not very strong, someone suggested that the company should sing to build up the psychic power in the room. While this was going on, the trumpet kept tapping the brother on the knee, arm and shoulder. It was so insistent that he said "I think we had better stop singing, as some person evidently is most anxious to speak to me."

He again asked who it was, and the voice, by now much stronger, replied "Eric Saunders." The brother asked where he had met him and he said "In the army." A number of places were mentioned, such as Aldershot, Bisley, France, and Palestine, to see if the communicant would take the bait, but Lowestoft was carefully not mentioned. The voice was not deceived. It replied "No, none of these places. I knew you near Lowestoft."

"Why do you say near Lowestoft?"

"You were not in Lowestoft then but at Kessingland."

"What company were you attached to?" But it not being possible to ascertain whether the reply was 'B' or 'C', the brother asked if he could remember the name of the company commander. The reply, 'McNamara' was correct for 'B' company.

As a test, Findlay's brother now pretended that he remembered the man and said "Oh, yes, you were one of my Lewis gunners, weren't you?" The reply was "No, you had not the Lewis guns then. It was the Hotchkiss." This was correct.

After several other correct answers to questions, the voice of Saunders said "We had great times there, sir: do you remember the general's inspections?" The brother laughed and said they had been continually being inspected by generals, to which one did he refer? The voice replied "The day the general made us all race around the guns." This was an incident which had caused a great deal of amusement to the men at the time. Then Sauders said he had been killed in France in the Big Draft in August, 1917. As there had been only one especially big draft, it had been something well remembered by both of them.

Findlay writes "He then thanked my brother for the gunnery training he had given him, and said it had been most useful to him in France. My brother asked him why he had come through to speak to him, and he said 'Because I have never forgotten that you once did me a good turn.' My brother has a hazy recollection of obtaining leave for one of the gunners, owing to some special circumstances, but whether or not his name was 'Saunders' he could not remember."

Since hundreds of men passed through his training, it had been difficult for the brother to know them individually, but all of them would have known him. About six months after the séance, the brother was in London, and met, by appointment, the corporal who had been his assistant with the light guns in his battalion. He asked him if he remembered 'Eric Saunders'. He did not, but he had his old pocket diary with him. In it he had been in the habit of keeping a full list of men under training, including the dates they went overseas. They looked in it for Company 'B' during 1917 and sure enough, there was 'Eric Saunders f.q. August '17.' F.q. meant fully qualified and red ink meant Saunders went out in August, 1917.

Direct voice talks to Feda during trance sitting (Gladys Osbourne Leonard)

Suzy Smith, in *The Mediumship of Mrs Leonard(209)* states that a direct voice developed during Mrs Leonard's trance sittings. The direct voice had the following functions: supplying the required word when Feda hesitated, or when Feda asked for it; supplying the correct word without its being asked for; addressing Feda; correcting Feda's mistakes or pronunciations, or even contradicting Feda. Researchers never identified the direct voice that assisted Feda in this way.

Examples of this are as follows:

Feda: That is when we usually av-av-
Direct Voice: *Avail.*
Feda: Avail ourselves of . . .

Feda: Here there is an inner urge towards meeting opportunities more than half-way; possibly it is due to – what?
Direct Voice: *Awareness.*
Feda: Awareness of the existence of all these opportunities.

On one occasion what the communicator wished to say was evidently, "It's like being put in charge of a Borstal institution (or reform school)."

Feda: It's like being put in charge of a department of boars. Pigs? Boars in an institution?

Direct Voice: *Borstal.*

Feda: I'm not quite sure. It's something to do with boars.

Feda: Willy – what? Who's he? Willy somebody – I can't get his other name. Willy – somebody is compelling you. Wait a minute. I've mixed that up.

Direct Voice: *It is not that at all.*

Feda: Willy – nilly? Is that right? Willy – nilly, you are now being compelled...

Feda: The conditions of my new life have impressed me more dr- dr-

Direct Voice: *Dramatically.*

Feda: Dramatically, he calls it, when they have people who ....

Feda: When I saw familiar things around me I said, "Thank God! Thank God! All the familiar and comforting things are here. I will live up to them, or I will live up to the benef- benef-

Direct Voice: *Beneficence which has given them to me.*

On occasion the direct voice corrected Feda's pronunciation:

Feda: It's an admiral idea, he says.

Direct Voice: *Admirable.*

Feda: It's just as if things become separate, like the spectrum, he calls it. (Then she added, as if to herself) A man once said Feda was a spectrum.

Direct Voice: *Specter, not spectrum.*

Sometimes the direct voice contradicted Feda:

Feda: The gentleman is not quite used to fitting in with what other people want him to do. If you suggest anything to him he doesn't jump at it. He waits to see if it was what he wants to do. He's just like that!

Direct Voice: *I am not!*

Feda: Yes, you are. He's a good, kind man, but it's just a habit. I feel he was an important person, that people thought a lot and paid much attention to his words. He says they didn't always pay attention, but it would have been better if they had done so sometimes. He's a funny gentleman!

Direct Voice: *Not funny!*

Feda: He's talking about the sinner that repeateth. I think the sinner that repeateth is an awful nuisance.

Direct Voice: *No, he isn't.*

Feda: Well, he sounds as if he is.

Feda: Your father says -

Direct Voice: *A few days out!*

Feda: A few days out? What, out of bed?

Direct Voice: *No, no, no, no!*

Feda: He says you must have good working – what? Hippopotamuses?

Direct Voice: *Hypotheses.*

Feda (more loudly): Hippopotamuses.

Direct Voice: *Hypotheses and don't shout.*

Feda: I'm not shouting. I'm only speaking plainly.

Specific evidence with no vague or general statements (Leslie Flint)

Victor Zammit (2005) again picks up on the accuracy of the information coming through in a Flint sitting. They were not, as some critics of mediums claim, vague suggestions which could apply to anyone. Take for example the following exchange given in Flint's autobiography, *Voices in the Dark*, between a young airman killed in World War II and his parents. He had initially appeared at a séance attended by Lord Dowding, giving his name as Peter William Handford Kite, and asking that his parents be contacted at an address he gave. The parents accepted an invitation to attend a second séance and for close on forty minutes Peter came through and in his own voice told them the following which his parents confirmed to be true:

- of a joke he made before he died about buying an Alsatian.
- that his mother had put a photograph of himself and photographs of his grave in Norway in her bag that morning.
- that he liked the cherry tree in the memorial garden they had planted for him.
- that his bedroom had not been changed in the six years since he died.
- that he had not liked the wallpaper in his bedroom.
- that his father was still driving his car although it was a too small for him.

In the following extract from Leslie Flint's autobiography *(169)* he describes his bitter disappointment in researchers:

> When first I began to allow myself to be tested I was naive enough to believe that if the tests were successful the scientists and researchers who had carried them out under their own conditions would proclaim to the world the truth of life after death. All too soon I learned the hard way that many of those who call themselves researchers have immutable values of their own which preclude belief in a meaning or purpose in man's existence or in the possibility of a life after death. Their concern was rather to disprove the reality of my voices and they would postulate any alternative however far-fetched or absurd sooner than admit the implication of their own successful experiment.

The return of the medium who was responsible for the death of Sherlock Holmes (Gladys Mallaburn)

Although perhaps not a great moment in modern mediumship, this is included to demonstrate how a story, if repeated often enough, can be accepted as true. Sir Arthur Conan Doyle, the literary creator of Sherlock Holmes, was a champion of Spiritualism. He also was a friend of medium Evan Powell and sat in many of his séances where he received specific evidence of survival. Though it is often quoted – including in Barbanell's *Spiritualism Today(31)* – that after one of Doyle's many sittings with Powell, Doyle announced he was killing off Sherlock Holmes, the fictitious detective, to devote the rest of his days to espousing Spiritualism, there is no direct evidence to support this, nor that Powell was often heard to say, jokingly, "I was responsible for murdering Holmes." – public clamour later prevented this 'slaying'.

This unsubstantiated, yet fabled, event is now woven into the lore of Spiritualism and accepted as fact when no sources support it[2]. It makes for an often quoted, good, but ultimately false, story.

Barbanell's link with the story comes at the end of a very long sitting with Gladys Mallaburn, from the North East of England, when the soft voice of Evan Powell spoke to Ralph Rossiter, whom he called his 'beloved son', saying 'I have met Holmes.'

Barbanell said he did not understand this comment until Rossiter explained the joke to him.

2. The fabled nature of this supposed event is fully explained in "Sir Arthur Conan Doyle and Evan Powell" by Paul J. Gaunt in *Psypioneer Journal,* Volume 7, No 7, July 2011, pages 219 – 227.

Emma Hardinge Britten

Emma Hardinge Britten

In the last analysis, it is our conception of death which decides
our answers to all the questions that life puts to us.
Dag Hammarskjold

Given her role in Modern Spiritualism, it is only fitting to
dedicate a special category for Emma Hardinge Britten.

Emma had complete trust in the spirit world. According to her
autobiography, when she went to America she was told by spirit
that someone would meet her. After waiting, someone did in fact
meet her and her mother. They could take them to arrange
accommodation, but they could not take her bags which contained
everything she owned. Emma was told by spirit to leave the bags
and someone would collect them later and bring them to her. She
left her bags and someone did in fact later collect them and bring
them to her.

Emma started as a 'test', or evidential, medium. In her day, 'test
mediums' were called so because they were tested in private sittings
for the accuracy of the evidence they brought. However, she gave
up this form of mediumship to be a 'speaking medium' or 'trance
orator', that is one who responded to a series of unrehearsed
questions. These questions were not easy questions that can be
answered off-the-cuff like 'How can we be a nice person?' No –
one of the inquiries Emma famously answered was 'Describe the
Geological Formation of the Earth'.

She knew that one form of mediumship (and in her day, mediums
tended to remain in one area/specialization of mediumship) is not
inherently better than any other and speaking with the voice of the
Spirit can inspire thousands.

When she spoke in trance, Emma spoke with a male voice
because this was acceptable to the audience of the time. But still,
lynch mobs often gathered where she was to speak with a sincere
desire to kill her – for her own good because it was unheard of for a
woman to speak in public and to especially speak on Spiritual
subjects. She not only spoke, she spoke in public, she spoke in public

on subjects that were completely objectionable – she spoke about the Spirit World to a very Christian audience. This was the height of vulgar, disgusting behaviour – out of class with being a lady. Yet, she bravely lived as a woman in a man's world. However, as a speaker, Emma changed the face of Spiritualism and moved continents. She also went into prisons and reminded prisoners of their soul and reminded them of the nature of their soul and why their soul was here.

She lived a plucky life for a Victorian woman and she is known as 'The Mother of Spiritualism'. She co-founded the Spiritualist National Union and started, and for five years edited, the *Two Worlds* newspaper coming a long way from her early days when she thought it very lower class to go to a séance.

Emma famously said that an emphasis on phenomena, especially public demonstrations of mediumship, would destroy Spiritualism turning it into a show with mediums as performers and celebrities. She also famously foresaw the future of Spiritualism and the danger of relying too much on phenomena. According to Emma, there were three phases or cycles of Spiritualism. In the first cycle, roughly 1848 – 1898, spirit communication would roll like a mighty flood across the world; it would be a period of steady growth and development. In the second cycle, roughly 1899 – 1949, it would record a decline in public effort due to lovers of sensationalism who would lower the standards that had been set up. The phenomena would displace the spirit teachings. Finally, in the third cycle, roughly 1949 – 1999, a new order would arise out of the materials provided by the second cycle and Spiritualism would be organically smaller, more compact, enduring and dynamic in character.

The steamer *Pacific* (Emma Hardinge Britten)

During a table séance on February 19, 1856, in which Emma laid out the letters of the alphabet on a table and her hand spelt out a message, a crew member of the mail steamer *Pacific*, Philip Smith, spoke through Emma. The *Pacific* was the ship on which Britten and her mother had originally travelled to America. They had got to know several members of the crew, including Smith. The extent to which the medium is affected by the psychic state of the communicator at the moment of death is well illustrated by the description of Emma Hardinge of her famous prediction of the loss of the steamer *Pacific*. She writes in her autobiography:

> That evening, just as my mother and myself were about to retire for the night, a sudden and unusual chill crept over me, and an irresistible impression possessed my mind that a spirit had come into our presence. A sensation as if water was streaming over me accompanied the icy chilliness I experienced, and a feeling of indescribable terror possessed my whole being. I begged my mother to light up every lamp we had at hand; then to open the door that the proximity of people in the house outside our room might aid to dissipate the horror that seemed to pervade the very air. At last, at my mother's suggestion, I consented to sit at the table, with the alphabet we had provided turned from me and towards her, so that she could follow the involuntary movements of my finger, which some power seemed to guide in pointing out the letters. In this way was rapidly spelt out "Philip Smith: Ship Pacific."
>
> For a few momonts this mode of manifestation ceased, and, to my horror I distinctly felt an icy cold hand lay hold of my arm; then distinctly and visibly to my mother's eyes, something pulled my hair, which was hanging in long curls; all the while the coldness of the air increasing so painfully that the apartment seemed pervaded by Arctic breezes. After a while my own convulsed hand was moved tremblingly but very rapidly to spell out "My dear Emma, I have come to tell you I am dead. The ship *Pacific* is lost and all on board have perished; she and her crew will never be heard from any more."

Emma couldn't sleep that night, although she doubted what she had been given. In the morning she went to house of a medium, who was a good friend, Mrs Kellogg. As she climbed the stairs to the apartment, Mrs Kellogg came out in a trance and spoke exactly the same words as the message Emma had received.

When Britten disclosed this tragedy, the owners of the vessel threatened to prosecute her. But it turned out that the facts presented by the spirit through Emma Britten were true; the *Pacific* had indeed sunk.

He recognised his General's voice (Emma Hardinge Britten)

In the mid-1860s Emma was invited to speak at a settlement on the Pacific Coast to deliver the Fourth of July Oration. Her host told her of the struggle he had had when he had booked 'a Spiritualist, a lady and *an Englishwoman*' to give the Oration.

She describes the scene that day:

"There was an immense concourse of people around the stand, some seated on the ground, others in traps, carts, or on horseback. ... What I had to say being upon the History of Nations, America in especial—The principles of true freedom—National life, and the history, power, and possibilities of the grand New World; all shades of politicians and religions in that immense assembly were satisfied, none hurt, none dissenting. The cheers grew into shouts; the clapping of hands into perfect leaps and yells of applause; and at the end of about an hour's address (without experiencing a shade of hoarseness), I was literally pelted with flowers. The women kissed my dress, and held up their dear little children for me to kiss."

Having arrived home, they were about to sit down to dinner, when Mrs Blood, her hostess, cried out, pointing to the front garden gate, "Look there!"

Round the gate was a party of at least a dozen men on horseback, who to Mr Blood's anxious enquiry of what they wanted, replied, that they wished to see the lady. Emma went out to them, and one of their party, doffing his hat, said "We are told, madam, that you claim to make all your public speeches through Spirit influence. May we ask, is that so?"

"Undoubtedly." she replied.

"Why we ask, madam", said the spokesman, "is this. We have a heavy wager on the matter. I say I know for a certainty who the Spirit is that spoke to-day. Others say it isn't so. Now, dear lady, won't you please decide the wager, and tell us who the Spirit was?"

"I will do so", Emma said, " if you write down the name of who you think it was. I will write the name of who I know it was. We will then compare notes." In a few seconds, Mr Blood procured pens, ink, and paper and she wrote "The Spirit that controlled me this morning was General Edward Baker."

The spokesman wrote "If that was a Spirit that spoke this morning, it was my former General, Ned Baker, killed at the battle of Bull Run."

When another of the party read out the two papers, consecutively, more shouts and cheers followed. Edward Baker was an Englishman, and a lawyer by profession. When the war broke out, being a warm partisan of the Northern side, he had entered the army, rose step by step, renowned for his bravery, until he was killed at the battle of Bull Run.

"He was my commander, Mrs Hardinge", said the first speaker, "but before the war I have heard him speak many and many a time. I knew his style, his manner, his very words, and if ever I heard Ned Baker in my life, I heard him this very morning on your platform."

Principles of Spiritualism (Emma Hardinge Britten)

In May 1871, Emma spoke on the subject of the spiritualists' 'creed' at Cleveland Hall in London. At the end of the lecture, she revealed that she had been given the 'ten commandments of spiritualism' by the late socialist and philanthropist Robert Owen. These evolved to become the Seven Principles of Spiritualism we know today. In the Cleveland Hall speech, directly after saying "These are some of the points of my creed, and all of them I have proved." Emma said her four Principles were: 1) I believe in God; 2) I believe in the immortality of the human soul; 3) I believe in right and wrong; and 4) I believe in the communion of spirits as ministering angels. Earlier in this lecture she referred to the now first two principles in saying "Spiritualism is wholly unselfish. It proclaimed from the first the fatherhood of God – that you all admit; and with it the brotherhood of man – and that you don't admit."

Note that her fourth principle was 'I believe in the communion of spirits as ministering angels', and a writer for the *Two Worlds* newspaper inadvertently substituted 'saints' for 'spirits'.

Threatened with lynching (Emma Hardinge Britten)

In New York, Emma offered her services as a medium, for which she refused payment. Afterward, she believed that she was ordered by the spirits to lecture, but in her Autobiography she says she 'shrank with disgust' at the idea of being a 'female preacher'. Eventually she relented, finding the task impossible to avoid, and was booked to speak at Troy, New York. She tried to write her lecture, or memorize it, but the spirits claimed they would take her sight and her memory, wanting her to speak *extempore*.

In the event, on 5th July 1857 she took to the platform and, inspired by the presence of her departed father, lost her fear and spoke from the heart. Her lecture was a success and she continued as the Sunday speaker in Troy for two years. Hardinge's speaking talents were such that spiritualists across the United States and Canada invited her to lecture, and she embarked on a tour. She spoke in churches and public halls, often facing hostile (mostly male) audiences of cowboys, miners, and settlers. Nevertheless, by her account, she spoke quietly and convincingly and many were converted to the cause. According to commentators she was 'dashing, brilliant and forceful' (*Two Worlds*, 13th October 1899). According to Emma Hardinge Britten's *Modern American Spiritualism*:

> A few weeks before the close of Mrs Hardinge's engagement in Memphis, she had agreed, according to her custom, to lecture for the benefit of the Leath Orphanage, an institution which was greatly in want of funds, and for which the guardians had solicited her willing aid. On the day fixed for the lecture, the proprietor of the hall was compelled to close the doors at the commands of a set of 'roughs', who, led on by several well-known clerical gentlemen, savagely threatened to lynch all parties concerned, if they dared to proceed with the lecture.
>
> The next day being Sunday, Mrs Hardinge, when preparing for her morning lecture, was advised by her spirit friends that she was threatened with some danger during the exercises, but that, if she had faith in their power and protection, nothing earthly could harm her.

Her funeral oration for Abraham Lincoln was delivered to over 3,000 people in New York, copied by shorthand and published in a pamphlet.

The Fox Sisters

The Fox Sisters

The sublime and the ridiculous are often so nearly related,
that it is difficult to class them separately.
One step above the sublime, makes the ridiculous;
and one step above the ridiculous, makes the sublime again."

Thomas Paine, *The Age of Reason*

Given their role in Modern Spiritualism, it is only fitting to have a special category for the mediumship of the Fox Sisters (Leah, Margaret [Maggie] and Catherine [Kate]). It was their mediumship, especially the events of 31st March 1848, that heralded the advent of Modern Spiritualism.

31st March 1848 (Kate and Margaret Fox)

From Fodor, in his book *These Mysterious People,* we learn that raps, knocks and noises of shifting furniture had been heard for several months by the Fox family in their cottage. These phenomena grew in intensity, and on 31st March it kept the whole family awake. Mr Fox got up and tried the window sashes to see if they were loose. As he shook them, raps seemed to reply. Little Kate noticed this and snapped her fingers. The raps snapped back. Kate then clapped, and there was an answering clap. Margaret joined in and counted: one, two, three, striking her palms. Claps came in answer. The girls' parents tested the knowledge and intelligence of the mysterious rapper. He rapped out the ages of all the Fox children, including one who had died. Rapping twice as the letters of the alphabet were called, he told a gruesome story.

He was a pedlar, Charles B. Rosma by name. He was given hospitality in the house for the night by a previous owner. He had five hundred dollars on him. At midnight, his host crept in and cut his throat with a butcher's knife. He dragged the body downstairs and buried it ten feet below in the cellar. The nightly raps continued and so the Fox family sent the girls to live with other family members. But the rapping followed the girls. Later, digging in the cellar of the cottage unearthed some hair and bones. Fifty-six years later, a rough wall, built a yard from the true wall, of the cellar crumbled. The new owner of the cottage, on excavating, unearthed an almost entire human skeleton with a pedlar's tin box near the bones.

The first public demonstration of mediumship (Kate and Margaret Fox)

After the events of 31st March 1848, Kate and Margaret went to live with different family members, but the rapping noises seemed to follow them and broke out in both places. Fodor(1934) records that these disturbances went on until Isaac Post, a visiting friend, suddenly remembered that Leah's brother, David, had conversed with the Hydesville spirits by using the alphabet. He tried the same and tremendous raps came in answer to the first question and the message was spelt out, "Dear Friends, you must proclaim this truth to the world. This is the dawning of a new era; you must not try to conceal it any longer. When you do your duty God will protect you and good spirits will watch over you."

From that time on communications began to pour through and the manifestations became orderly. The table rocked, objects moved, guitars were played and psychic touches were experienced. The spirits instructed Isaac Post and his cousin George Willets to rent Rochester's largest hall and for three nights and charge the public 75 cents each to witness the Fox sisters' mediumship. Eilab Capron, a Congregational Friend from Auburn, New York was assigned by spirits to deliver an address explaining the nature of the manifestations.

On 14th November 1849, four hundred people filled Corinthian Hall to hear mysterious noises. A committee of five distinguished citizens was appointed to judge the authenticity and source of the raps. The committee would not explain the phenomena as fraud and another committee was formed. This one also reported that when the girls 'were standing on pillows with a handkerchief tied round the bottom of their dresses, tight to the ankles, we all heard rapping on the wall and floor distinctly'. Other accounts of that evening confirm the authenticity of the raps as well as the hostility of the crowd.

According to Arthur Conan Doyle's *History of Spiritualism*:

> The examination of the Fox sisters was thorough to the length of brutality, and a committee of ladies was associated with it.

The latter stripped the frightened girls, who wept bitterly under their afflictions. Their dresses were then tied tightly round their ankles and they were placed upon glass and other insulators.

And in Emma Hardinge Britten's book *Modern American Spiritualism:*

> The two first committees had frankly declared their opinions of their perfect honesty; but it was evident they disliked the task of presenting themselves before the excited crowds that had threatened to 'lynch the rappers and their advocates too'. They had heard the sounds and failed utterly to discover their origin. They had proved that neither machinery nor imposture had been used, and their questions, many of them being mental, were answered correctly.

Passion rose to fury heat, the girls were nearly lynched, but in spite of the hostile atmosphere and denunciation in the newspapers the girls continued and the movement kept on growing.

Spiritualism predicted on 31st March 1848 (Andrew Jackson Davis)

Andrew Jackson Davis is said to have predicted the birth of Spiritualism on the same day that the phenomena occurred in the Fox family home. On 31st March 1848, Jackson, who became known as the 'Poughkeepsie Seer', wrote in his journal "About daylight this morning a warm breathing passed over my face and I heard a voice, tender and strong, saying 'Brother, the good work has begun. Behold a living demonstration is born.' I was left wondering what could be meant by such a message. This was the exact date of the Hydesville Rappings."

Rapping mediums (Leah and Kate Fox)

According to Robert Dale Owen, of the three sisters Leah Fox was the best medium for raps. He recorded some very curious experiments in raps with Mrs Underhill [Leah] in 1861. He heard raps at the seaside in a ledge of rock. He wrote:

Placing my hands on the same ledge, a few steps from Mrs Underhill, and asking for raps, when this came audibly I felt, simultaneously with each rap, a slight but unmistakably distinct vibration or concussion of the rock. I heard raps on board of an excursion boat and later in a sailing boat sounding from underneath. I also obtained them in the open air on the ground. They sounded like, 'a dull sound, as of blows struck on the earth; then I asked Mrs Underhill to touch one of the trees with the tips of her fingers and applying my ear to the tree I heard the raps from beneath the bark'.[1]

Leah wrote in *The Missing Link,* that during the funeral of her second husband, Mr Calvin Brown, raps were heard all over the room while S. B. Brittan delivered the funeral sermon and Judge Edmunds the eulogy.

However, it was Kate Fox who visited England where she was investigated in connection with her phenomenon of raps. Sir William Crookes carried out a full investigation with Kate Fox. Crookes tested Kate in his own laboratory and he states in *Researches in the Phenomena of Modern Spiritualism* that although he had experienced the raps in connection with many other mediums, and at different times in his experiments had heard:

...delicate ticks, as with the point of a pin; a cascade of sharp sounds as from an induction coil in full work; detonations in the air; sharp metallic taps; a cracking like that heard when a frictional machine is at work; sounds like scratching; the twittering as of a bird, etc. But for power and certainty, I have met with no one who at all approached her.

Crookes continued:

For several months I enjoyed almost unlimited opportunity of testing the various phenomena occurring in the presence of this lady and it seems only necessary for her to place her hand on any substance for loud thuds to be heard in it, like a triple pulsation, sometimes loud enough to be heard several rooms off. In this manner I have heard them in a living tree—on a

1. From 'Raps' in the *Encyclopedia of Occultism & Parapsychology*.2001 (http://www.encyclopedia.com)

sheet of glass—on a stretched iron wire—on a stretched membrane—a tambourine—on the roof of a cab—and on the floor of a theatre. Moreover, actual contact is not always necessary; I have had these sounds proceeding from the floor, walls, etc., when the medium's hands and feet were held—when she was standing on a chair—when she was suspended in a swing from the ceiling—when she was enclosed in a wire cage—and when she had fallen fainting on a sofa. I have heard them on a glass harmonicon—I have felt them on my own shoulder and under my own hands. I have heard them on a sheet of paper, held between the fingers by a piece of thread passed through one corner.

I have tested them in every way I could devise, until there is no escape from the conviction that they were true objective occurrences not produced by trickery or mechanical means.

J. J. Morse in *Two Worlds* (Vol. 19, p. 340), writes of Kate Fox, "I have been present with Kate Fox when the raps were heard on a sheet of paper, held between the thumb and forefinger of another person standing beside the medium, the paper visibly shaking from the violence of the raps produced upon its surface."

Spirit lights (Leah Fox)

To Robert Dale Owen, we owe the description of a luminous instrument that seemingly produced the raps. Fodor(1934) reports that Owen was present in a séance with Mrs Underhill on 22nd February 1860 and wrote:

The spirit lights which seemed to produce (or at least were highly incidental to) the rapping noises are observed in the séances of Leah Fox. In a séance with her, while I was looking intently at such a light, about as large as a small fist, it rose and fell, as a hammer would with which one was striking against the floor. At each stroke a loud rap was heard in connection. It was exactly as if an invisible hand held an illuminated hammer and pounded with it.

Such psychic lights may indeed directly relate to raps and may represent an initial stage of materialization.

One of the earliest instances of absent healing (Leah Fox)

Ray Buckland, in *The Spirit Book*, writes that one of the earliest instances of distant healing connected with Spiritualism occurred when a Mr E. W. Capron visited the Fox Family at Rochester, New York. He mentioned to an entranced Leah Fox that his wife, Rebecca, was suffering from a severe and persistent cough. While in trance, Leah said "I am going to cure Rebecca of her cough." She went on to give a very accurate description of Capron's wife and then pronounced her cured. On returning home, Capron found that his wife was indeed cured and the cough never returned.

The Fox Sisters and their public mediumship   (Kate and Margaret Fox)

Success and tragedy followed the Fox sisters throughout their lives. They achieved notoriety as mediums but couldn't handle the pressures of the fame that came with it. Their first public sittings were soon followed by a propaganda tour to Albany in May 1850, then to Troy, where their life was threatened, and on 4th June 1850, they brought the message of spiritualism to New York City. Rooms were rented in the Barnum's Hotel where thrice daily public demonstrations were advertised with an admission price of one dollar.

These demonstrations attracted enough attention to create a demand for private séances for select audiences. In a biography[2] of Kate and Margaret taken from Fodor's Encyclopedia we read that Horace Greeley, the editor of the *New York Tribune*, was their first caller and he received an evidential spirit contact from his son. Fearing for their safety, he advised them to charge five dollars admission fee.

Later, under the aegis of the Society for the Diffusion of Spiritual Knowledge, free public sittings were initiated for which Mr H. H. Day and Mr Greeley paid 1,200 dollars a year to Kate. Interest ran high from the very first. In a single sitting, the following celebrities gathered around the séance table: The Rev. Dr Griswold, James Fenimore Cooper (who received accurate answers to questions about a sister killed fifty years before), George Bancroft, the historian, The

2. To be found on www.survivalafterdeath.info

Rev. Dr Hawks, Dr J. W. Francis, Dr Marck, Willis and Bryant, the poets, General Lyman and Bigelow of the *Evening Post*. Most were convinced of the authenticity of the mediumship.

Horace Greeley reported in *The Tribune*:

> We devoted what time we could spare from our duties out of three days to this subject, and it would be the basest cowardice not to say that we are convinced beyond a doubt of their perfect integrity and good faith in the premises. Whatever may be the origin or cause of the 'rappings', the ladies in whose presence they occur do not make them. We tested this thoroughly and to our entire satisfaction.

Although the phenomena in these first séances were not powerful, raps occurred, the table and chairs moved and the sitters were touched by invisible hands. Perhaps their most powerful early manifestation was recorded in 1853 by Governor Talmadge. It was the complete levitation of the table with him on top. He also claimed to have received a communication in direct writing from the spirit of John C. Calhoun. In 1854, William Lloyd Bryant witnessed a similar event at a table tipping séance. Spirit lights and materializations were a comparatively late development. They were obtained both with Kate and Leah Fox.

Four hundred séances (Kate Fox)

According to *Encyclopedia of Psychic Science* by Nandor Fodor, between 1861 and 1866, Kate Fox was engaged exclusively for Charles F. Livermore, a rich banker of New York, whose wife, Estelle, had died in 1860. Kate sat for him in nearly four hundred sittings of which detailed records were kept. The doors and windows were carefully locked and the séances, witnessed by prominent men, were often held in Livermore's own house. While the medium retained consciousness Estelle gradually materialized. She was not recognised until the forty-third sitting when she was illuminated by a psychic light. Later, the materialization became more complete but the figure could not speak, except a few words.

The communication took place through raps and writing. Estelle and another spirit named Benjamin Franklin, wrote on cards brought by Livermore. Whilst she wrote the hands of Kate Fox were held.

The script was a perfect reproduction of the characters she used when on earth.

In his book *These Mysterious People* Fodor tells us that in the records of 22nd February 1862, there is a unique description of the materialization of flowers. It reads:

Appearance of flowers. Cloudy. Atmosphere damp. Conditions unfavorable. At the expiration of half an hour a bright light rose to the surface of the table, of the usual cylindrical form, covered with gossamer. Held directly over this was a sprig of roses about six inches in length, containing two half-blown white roses, and a bud with leaves. The flowers, leaves and stem, were perfect. They were placed at my nose and smelled as though freshly gathered; but the perfume in this instance was weak and delicate.

We took them in our fingers and I carefully examined the stem and flowers. The request was made as before to be very careful. I noticed an adhesive, viscous feeling, which was explained as being the result of a damp, impure atmosphere. These flowers were held near and over the light, which seemed to feed and give them substance in the same manner as the hand. By raps we were told to 'notice and see them dissolve'.

The sprig was placed over the light, the flowers dropped, and in less than one minute melted as though made of wax, their substance seeming to spread as they disappeared. By raps, 'see them come again'. A faint light immediately shot across the cylinder, grew into a stem; and in about the same time required for its dissolution, the stem and the roses had grown into created perfection. This was several times repeated, and was truly wonderful.

Concerning these séances, Dr John F. Gray of New York testified:

Mr Livermore's recitals of the séances in which I participated are faithfully and most accurately stated, leaving not a shade of doubt in my mind as to the truth and accuracy of his accounts of those at which I was not a witness. I saw with him the philosopher Franklin, in a living, tangible, physical form, several times; and, on as many different occasions, I also witnessed the production of lights, odours, and sounds; and also the formation of flowers, cloth-textures, etc., and their disintegration and dispersion.

At the 388th séance, Estelle declared that she appeared for the last time. Livermore never saw her any more. In gratitude for the consolation he derived from these sittings, he enabled Kate Fox to visit Britain in 1871. In a letter to Benjamin Coleman, he praised her irreproachable character and detailed her idiosyncrasies.

The best test, rapping and physical medium I have ever met (Leah Fox)

In her autobiography Emma Hardinge Britten(*106*) writes this of the Fox sisters:

> From my first entrance into American Spiritualism, I became well acquainted with Mrs Fox and her daughters, Katey and Margaretta, the so-called "Rochester Knockers", and one of my most esteemed friends was Mrs Leah Fox Underhill, the eldest of the renowned Fox sisters.

> This lady was the best test, rapping and physical medium I have ever met, as well as one of the kindest and noble-hearted of women.

> After her marriage with Mr Daniel Underhill, ... although she was placed in wholly independent circumstances, she never flagged in her devotion to the cause she had espoused but opened her handsome house in 37th Street, New York for winter evening receptions in which, when ever I was in the city, she kindly invited me to become her associate. ...

> After the general receptions broke up, a few privileged friends would remain to share a social supper on the famous old Rochester dinner table at which the first Spirit circles of the age were held, under the auspices of the Fox sisters.

> At these séances of Mrs Underhill's, the manifestations were so powerful and startling that they would seem in cold recital too incredible to justify repetition.

Inspirational Trance
Speaking

Inspirational Trance Speaking

I can hardly wait to die.

Richard Hodgson, Psychical Researcher

Mediums have given public addresses in various degrees of trance since the mid-19th century. This is most definitely a form of mediumship. Their topics are often chosen by the audience immediately before the medium speaks. The contents of the address greatly surpass the medium's normal intellectual power and knowledge.

As inspirational speakers, women became sources of religious truth and, as such, assumed the authority of religious leaders. In this way, mediumship circumvented the structural barriers that excluded women from religious leadership. By communicating directly with spirits, mediums bypassed the need for education, ordination, or organizational recognition, which secured the male monopoly of male religious leaders. While men might bar women from church councils or from theological education, human authority could not supersede that given to mediums by the spirits who spoke through them. Thus, spirit communication carried its own authority. If one accepted the message, one had little choice but to accept the medium.

Spiritualism also changed the accepted norms by encouraging women to speak in public. Men called meetings to order, forcefully presiding over gatherings that could number in the thousands. They addressed audiences in a 'normal' state, expressing their own views on Spiritualist subjects. In contrast, a woman would write a speech and let a man deliver it, like in graduation address, but female mediums could speak from the podium because they were unconscious. These women presented not their own views but those of the spirits who spoke through them. An example of this dichotomy was the first woman to be ordained, Congregationalist Antoinette Brown Blackwell. In 1853, her speaking brought a religious convention to halt, but from 1853-1859 the lecture circuit was predominantly filled with female trance speakers. Later, she tried to secure an arrangement whereby she could preach weekly reform sermons for free in New York City in 1859, but no backer would underwrite the cost of the hall. In contrast, a relatively obscure medium, Ella E. Gibson filled a concert hall in Augusta, Maine for six consecutive evenings.

Horace Greeley's *New York Tribune* alone among New York papers reported women's rights lectures, but, in 1858, Greeley found this practice too controversial to continue. Yet trance speakers received extensive press notices, both positive and negative.

Trance speakers enjoyed the support of the mass of believers during the 1850s. At that time, these mediums were generally women; they did not give private sittings, and did not receive messages from individually identifiable spirits. For audiences that had never witnessed a woman speaking in public, the spectacle of a woman or a teenage girl at the podium must have appeared impressive, if not miraculous.

Ursula Roberts in her autobiography *Living in Two Worlds* describes the effect on her when she witnessed the trance mediumship of Meurig Morris:

> So we went to listen to Mrs Morris who was appearing in a large hall in Brighton. I watched her with avid curiosity. There she sat, a gentle, young woman who nervously took endlessly sips from a glass of water, and who offered a prayer in a voice which was only just audible to my acute hearing. Yet later when she stood to address the large audience a voice of enormous volume filled the hall, and with the voice a feeling of tremendous power and peace flowed into me with absolute healing. I was listening to the voice of a spirit called 'Power' and as the spirit spoke through her I knew that from 'Power' radiated a living quality similar to the Power that had revealed to me the glories of nature. This was the living quality of the Spirit and I knew that this was what I must seek. As it was not to be found in the Church, I would search for it in Spiritualism and I hoped spirits such as 'Power' could restore to me the contact with Universal Beauty.

First inspirational speech at age six (Cora L. V. Scott Hatch Daniels Tappan Richmond)

Cora was said to have been born with a veil over her face which indicated a special gift. She first spoke in trance at age of six for one and half hours. Her first public address was at age eleven. At a time when women did not speak in public, Afro-American churches in Washington DC welcomed Cora Hatch[1] to their pulpits when no non-Afro-American church ever did. According to observers, it was Cora Hatch's practice to enter the hall already in trance. The subjects of her speeches were picked by the audience just before she spoke and were said to include materialization or the history of occult.

Emancipation Proclamation (Henrietta 'Nettie' Sturdevant Colburn Maynard)

Trance speaker Henrietta Maynard had a special claim to fame since her oratory reportedly influenced Abraham Lincoln on the issue of emancipation. She was known as 'Lincoln's Medium' Maynard described her meetings with the president in her book, *Was Abraham Lincoln a Spiritualist?* which began when she visited Washington D.C. in the spring of 1862 in order to see her brother, then in a Federal Army hospital. Lincoln's wife had a sitting with Maynard and was enormously impressed. The following day, she sent a carriage to collect the medium. In a state of trance, the medium delivered a powerful address in front of the President relating to the forthcoming Emancipation Proclamation, The speaker urged Lincoln 'not to abort the terms of its issue and not to delay its enforcement as a law beyond the opening of the year'; and he was then assured that it was to be the crowning event of his administration and his life even though he was being strongly counselled by certain individuals to defer the matter. According to reports, President Lincoln acknowledged the pressures upon him and was deeply impressed by the medium's message. This is Nettie's description of her first meeting with President Lincoln:

> I was led forward and presented. He [Lincoln] stood before me, tall and kindly, with a smile on his face. Dropping his hand upon my head, he said, in a humorous tone "So this is our little Nettie that we have heard so much about?" I could only smile and say, "Yes, sir." like any school girl; when he kindly led me

---

1. Cora L. V. (these initials are listed as either "Lavina Victoria" or "Lodencia Veronica") Scott was married four times, so her name is listed in a variation of "Cora L. V. Scott Hatch Daniels Tappan Richmond."

to an ottoman. Sitting down in a chair, he began asking me questions in a kindly way about my mediumship; and I think he must have thought me stupid, as my answers were little beyond 'Yes' and 'No'. His manner, however, was genial and kind, and it was then suggested we form a circle. He said "Well, how do you do it?" looking at me. Mr Laurie came to the rescue, and said we had been accustomed to sit in a circle and join hands; but he did not think it would be necessary at this instance. While he was speaking, I lost all consciousness of my surroundings and passed under control.

For more than an hour I was made to talk to him, and I learned from my friends afterward that it was upon matters that he seemed to fully understand, while they comprehended very little until that portion was reached that related to the forthcoming Emancipation Proclamation. He was charged with the utmost solemnity and force of manner not to abate the terms of its issue, and not to delay its enforcement as a law beyond the opening of the year; and he was assured that it was to be *the crowning event of his administration and his life*; and that while he was counselled by strong parties to defer enforcement of it, hoping to supplant it by other measures and to delay action, *he must in no wise heed such counsel, but stand firm to his convictions and fearlessly perform the work and fulfill the mission for which he had been raised up by an overruling Providence*. Those present declared that they lost sight of the timid girl in the majesty of the utterance, the strength and force of the language, and the importance of that which was conveyed, and seemed to realize that some strong masculine spirit force was giving speech to almost divine commands.

I shall never forget the scene around me when I regained consciousness. I was standing in front of Mr Lincoln, and he was sitting back in his chair, with his arms folded upon his breast, looking intently at me. I stepped back, naturally confused at the situation... not remembering at once where I was; and glancing around the group, where perfect silence reigned. It took me a moment to remember my whereabouts.

A gentleman present then said, in a low voice, "Mr President, did you notice anything peculiar in the method of address?"

Mr Lincoln raised himself, as if shaking off his spell. He glanced quickly at the full length picture of Daniel Webster, that hung above the piano, and replied "Yes, and it is very singular, very!" with a marked emphasis.

Mr Somes said "Mr President, would it be improper for me to inquire whether there has been any pressure brought to bear upon you to defer the enforcement of the Proclamation?" To which the President replied "Under these circumstances that question is perfectly proper, as we are all friends (smiling upon the company). *It is taking all my nerve and strength to withstand such a pressure.*" At this point the gentlemen drew round him and spoke together in low tones, Mr Lincoln saying least of all.

At last he turned to me, and laying his hand upon my head, uttered these words in a manner that I shall never forget "My child, you possess a very singular gift; but that it is a gift from God, I have no doubt. I thank you for coming here tonight. It is more important than perhaps anyone present can understand. I must leave you all now; but I hope I shall see you again." He shook me kindly by the hand, bowed to the rest of the company, and was gone." We remained for an hour longer, talking with Mrs Lincoln and her friends, then returned to Georgetown. Such was my first interview with Abraham Lincoln, and the memory of it is *as clear and vivid as the evening on which it occurred. [italics in the 1956 edition text]*

In his book, an esteemed witness, Colonel Simon Kase, describes the scene this way:

They exchanged the courtesies of the day and chatted for about ten minutes. The young girl then walks up to Lincoln with closed eyes giving him the following message "Sir, you have been called to the position that you now occupy for a very great purpose. The world is in universal bondage; it must be physically set free, that it may mentally rise to its affairs of this nation as well as a Congress at Washington. This Republic is leading the van of Republics throughout the world." Nettie Colburn Maynard continued to address Lincoln for over an hour on the significance of liberating the slaves. She argued that the Civil War would go on until slavery was abolished because, "God destined all men to be free." Colonel Kase described her words, 'Her language was truly sublime, and full of arguments, grand in the extreme, that from the time his proclamation of freedom was issued, there would be no reverse to our army'.

'The Preaching Woman' (Achsa White Sprague)

During her lifetime, she became one of the best known women in eastern America. Boston, Providence, New York, Philadelphia and Hartford all issued frequent demands for her entranced speaking appearances. Achsa's first appearance as a public speaker was in the Union Church at South Reading. Within a few months of her first lecture, she was filling halls in Boston, where local Spiritualists implored her to extend her visit. For more than seven years from 1854 to 1861, she travelled alone by railroad, stagecoach, and steamboat throughout New England and as far west as Chicago, Milwaukee and St. Louis, where newspapers carried accounts of her lectures before audiences of thousands. Below are some newspaper accounts of her trance speaking:

This excellent woman and gifted medium delighted a large and respectable audience in Concert Hall on Sunday afternoon and evening, with religious and philosophical teachings of the highest order pouring forth in a perfect torrent of eloquent speech – *L. G. B., Burlington, Vt., June 4th.*

It is surprising how a lady, with less than the educational advantages of the clergyman or the lawyer, can pour forth, for an hour and a half or more, such beautiful sentences with such eloquent and impressive elocution, as no clergyman or lawyer, of our acquaintance, can equal. – *Terre Haute Daily Evening Journal, Indiana, Jan. 25th.*

Miss Sprague delivered a lecture on Spiritualism last evening in Republican Hall, which was packed to suffocation with hearers. She spoke under mesmeric influence for an hour and a quarter saying death was only a change, a removal, a transition to a different state, at whose approach we should have no fears. – *Providence, R. I.*

Trance address which leaves a mark on medium (Mona van der Watt)

George Cranley relates that through the mediumship of Mona van der Watt, the spirit of Nobel Prize laureate, Wilhelm Röntgen, the discoverer of X-Rays, gave a talk on the healing rays used by spirit doctors and guides and, as evidence of his presence, said he would leave a mark on the medium which would disappear within twenty minutes. When Mona came out of trance, clearly visible on her hand was the raised shape of an X which gradually subsided and disappeared.

'Power' and the swinging microphone[1] (Louisa Anne Meurig Morris)

Meurig Morris was a charming but extremely simple British woman with a limited education. So deep was her entrancement (assumed to be in the delta state of brain waves), she possessed a totally different personality. Her controls included 'Little Sunshine', 'Sister Magdelene', and 'Power'. 'Power' never revealed his true identity. His desire was to remain impersonal as it was the teaching and not the teacher which counted. And so overwhelming was his personality that people learned to approach him in a spirit of reverence. Sir Oliver Lodge had met him, and from the conversation on the immediate future of humanity, the great scientist emerged with tears in his eyes.

This great moment occurred at the British Movietone Company when a film was being made of 'Power's' oratory. Mrs Morris was giving a trance address and the microphones were held by seventy people high up in the air on new half-inch ropes. A rope suddenly snapped and a terrific crash startled all present. Within half an inch of Mrs Morris' entranced face, the microphone swung across swaying to and fro. A foreman rushed up and dragged the rope aside to keep it out of the sight of the camera.

The cameraman never stopped filming and neither did Mrs Morris, in spite of the obvious danger to her life, falter and her trance speech went on undisturbed. According to 'Power', the rope was

1. This account and the following one about Meurig Morris are from Fodor's *These Mysterious People* Ch25 (www.survivalafterdeath.info)

super-normally severed to prove, by the medium's demeanour that she was indeed in trance, as no human being could have consciously exhibited such self-possession as she did when the accident occurred. This moment is preserved thanks to YouTube.

'Power' overcomes technical difficulties (Louisa Anne Meurig Morris)

Another amazing moment in modern mediumship concerning 'Power' and Mrs Morris was a veritable technical miracle which occurred at the Columbia Gramophone Company's studio in the course of recording 'Power's' voice. According to the publicly rendered account of C. W. Nixon (of the Columbia Gramophone Company), an incident occurred at the very commencement of the operation which, by all the rules, should have spoiled the first side of the record. Mr Ernest Oaten, President of the International Spiritualist Federation, was in the chair, and being unaware that the start was to be made without the appearance of the usual red light, he told Mrs Morris as she stood up "Wait for the signal." These words were picked up by the microphone and were heard by the engineers in the recording-room after the apparatus had been started. It was believed that they must be on the record.

Later, when the second side of the record was to be made, there was confusion in starting. Toward the end, as if to make technical failure a certainty, Mrs Morris turned and walked several paces away from the microphone. A week before the record was ready for reproduction Cowen rang Nixon and told him that 'Power' asserts that notwithstanding the technical mistakes the record would be a success, that Mr Oaten's words would not be reproduced and that the timing and volume of the voice would not be spoiled by the later accidents. This statement was so extraordinary and appeared to be so preposterous that Nixon had it taken down word by word, and sent it in a sealed envelope to Mr Oaten in Manchester with the request that he would keep it unopened until the record was ready and the truth or otherwise of the prediction could be tested. The record was played in the Fortune Theatre on 25th April 1931. It was perfect. The letter was opened. The prediction was found to be true in every detail.

Books dictated by an illiterate while in trance (Andrew Jackson Davis)

In 1845, at age nineteen, Andrew Jackson Davis felt the need to speak and write. According to J. H. Brennan's book, *Whisperers: The Secret History of the Spirit World* (198), Davis' 157 entranced lectures given while he was on a series of public demonstrations in New York so impressed a wealthy patron named Silone Dodge that he arranged to have his lectures published in book form. But being essentially illiterate (by this point in his life he had only had 5 months of schooling and never read more than a half dozen books), Davis was teamed up with a Dr Lyon, from Bridgeport, as hypnotist for this work. Lyon took the young man to New York, where a Reverend William Fishbough acted as secretary and took the dictation Davis gave while in trance.

In November, 1845, an entranced Davis began to dictate his great work *The Principles of Nature, Her Divine Revelations*, and a *Voice to Mankind*. The dictation lasted for fifteen months, and the book was published in 1847. Dr George Bush, Professor of Hebrew at the University of New York, was present at many of the trance utterings. He later said:

> I can solemnly affirm that I have heard Davis correctly quote the Hebrew language in his entranced dictation, and display a knowledge of geology which would have been astonishing in a person of his age, even if he had devoted years to the study. He has discussed, with the most signal ability, the profoundest questions of historical and Biblical archeology, of mythology, of the origin and affinity of language, and the progress of civilization among the different nations of the globe, which would do honour to any scholar of the age, even if in reaching them he had the advantage of access to all the libraries of Christendom.
>
> Indeed, if he had acquired all the information he gives forth in these lectures, not in the two years since he left the shoemaker's bench, but in his whole life, with the most assiduous study, no prodigy of intellect of which the world has ever heard would be for a moment compared with him, yet not a single volume or page has he ever read.

Later in life, when a New York law banned mesmeric healers, Davis enrolled in the United States Medical College where he earned degrees in both anthropology and medicine – the latter of which allowed him to continue his healing practice – despite being functionally illiterate.

Levitation

Levitation

The phenomena I am prepared to attest are so extraordinary, and so directly oppose the most firmly rooted articles of scientific belief— amongst others, the ubiquity and invariable action of the force of gravitation—that, even now, on recalling the details of what I witnessed, there is an antagonism in my mind between reason, which pronounces it to be scientifically impossible, and the consciousness that my senses, both of touch and sight—are not lying witnesses when they testify against my preconceptions.

Sir William Crookes

Levitation is the movement upward of an object or objects without normal means of support. It can occur in darkness, red-light or full light[1] conditions. According to Spiritualist theories, this can be done by either telekinesis or by the use of ectoplasm.

Sir Arthur Conan Doyle suggested that in a séance, ectoplasmic rods are created, act as a conductor, and are used to levitate objects such as a table. The rods can form out of the solar plexus and stomach area of the medium's body, but then can be connected to other sitters as well if needs be. The medium is the significant source of ectoplasm, but some regular sitters are used as extra energy resources.

In Britain, Sir William Crookes narrated his own experiences:

On one occasion, I witnessed a chair, with a lady sitting on it, rise several inches from the ground. On another occasion, to avoid the suspicion of this being in some way performed by herself, the lady knelt on the chair in such a manner that its four feet were visible to us. It then rose about three inches, remained suspended for about ten seconds and then slowly descended.

At another time two children, on separate occasions rose from the floor with their chairs, in full daylight under (to me) most satisfactory conditions; for I was kneeling and keeping close watch upon the feet of the chair, observing distinctly that no one might touch them. (*Researches (99)*)

---

1. D. D. Home seldom sat in darkness. Eusapia Paladino once levitated a table in blazing sunshine.

Levitating objects rapping out answers (D. D. Home)

Concerning other levitations associated with Daniel Dunglas Home, Nandor Fodor writes in his *Encyclopedia of Psychic Science* of Sir William Crookes' observations:

> One of the most amazing things I have seen was the levitation of a glass water-bottle and tumbler. The two objects remained suspended above the table, and by tapping against each other answered 'yes' to questions. They remained suspended about six to eight inches above the table for about five minutes, moving in front of each person and answering questions.

Another note of Sir William Crookes *(106)* is still more interesting:

> During a séance with Mr Home a small lath moved across the table to me in the light and delivered a message to me by tapping my hand; I repeating the alphabet and the lath tapping me at the right letters. The other end of the lath was resting on the table, some distance from Mr Home's hands. The taps were so sharp and clear and the lath was evidently so well under control of the invisible power which was governing its movements, that I said "Can the intelligence governing the motion of this lath change the character of the movements, and give me a telegraphic message through the Morse alphabet by taps on my hand."
>
> Immediately I said this the character of the taps changed and the message was continued in the way I had requested. The letters were given too rapidly for me to do more than catch a word here and there and consequently I lost the message; but I heard sufficient to convince me that there was a good Morse operator at the other end of the line, wherever it might be.

Table levitates before and after séance (Mr and Mrs L. R. Hodges)

The power of spirit to manifest in ordinary home circles with virtually unknown mediums has always existed. Mr and Mrs L. R. Hodges, of Brighton, sat once a week for four years with no indication that any power was being developed in either one of them. Patiently, they continued to sit only for the phenomena of direct voice. Finally, cool psychic breezes were felt, then the sounds of snapping fingers. When direct voices were finally heard they had the distinctive characteristics of their owners and husband and wife remained normal and conversed with them naturally. Maurice Barbanell in *Power of the Spirit(60)*, writes:

> Before the sitting, when we were having tea, the heavy table on which all the food was laid – and I am referring to the pre-war days – was levitated in full light! It rose several inches clear of the ground. After the séance while we were discussing the phenomenon, the table was levitating again. I tried to raise it myself, but could shift it only a little with the utmost effort.

Flying trumpet and levitating table (Kathleen Goliger)

In his article *The Mystery of Ectoplasm Part 5* Michael Tymn records that during December 1915, Professor William Crawford invited Sir William Barrett, Professor of Physics at Royal College in Dublin, to join him in investigating the mediumship of Kathleen Goliger. At first, they heard knocks, and then messages were spelled out as one of the sitters recited the alphabet. Barrett then reported observing a floating trumpet, which he tried unsuccessfully to catch. Barrett wrote "Then the table began to rise from the floor some 18 inches and remained suspended and quite level. I was allowed to go up to the table and saw clearly no one was touching it, a clear space separating the sitters from the table."

Barrett put pressure on the table to try to force it back to the floor. He exerted all his strength but was unable to budge it. He continued "Then I climbed on the table and sat on it, my feet off the floor, when I was swayed to and fro and finally tipped off. The table of its own accord now turned upside down, no one touching it, and I tried to lift it off the ground, but it could not be stirred; it appeared screwed down to the floor." When Barrett stopped trying to right the table, it righted itself on its own accord.

Table tilts in a restaurant (Mina 'Margery'Crandon)

The mediumship of Mina 'Margery' Crandon began to accelerate in 1923. At that time, she was sitting weekly for table tilting and levitation. According to J. Malcolm Bird in *"Margery":The Medium* levitations started in earnest in June 1923 with sound phenomena occurring with hands on and off the table. In July 1923, levitations of the table a foot and a half off the ground started to occur. On 28th July the table levitated a foot and a half off the ground for twenty one seconds. On 4th August it levitated with a man sitting on it, spilling him to the floor. Again on 11th August, there was levitation without contact, and a man was twice dumped off the table. On 18th October, Margery entered a restaurant at three o'clock in the afternoon, and sat down at one of the smaller tables. After her order was served, the lady opposite her called the waitress and asked her to put something under the table that it was making her seasick. It was in fact tilting sharply first to one end and then to the other. Margery withdrew in embarrassment, leaving her meal half eaten.

The many levitations of Daniel Dunglas Home (D. D. Home)

Home's first levitation occurred 8th August 1852, in Ward Cheney's house at Manchester, Connecticut. *The Hartford Times* recorded the event:

> Suddenly and without any expectation on the part of the company, Mr Home was taken up in the air. I had hold of his hand at the time, and I felt his feet – they were lifted a foot from the floor. Again and again he was taken from the floor, and the third time he was carried to the ceiling of the apartment with which his hands and feet came in gentle contact. I felt the distance from the soles of his boots to the floor, and it was nearly three feet. Others touched his feet to satisfy themselves.[2]

On over 100 occasions during the 1860s and into the late 1870s Home was levitated up to the ceiling and often around the room above the heads of witnesses. With no other medium was bodily levitation so often and so reliably attested to as with Home.

Again Sir William Crookes narrated his own experiences:

> The most striking cases of levitation which I have witnessed have been with Mr Home. On three separate occasions have I seen him raised completely from the floor of the room. Once sitting in an easy chair , once kneeling on the chair and once standing up.

---

2. Fron *The Levitations of D.D.Home* on http://parapsychologyinfo.com)

On each occasion I had full opportunity of watching the occurrence as it was taking place. There are at least a hundred instances of Mr Home's rising from the ground, in the presence of as many separate persons, and I have heard from the lips of the three witnesses to the most striking occurrence of this kind – the Earl of Dunraven, Lord Lindsay and Captain C. Wynne – their own most minute accounts of what took place. To reject the recorded evidence on this subject is to reject all human testimony whatever; for no fact in sacred or profane history is supported by a stronger array of proofs. *(Researches:99)*

In the *Journal of the Society for Psychical Research* (Vol. 6, no. 15, [1889]), Crookes further stated:

On several occasions Home and the chair on which he was sitting at the table rose off the ground. This was generally done very deliberately, and Home sometimes tucked up his feet on the seat of the chair and held up his hands in full view of all of us.

On such an occasion I have got down and seen and felt that all four legs were off the ground at the same time, Home's feet being on the chair. Less frequently the levitating power was extended to those sitting next to him. Once, my wife was thus raised off the ground in her chair.

Out one window and in by another (D. D. Home)

This was the most famous case in history of levitation and was witnessed on 13th December (or 16th December, as first printed in Lord Adare's book), 1868, at Ashley House, Victoria Street, London. It was this Ashley Place levitation that ensured Home's lasting place in the history of Spiritualism.

Two of the three witnesses were leading members of London society – Lord Lindsay (late earl of Crawford) and Viscount Adare (later Earl of Dunraven). The other witness was Captain Charles Wynne, Adare's cousin. Sir Arthur Conan Doyle declared the testimony of the three witnesses 'unimpeachable'.

The three witnesses wrote up an account of the incident, which became the talk of London. Home had levitated, floated out of a third story window and come in through the window of another room.

Lord Adare noted:

He [Home] then said to us "Do not be afraid, and on no account leave your places." and he went out into the passage. Lindsay suddenly said "Oh, good heavens! I know what he is going to do; it is too fearful." Adare said "What is it?" Lindsay replied "I cannot tell you, it is too horrible! Adah [the spirit of a deceased American actress] says that I must tell you; he is going out of the window in the other room, and coming in at this window."

We heard Home go into the next room, heard the window thrown up, and presently Home appeared standing upright outside our window; he opened the window and walked in quite coolly "Ah", he said, "you were good this time." – referring to our having sat still and not wished to prevent him.

He sat down and laughed. Charlie asked "What are you laughing at?" Home said "We [the spirits – Home always was spoken of in third person when in trance] are thinking that if a policeman had been passing and had looked up and had seen a man turning round and round along the wall in the air he would have been much astonished. Adare, shut the window in the next room."

So I [Adare] got up, shut the window, and in coming back remarked that the window was not raised a foot, and that I could not think how he managed to squeeze through. He arose and said "Come and see." I went with him; he told me to open the window as it was before. I did so; he told me to stand a little distance off; he then went through the open space, head first, quite rapidly, his body being nearly horizontal and apparently rigid. He came in again, feet foremost, and we returned to the other room. It was so dark I could not see clearly how he was supported outside. He did not appear to grasp, or rest upon, the balustrade, but rather to be swung out and in.

Outside each window is a small balcony or ledge, 19 inches deep, bounded by stone balustrades, 18 inches high; the balustrades of the two windows are 7 feet 4 inches apart, measuring from the nearest points. A string-course, 4 inches wide, runs between the windows at the level of the bottom of the balustrade; and another 3 inches wide at the level of the top.

Between the window at which Home went out, and that at which he came in, the wall recedes 6 inches. The rooms are onthe third floor. I asked Lindsay how Adah had spoken to him on the three occasions. He could scarcely explain; but said it did not sound like an audible human voice; but rather as if the tones were whispered or impressed inside his ear. When Home awoke he was much agitated; he said he felt as if he had gone through some fearful peril, and that he had a horrible desire to throw himself out of the window; he remained in a very nervous condition for a short time, and then gradually became quiet.[3]

Another witness, Lord Lindsay, gave an account of the incident before the Committee of the Dialectical Society in London in 1869 and wrote out an account in 1871. Before the society, he stated:

I saw the levitations in Victoria Street, when Home floated out of the window; he first went into a trance and walked about uneasily; then he went into the hall; while he was away, I heard a voice whisper in my ear "He will go out of one window and in at another." I was alarmed and shocked at the idea of so dangerous an experiment. I told the company what I had heard, and we then waited for Home's return. Shortly after he entered the room, I heard the window go up, but I could not see it, for I sat with my back to it. I, however, saw his shadow on the opposite wall; he went out of the window in a horizontal position, and I saw him outside the other window [that in the next room] floating in the air.

It was eighty-five feet from the ground. There was no balcony along the windows, merely a string course an inch and a half wide; each window had a small plant stand, but there was no connection between them.

In his letter dated 14th July 1871, published in the *Spiritualist* newspaper, there was a further addition to the story:

"The moon was shining full into the room; my back was to the light, and I saw the shadow on the wall of the window sill, and Home's feet about six inches above it. He remained in this position

3. Source: Viscount Adare. *Experiences in Spiritualism with D. D. Home*. London: privately printed, 1870. (retrieved from http://parapsychologyinfo.com)

for a few seconds, then raised the window and glided into the room feet foremost, and sat down."

Given the space between the two windows was over seven feet, the window ledges were only four inches wide, and the windows some seventy feet above the ground, makes trickery an unlikely explanation.

Dancing piano with President Lincoln (Mrs Belle Miller)

In L. B. Jefts' pamphlet, *Lo, I am with you always*, we read:

> Many years ago a remarkable feat of telekinesis was accomplished in the presence of President Abraham Lincoln. Many séances were actually held in the White House by a medium named Nettie Colburn, who was known later as Nettie Colburn Maynard. At one séance held at a friend's house in Georgetown which was attended by President and Mrs Lincoln, the concert grand piano, weighing nearly a ton, started to levitate.

In Nettie Colburn Maynard's own book *Was Abraham Lincoln a Spiritualist?(81)* she tells us:

> ... that evening the daughter of the house Mrs Belle Miller gave an example of her power as a 'moving' medium and highly amused and interested us by causing the piano 'to waltz around the room' ... Mrs Miller played upon the piano (a three-corner grand), and under her influence it rose and fell, keeping time to her touch in a perfectly regular manner ...
>
> The President with a quaint smile, said "I think we can hold down that instrument." Where upon he climbed upon it, sitting with his legs dangling over the side, as also did Mr Somes, S.P. Kase, and a soldier in the uniform of a major from the army of the Potomac. The piano notwithstanding this enormous added weight continued to wabble about until the sitters were glad 'to vacate the premises'.

Nettie Colburn continues:

> We were convinced that there were no mechanical contrivances to produce the strange result, and Mr Lincoln expressed himself perfectly satisfied that the motion was caused by some 'invisible power'.

Squadron mates lift medium up as a prank (Albert Best)

This account of levitation was given to medium Gordon Smith by a Catholic priest who had been invited to a demonstration of mediumship in a friend's house in Glasgow. (*posted in Oct 2011 on the forum of www.spiritualismlink.com.*)

Mr Best sat in a large and very heavy-looking armchair at the far end of the well-lit sitting room, whilst the rest of the group was seated around the room in a sort of circle formation. Mr Best closed his eyes and fell into a sort of trance and a voice spoke through him in an accent which was hard to distinguish as any exact nationality. He began to give what I believe was a message from the spirit on the other side to one of my colleagues, who was confirming what he was hearing when, without warning, the chair on which Mr Best was sitting began to shake furiously. Mr Best snapped out of his trance state and began to protest to unseen forces around him, saying "Stop that!" and "Put me down!"

If I had not been in the company of people who I consider sane of mind, I would not have believed my eyes, as the chair, along with Mr Best, lifted up, till the little man's head was near ceiling height. No sooner had this happened that voices could be heard, which I can say came from no one seen sitting in that room. The chair slowly returned to the floor with Mr Best still calling out to the invisible forces around him and the session ended soon after.

The medium explained that he was unharmed and never in any danger, but he did not like it when they played games like that just to impress people. He said that the spirits who had played this prank on him were men who had been part of his squadron during the war and who had died in Africa in 1943. This was Mr Best's account; quite honestly, I along with the most of my group, even those among us with a background in physics, have absolutely no explanation for what we experienced.

Levitating dinner table and piano (Florence and Katie Cook)

Florence Marryat writes in her book *There is No Death* that the first time she met Florence Cook was at the private house of Mr Dunphy of *The Morning Post*.

On that occasion, as we were sitting at supper, after the séance, – a party of perhaps thirty people – the whole dinner table, with everything upon it, rose bodily in the air, to a level with our knees, and the dishes and glasses swayed about in a perilous manner, without, however, coming to any permanent harm.

Florence Marryat also had a number of sittings with Florence Cook's younger sister Katie, also a powerful medium but worked more privately than Florence. She writes of another levitation, this time with Katie, in the house of a Mr Blackburn in Elgin Crescent, London.

We sat in a small breakfast room on the basement floor, so small indeed for the size of the party that as we encircled a large round table, the sitters' backs touched the wall on either side, this entirely preventing anyone crossing the room whilst we were established there. The only piece of furniture of any consequence in the room besides the chairs and table was a trichord cabinet piano, belonging to Mrs Cook (who was keeping house at the time for Mr Blackburn) and which she much valued.

Katie Cook sat amongst us as usual. In the middle of the séance her control 'Lily', who was materialized, called out "Keep hands fast. Don't let go whatever you do!"

And at the same time without seeing anything (for we were sitting in complete darkness), we became conscious that something large and heavy was passing or being carried over our heads. One of the ladies of the party became nervous and dropped her neighbour's hand with a cry of alarm and at the same moment a weighty body fell with a fearful crash on the other side of the room...

When lights were struck we found the cabinet piano had actually been carried over our heads to the opposite side of the room where it had fallen on to the floor and been seriously damaged [much to Mrs Cook's dismay]. The two carved legs were broken off and the sounding board smashed in.

Materialization

Materialization

It is all very well for you, who have probably never seen
any spiritual manifestations, to talk as you do;
But if you had seen what I have witnessed you would hold
a different opinion.

W. M. Thackeray

The materialization of animate objects is an extremely rare occurrence in mediumship. Ectoplasm and darkened or red-light conditions are usually required, although in still rarer incidences it has occurred in full light.

The word Ectoplasm, from the Greek ektos, meaning 'outside', and plasma, meaning 'something formed or moulded', is a term coined by Charles Richet to denote a substance or spiritual energy 'exteriorized' by physical mediums. Around 1913, the German Baron von Schrenk-Notzing called ectoplasm 'teleplasma' and produced a chemical analysis of it as follows: 'colourless, slightly cloudy fluid with slightly alkaline reaction, traces of sputum, mucous membrane granules, potash, cell detritus, skin discs and minute particles of flesh'. His analysis was similar to that described by Dr Dombrowski of the Polish Society for Psychical Research in 1916.

According to Nandor Fodor in his *Encyclopedia of Psychic Science*, the discovery of ectoplasm is not new, as Foster Damon, of Harvard University, found in the works of the philosopher Vaughan, who lived around 1650, a description of a substance under the name of 'first matter' or 'mercury', drawn from the body, which has all the characteristics of ectoplasm.

Barbanell in *Spiritualism Today(33)* describes seeing two kinds of ectoplasm, one coloured white and the other brown. The white strip streamed from the medium's nose and the brown strip from one ear – later there were two brown strips, one from each ear [seen by *ultra-violet* light]. Yet when the red lamp was switched on, only one colour, a whitish hue, is visible. The brown ectoplasm was said to be of a 'lower vibration', composed out of the material in the room, furnishings, carpets, curtains, etc. The white ectoplasm came from the medium's body.

The ectoplasm from the medium's body, when handled, has been described as 'bone dry and like fine cloth' but can be used by spirit chemists to form any texture – skin, hair, beards, feathers, rough cloth. It has also been seen to form a rod-shaped structure which when attached to the trumpet enables it to move and voices travel along it.

According to Ramadahn, the spirit guide to Ursula Roberts, when a blending of the medium and the spirit guide occurs, ectoplasmic substances can be formed. When the conditions were perfect – clear, dry weather, which is so important to physical manifestations – and experienced and sympathetic sitters were present, the medium seemed to experience little or no fatigue. But séances for physical manifestations can put a strain on the medium. As Gladys Osbourne Leonard describes in her book *My Life in Two Worlds*, – one of the séances she sat in was called a halt because too much energy was being created by the sitters who were forming a battery by holding hands and this put a tremendous strain on the medium. Afterwards, he 'could scarcely stumble out of the room'.

During the manifestations, the medium usually sits within an enclosed area, called a cabinet. The cabinet is basically anything which allows a physical medium to sit away from the sitters, to help focus the energies and create a type of battery from which the phenomena can be formed and energized. There is usually a curtain in front of the cabinet, which can be spread apart in order for people to see what is going on within the cabinet.

According to Nandor Fodor in his *Encyclopedia of Psychic Science*, the exteriorization of ectoplasm requires a state of passivity on the part of the medium and complete materializations are the final product of the ectoplasmic process. Nobel laureate Professor Charles Richet, in *Thirty Years of Physical Research*, describes materialization as the production of a being formed of living matter which has its proper warmth, apparently a circulation of blood, and a psychological respiration. A psychic personality having a will distinct from the will of the medium, in a word, a new human being!

Richet went on to describe these details of materializations:

"I have seen admirably modelled fingers with nails, I have seen a head and felt the skull under thick black hair, a well materialized hand has the functional capacity of a normal hand."

He states that these materialized forms have a circulation of blood and also respiration. He goes on to say that in his experiments he has found that the spirit form has a will and a personality entirely separate from that of the medium.

Animals as well as humans have been known to materialize. Many incidents of a pet materializing have occurred. Maurice Barbanell witnessed several materialized animals including the favourite dog of one of the sitters and its tail was heard wagging against the leg of a chair. He also wrote about a pet cat that scratched at the carpet and a bird, which the medium had taken in when she found it injured, that used to materialize and fly about the séance room. McNamara writes on www.ghostcircle.com: "One of the most interesting phenomenon seen during materialization is the physical link between the materialized form and the medium. After a spirit materializes and walks away from the medium, cord of ectoplasm linking the spirit form with the physical medium can often be seen. This ectoplasmic cord can be likened to the umbilical cord of a foetus. Through it, the spirit operator receives a supply of etheric energy-matter from the medium. The spirit dematerializes by the ectoplasm withdrawing back into the medium's body."

Interlocking rings of different types of wood (Mina 'Margery' Crandon)

Hannen Swaffer in *My Greatest Story(208),* writes:

When I first visited the Crandons I saw the greatest psychical exhibit in history. Two years later when I returned I found that it had been destroyed as mysteriously as it had been produced.

In 1934, Button [William Button, then President of the American Society for Psychical Research] asked Walter [Margery's control] for a piece of evidence that, regardless of the way it was obtained, would be, in itself, scientific proof, of spirit power. If two rings were interlocked by Walter, he said, they could go anywhere. They could not be explained by trickery. Well, the rings were obtained and, in a few minutes, interlocked by Walter in the séance room. Then, told of the experiment, Sir Oliver Lodge suggested an even more convincing one – two different kinds of wood. So one ring made of white wood and one made of red mahogany. These, like the others, were soon joined up by Walter. So were other pairs. The test was made time after time.

Then, except for the original pair of rings of different colours, all the pairs of rings were taken apart as mysteriously as they had been joined. Walter would play games with them. Sometimes in the séance room sitters would see the rings looking as though parts of them had been eaten away. Sometimes Margery saw sawdust lying on the table and part of the rings missing. Sitters have seen them grow again.

Ectoplasm being reabsorbed by the medium (Helen Duncan)

Dr John Winning, in his article from August 1938, 'Materialization: How is it done? What are the methods?' reproduced in *Psypioneer Journal* Volume 9, No 06: June 2013 states:

Last week, I was again privileged to sit with Mrs Duncan[1]. There would be about fifteen sitters. The room was lit by a red lamp of sufficient radiance to permit one seeing the outline of all the other sitters. I sat in front, about three feet away from the opening of the cabinet. Within a few seconds of the white lights going out and the room being lit by the red lamp, Albert, the guide of Mrs Duncan, greeted us. Then followed, in the space of less than an hour, the appearance of more than a dozen materialized spirits. First, came a young girl greeting her mother. It was very touching to see that reunion. But Daisy was not content to show herself to her mother only. She came to the centre of the cabinet and almost outside, revealing to us the loveliness of her form and dress.

Her robes were beautifully white and silvery and must have contained many yards of material. She seemed to dematerialize right through the floor in front of us. Many others materialized and gave words of comfort to relatives. Later, a lady came out carrying a baby. She was recognised by one of the sitters.

1. Helen Duncan's full name was "Victoria Helen McCrae Duncan (née Mac-Farlane)."

Albert told us that she had passed to his side during child-birth, which fact was admitted by the relatives in the meeting. Shortly after that a little boy came out to speak to his own folks on earth. He told us his name was Colin and that he was very happy in his new life.

Peggy, the inimitable guide of Mrs Duncan, came next, and in her sweet childish manner chatted for some time with us. I noted the materialized forms very carefully. Some were taller than Mrs Duncan, some smaller, and all slimmer. The gracefulness of Daisy, the stature of Colin, and the liveliness of Peggy could not have been simulated by Mrs Duncan. Just before the finish, Albert opened wide the curtains and brought Mrs Duncan right to the front. She was still deeply entranced, and was perfectly visible to us all. Soon there appeared a mass of white substance[2] in front of Mrs Duncan's face. It assumed the shape of a roll of cloth thirty inches wide. This suddenly unrolled as a sheet of white shimmering material five to six feet long.

Albert told us to watch carefully, and we saw the mass being gradually absorbed into the medium's body through her mouth. Then Albert said "We sometimes have to use a trumpet to make our voices heard. Here is the trumpet." He brought Mrs Duncan forward again, showing a long round trumpet about two feet long and four inches in diameter protruding from her mouth. This also was seen to be slowly absorbed into the medium's mouth.

Billet dematerializes (Helen Duncan – for Estelle Roberts)

Billet reading, as explained earlier, is a form of psychometry, which may or may not be a form of mediumship but when it involves spirit communication it is. This great moment of modern mediumship is an example of Billet reading with dematerialization by spirit intelligences. Barbanell, in *Power of Spirit(46)*, writes:

---

2. Maurice Barbanell (*Power of the Spirit*), witnessed ectoplasm stream out of Helen Duncan, from her nostrils, mouth and ears, "in waving billows of luminosity." He further testified that the medium and all the sitters swallowed tablets of methylene blue to dye blue the contents of everyone's stomach, and yet when the materializations appeared, they were snowy white.

Helen Duncan, in addition to being a materialization medium, is able to read written questions which have been placed in sealed envelopes [billets][3], and to supply the answers. I have tested her many times. Once I wrote a question concerning a woman with a most unusual hyphenated name. Mrs Duncan did not see what I wrote, but she was able to repeat the question, including the name, and to give me the reply.

I happened to mention this phenomenon to Estelle Roberts, who expressed the desire to see it and I arranged a meeting between the two mediums. I handed Estelle a sheet of paper on which she wrote a question which nobody else could see. She folded the paper and placed it in an envelope which I handed her. This was sealed by her and handed to Helen Duncan. Before attempting to 'read' the question, Mrs Duncan followed her usual procedure. Slowly she rubbed the envelope on her temple and then at the base of her spine. She said it was always necessary to do that before she could 'read' the wording on the folded paper.

Then, slowly, she exclaimed "When – will – I – hear – from – my —?" Here a puzzled expression came over Mrs Duncan's face. "It's gone!" she exclaimed. Estelle commented "That was very good. You have read my question all except the last two words." Still looking puzzled, Helen Duncan repeated "It's gone!" Estelle assured her that it was accurate as far as Mrs Duncan had gone, and to confirm her statement opened the envelope with the intention of showing her the paper. Then we were all surprised, for the paper had gone! The envelope was empty!

So far as I know it has never reappeared. Estelle had asked a question concerning someone who had passed on and recalled that Red Cloud had told her not to ask for information concerning this individual until a certain time had elapsed, and that had not yet occurred.

---

3. According to Ray Buckland, who writes in his book, *The Spirit Book*, "Billets, from the French billet meaning 'note', are pieces of paper usually about the size of a playing card. People are asked to write a name on the piece of paper—the —or they might be asked to write any question they have. The paper is folded up, collected, and handed to the medium, who will go on to name the name (and, perhaps, contact the spirit of the person named) or answer the question. This is done without the medium opening the folded billet."

A buzzard, lion, ape-man and weasel materialize   (Franek Kluski, pseudonym of Teofil Modrzejewski)

Franek Kluski, an educated man, banker and journalist, had a short period of mediumship which lasted only seven years. The amount of information detailing his activity is therefore limited, but Dr Gustave Geley, a French physician and leading psychical researcher and Director of the Institut Metapsychique International of Paris, called him 'The King of Mediums'. Dr Charles Richet and Camille Flammarion also investigated Kluski. *In Clairvoyance and Materialization: A Record of Experiments*, Geley and DeBrath state "All of us who participated in the experiments know full well that there has been no fraud, and that our confidence in the obvious honesty of Mr Franek Kluski has never been abused. We know, too, that our close control did not permit trickery."

In 1920, Kluski was studied on ten occasions at the International Metapsychic Institute managed by Dr Geley in Paris. Three of the sittings were considered failures, apparently due to the 'overwrought' state of Kluski, but the other eight sittings produced significant phenomena. As detailed by Geley, the sittings in his laboratory were behind locked doors and in red light. Kluski was searched and required to empty all of his pockets before being seated in an ordinary chair in front of a dark cabinet, the curtains of which were open, but Geley reported that the cabinet, which is generally used to permit the condensation of ectoplasm, was not necessary. Kluski's hands were held by Geley's assistants on each side of him.

Reporting on him in *Psychic Science* (October 1925), Professor F. W. Pawlowski, Professor of Aeronautical Engineering, wrote a vivid account (The mediumship of Franek Kluski in the *Journal of the American Society of Psychical Research,* Sept 1925) of his experiences in Kluski's séance room. He writes "On one occasion a large bird similar to a hawk or buzzard appeared." The bird was heard to stretch its wings with a whirring sound, accompanied by blasts of wind. Professor Pawlowski states in his article that the buzzard 'flew around, beating his wings against the walls and ceiling, and when he finally settled on the shoulder of the medium he was photographed with a magnesium flash'.

Kluski's 'lion' is described in Geley's *L'Ectoplasmieet la Clairvoyance*, English translation *Clairvoyance and Materialization*.

This animal is sometimes rather menacing. On one occasion the frightened sitters, unable to control the animal broke up the séance by waking the medium, who 'was deeply entranced'.

The lion liked to lick the sitters with a moist and prickly tongue, and gave forth the odour of a great feline, and, according to *Psychic Science* (April 1926), even after the séance the sitters, and especially the medium, were impregnated with this acrid scent as if they had made a long stay in a menagerie among wild beasts.

Also appearing at several séances was a creature Geley called 'Pithecanthropus' which was a hairy man or ape figure that frightened a number of sitters. According to those present, it smelled like a wet dog. Geley and DeBrath write in *Clairvoyance and Materialization: A Record of Experiments(234)*:

> It is impossible for anyone to deny or to reject these phenomena, or to explain them by ascribing them to sleight-of-hand performances. I realize perfectly that it will be difficult for most people to believe them; that it is hard to conceive of the possibility of the coming into existence, within a few minutes, of living human beings, whose bones can be felt through their flesh, whose heart-beats can be heard and felt.
>
> I admit that all of these things are beyond our comprehension. To admit the possibility of these things would revolutionize our entire viewpoint of life and death as well as our entire attitude toward philosophy and science. This ape-man moved the furniture and behaved rather roughly with regard to the sitters, trying to lick their hands or faces; often the séance had to be prematurely ended when it became over-enthusiastic. Pawlowski related how it grabbed one woman's hand to rub against its face, and this frightened her considerably and caused her to shriek.

"One of us", writes Dr Geley, "at the séance of 20th November 1920, felt its large shaggy head press hard on his right shoulder and against his cheek. The head was covered with thick, coarse hair; a smell came from it like that of a deer or a wet dog.When one of the sitters put out his hand the Pithecanthropus seized it and licked it slowly three times. Its tongue was large and soft. At other times we all felt our legs touched by what seemed to be frolicsome dogs."

According to Col. Norbert Ocholowicz: "This ape was of such great strength that it could easily move a heavy book-case, which was filled with books through the room, carry a sofa over the heads of the sitters, or lift the heaviest persons with their chairs into the air to the height of a tall person. Though the ape's behaviour sometimes caused fear, and indicated a low level of intelligence. It was never intentionally malignant. Indeed, at times it often expressed goodwill, gentleness and readiness to obey..."

It was seen for the last time at the séance of 26th December 1922, in the same form as in 1919, and making the same sounds of smacking and scratching. It also was associated with a very acrid scent. Another small animal, reminding the sitters of a weasel, was described by Mrs Hewat McKenzie, widow of the founder of the British College of Psychic Science as follows:

"It used to run quickly over the table on to the sitters' shoulders, stopping every moment and smelling their hands and faces with a small, cold nose; sometimes, as if frightened, it jumped from the table and rambled through the whole room, turning over small objects, and shuffling papers lying on the table and writing-desk. It appeared at six or seven séances, and was last seen in June 1923."[4]

Materialized child eats half a banana (Helen Duncan)

From *Living in Two Worlds: The Autobiography of Ursula Roberts*, we read about the materialization of Helen's child control, Peggy. She acted as a helping messenger at the séances and on one occasion began chatting with a man she knew from previous meetings. The man said he had a gift for her. Peggy was then seen unwrapping it with her materialized hands and discovered it was a banana. She proceeded to eat half of it and hand it back to the man.

After the séance, it was discovered to have the tiny teeth indentations of a child on it. Also witnessed through the mediumship of Mrs Duncan was a materialized spirit who drank a glass of water and later dematerialized without leaving a wet mark on the floor.

Note that this was not the only time Peggy materialized and ate something. During the séance in which Agnes Sakoshansky

4. Much detail taken from Fodor's *These Mysterious People* Ch 6 on (www.survivalafterdeath.info)

materialized in her wedding dress, Peggy came out and sang to them. A sitter handed her a box of chocolates. Peggy ate some, and then very generously suggested that the other sitters might like to join her. She insisted that the sitters have a chocolate each.

Father materializes and shows a scar he had in life (Keith Rhinehart)

George Cranley on his website writes that Keith Rhinehart produced phenomena under controlled conditions which deeply impressed scientists in Japan. Physicists and chemists from faculties of the universities of Tokyo and Osaka and from electro-technical laboratories publicly expressed their surprise in films that have been televised in Japan and the United States. Rhinehart's manifestations in Japan occurred during a time when he was securely locked in a specially constructed chair, so designed that if the occupant so much as moved an inch it would be recorded. Before being placed into the chair Rhinehart had been stripped and thoroughly examined, then given a simple dark kimono to wear. He was also carefully weighed, and measured, his blood pressure taken, his urine analyzed and many other tests made. (These tests were repeated after the séance, and the results have been published; indicating that amazing physiological changes occur during mediumship.)

Rhinehart was then placed into the chair and tied securely. Both of his arms lay in wooden enclosures in which he could not move them without having his motions recorded. The chair arms were studded with small buttons connected to red lights, and if his arms were raised off the buttons, the red lights would flash on. There was also an automatic weighing device fitted into the chair, which had been especially constructed by scientists for the visit of this prominent American medium. The weighing device was wired to an electrical graph-chart that recorded any of his movements.

Under these test conditions many physical phenomena showing ectoplasm in various forms were produced under white light and photographed with still and movie cameras. During the Japanese tests ectoplasm flowed from Rhinehart's nose, ears, throat, and solar plexus, levitating trumpets and producing partial materializations.

Some of the phenomena were photographed on infrared motion picture film, later televised in Japan.

At séances arranged under these controlled conditions in Tokyo and Kyoto during Rhinehart's visit to Japan in 1958, materialized spirits appeared. One was recognized as the deceased father of Professor Iki Goto, D.E., of Tokyo, an investigator at the séance. The spirit walked out of the cabinet down the room, turned around, and walked slowly back into the cabinet.

Some fifteen minutes later, the spirit appeared again. This time, he had his sleeves rolled up and showed a scar he had received in his earthly life. This phenomenon, illuminated by white light was witnessed by some three hundred sitters who 'marvelled and wondered', according to the widow of the late Wasaburo Asano, founder of modern psychical research in Japan and first president the Japanese Psychic Science Association. It was at this séance that hundreds of apports were manifested (see section titled 'Apports').

Husband kisses his beloved wife again (Minnie Rose Harrison)

Minnie was the medium of the 'Saturday Night Club', a circle of friends and family that met weekly in a home circle for about ten years starting in 1946. Lt. Colonel Roy Dixon-Smith, a British career military officer serving in the Indian army, was one of many guests who sat with the Saturday Night Circle after guests were allowed in 1948.

His wife Betty had died when she was in her early thirties in 1944 while they were living in India. Dixon-Smith wrote in his book, *New Light on Survival* "For evidential reasons I revealed no details of my private life before the séance was over, and for the same reason they would have refused to have listened to them since they were just as anxious as I for genuine evidence."

The first phase of the sitting was the 'direct voice' in which a trumpet hovered in front of the sitter to be addressed. When the trumpet settled in front of Dixon-Smith, Sunrise, Minnie's main spirit guide, gave an excellent description of Betty and then allowed her to speak directly.

"Betty then attempted to speak to me," Dixon-Smith recorded. "After prolonged and seemingly painful effort and a few exclamations to the effect that she couldn't do it, she managed to say 'I am your Betty'."

At the conclusion of the direct-voice phase, the red light was turned on and the room was well illuminated, so that Dixon-Smith had no difficulty in observing forms and faces. Minnie Harrison, who had been in trance within the circle during the direct-voice phase, then came out of trance and her son guided her to her place behind the curtain. Dixon-Smith observed a half-dozen materializations of friends and relatives of the other sitters. He records:

> I rose from my chair, walked up to them and shook them by the hand, and we made conventional remarks to each other just exactly as everyone does when first meeting a stranger. They were swathed in white muslin-like draperies and cowls...They were solid, natural, and except for their apparel, *exactly like ordinary living people.* In fact, had everyone been dressed similarly, it would have been quite impossible to distinguish these materialized forms from the rest of the company. Their hands felt perfectly natural and life-like in every respect and their handgrips were very firm. They smiled, laughed, and chatted to me and the others; all their features, complexions, and expressions being perfectly clear in that ample light... There were mutual cheery good-byes as they departed, sinking apparently through the floor in precisely the same manner as the forms at Buckie.

Buckie was a reference to being in Scotland where Dixon-Smith had sat with another materialization medium just before sitting with the Saturday Night Club. Then the guide announced the coming of Betty and asked them to sing, 'I'll walk beside you'. As they sang, Betty emerged from the curtain and stood silently in full view. Dixon-Smith wrote:

> I rose from my chair and walked up to the figure, taking the extended hand in mine. I examined the hand, and it was just like Betty's and quite unlike the medium's. I stared into the face, and recognized my wife. We spoke to each other, though what we said I cannot remember, for I was deeply stirred and so was she and her voice was incoherent with emotion.

"Can he kiss you?" someone asked and Betty murmured "Yes." I then kissed her on her lips which were warm, soft, and natural, Thereupon she bent her head and commenced to weep, and in a moment or two she sank. I watched her form right down to the level of the floor at my feet where it dissolved, the last wisp of it being drawn within the cabinet.

Pieces of ectoplasm cut from Aunt Agg's robes (Minnie Harrison)

In *Visits By Our Friends From the 'Other Side'(32)* we read:

At the close of our fifty-second sitting on 26th April 1947, during which we had received the ectoplasmic feather, Sunrise, [Minnie's spirit circle leader], had promised us that within a few weeks we would have the opportunity of cutting a piece of ectoplasm from Aunt Agg's robes. True to his promise, three weeks later, Aunt Agg[5] spoke to Mr Jones [a surgeon] and asked him to have his scissors ready for the following week. Usually Granny Lumsden was the first to materialize each week, but this particular week, 24th May, Aunt Agg came first. She came out from the cabinet, stood in front of Mr Jones and invited him to cut off a piece of her ectoplasmic robes which she held up towards him. As he cut off a piece about the size of a small pocket handkerchief we all saw Aunt Agg cringe a little and heard a slight gasp from my mother behind the cabinet curtain.

Being an experiment approved by our Spirit helpers my mother suffered no ill effect; but here again I can only emphasize the importance of such approval in relation to the safety of the medium. Materialization mediums in deep trance place their trust in the hands of the sitters and that trust is sacrosanct!

The piece of ectoplasm was passed around the sitters and then I placed it on the mantelshelf alongside me. After Aunt Agg went, Sunrise spoke to us and said that they too were experimenting this week and did not expect the ectoplasm to be still there when the circle closed. He asked us not to be

5. The 'Aunt Agg', to whom Tom Harrison frequently refers, was his mother's sister, Mrs Agnes Abbott who gave trance sittings to Arthur Findlay and demonstrated in the large halls in London with other mediums from the London Spiritualist Alliance in the 1930-40s. She was herself a trumpet medium within her own home circle until her passing in 1942.

too disappointed however as we would be able to repeat the experiment next week, when we should have another small jar ready to receive it – as we had done with the ectoplasmic feather. But this time, he said, just provide the empty jar and the Spirit chemists would put in some liquid to try to keep the Ectoplasm a little longer.

After a number of other materializations we closed at 9.20 pm. and as expected, when the room lights went on there was no Ectoplasm to be seen. But we were all looking forward to the following week of course!

The following week, 31st May, it happened that we had previously arranged to have two guest visitors – a Chartered Accountant friend of Sydney's and the Matron of a large local hospital who had worked with Mr Jones for many years. We asked Sunrise if we ought to re-arrange their visit but it was agreed we should go ahead as usual – much to our visitors' delight when we explained to them before we started. We had our usual excellent Trumpet voice phenomena and some flower apports were given to our visitors, including a rose and two carnations.

After about half an hour my mother went into the cabinet and our materialization phenomena followed. Firstly there was a close nursing colleague from the same hospital as Mr Jones and the Matron, followed by the accountant's mother. In both cases the visitors were quite certain of the identity of the materialized spirits and were extremely thrilled and happy to be able to meet and talk to them again. Then Aunt Agg came, and after chatting to our visitors in her usual friendly manner, she turned to Mr Jones to repeat last week's cutting. The piece of ectoplasm was again passed round the sitters, including our visitors, and then I unscrewed the lid of the jar, which had been standing on the mantelshelf all evening, put in the ectoplasm and screwed on the lid. At no other time was the lid not screwed on the jar, but as I put in the ectoplasm I was aware of the same 'bleach-like' odour as the jar with the ectoplasmic feather some five weeks earlier. I was also able to see sufficiently in the dim red light, that the jar was about one third full of liquid—again supplied by the Spirit chemists as Sunrise had said.

Another remarkable apport!

When the room lights went on at the close of the sitting the piece of ectoplasm was still there in the liquid in the jar. Again we all examined it very closely, especially my mother of course, and agreed it looked like very, very fine cotton material, with one of the ladies commenting that it reminded her of 'chiffon' – a gossamer-like material.

Naturally we were very excited to have been privileged to carry out such a unique experiment – especially in the presence of our two visitors who were so thrilled to have been part of it. By the time we left Syd and Gladys's the ectoplasm was still in the jar and had dissolved only very slightly – quite different from the ectoplasmic feather which completely dissolved into the liquid within two and a half hours. The jar was left on the mantelshelf and the ectoplasm gradually dissolved over the next four days until by the following Wednesday there was only the yellowish liquid with a few minute specks suspended therein.

Son who had grown up in the spirit world appears and a father materializes to apologize (Minnie Rose Harrison)

Tom Harrison writes in V*isits By Our Friends From the 'Other Side'(16)* of a special event that occurred on Aunt Agg's son's wedding day on Saturday, 14th June 1947, her birthday anniversary:

We started in our usual way with trumpet voice phenomena. The first voice we heard was very faint "Bruce ... Bruce" and nothing more. Sunrise, [the circle spirit leader], then took the trumpet and told us that the voice belonged to a young boy who was accompanied by another boy, whose names were Bruce and Robert. He then added that 'burning' was connected with both of their passings to the spirit world but they were unable to use the trumpet to speak to us themselves. Mr and Mrs Mackenzie immediately recognised them as their son Bruce and his cousin Robert. Robert had been burned to death some years ago as a boy, and Bruce had been so badly scalded in an accident in their home when he was only 11 months old that he passed to the spirit world. ... Bruce's accident had happened nine years ago while Mac (Mr Mackenzie) had been attending to him, and ever since that sad day he had blamed himself for not keeping a closer watch. Sunrise then told Mac that Bruce wanted his father to know that he must not blame himself and that Bruce knew how much he had suffered over the past nine years. This certainly appeared to ease Mac's mind, as he said at the time.

After Sunrise had told us about Bruce and Robert, another gentleman then spoke through the trumpet—said he was also James McKenzie, Mac's father. He spoke quite clearly, with a slight Scottish accent and in short clipped phrases. More good evidence was given to Mac from his father. Later Sunrise said that Mac had felt very bitter about the way his father had acted whilst on the earth, but recently had forgiven him as he felt he had 'worked out his own salvation'.

Mac immediately confirmed this was absolutely true—but we in the Circle had certainly not been aware of it. His father had left his wife and their children when Mac was only six years old – a fact known only to the McKenzies in that room that evening! It is interesting that at another sitting, months later when Mac was a visitor again, his father materialized and they met face to face. Whilst they stood together shaking hands and talking, his father begged forgiveness. In a very emotional moment for both of them, Mac had no hesitation in offering that forgiveness.

But better still, later during that sitting of 14th June, Bruce materialized as a young man who had grown up in the spirit world. He was able to talk to his father face-to-face and comfort him in the most personal way possible. Although Mac had experienced materialization phenomena previously he was quite overcome – but went home a very happy father indeed.

Hair cut from Archael (Estelle Roberts)

The cutting of Archael's hair is reported in the 27th March 1937 edition of the *Psychic News* as well as Estelle Roberts' autobiography, *Fifty Years a Medium(96)*:

A fortnight after this we held another materialization séance. On this occasion two spirit figures materialized, Red Cloud and another guide known to us as Archael. Archael, playing the more prominent part, was materialized for an hour, permitting each of the sixty sitters present to file past within two feet of him. Throughout this time he held a red torch so that its rays shone on his head and shoulders.

When everybody was again seated Red Cloud called upon Constance Treloar to hand him a pair of scissors. He then cut a lock of hair from Archael's head and handed it to her. It was about six inches long, fine and silky and, for the benefit of the skeptics among my readers, bore no resemblance to my own. Archael's hair was straight, quite different from mine in texture, and unmistakably fairer than my own, with its signs of greyness and its permanently waved curls. The lock was subsequently examined by Clarksons, the theatrical wig-makers, and pronounced to be genuine hair. I have it in my possession today and also a document signed by all those present testifying to what they had seen.

This hair is now on exhibition at the Emma Hardinge Britten Museum at the Arthur Findlay College for the Advancement of Spiritualism and Psychic Sciences.

It seems that materialized spirits often gave locks of hair as souvenirs. Katie King did it several times. Once within the cabinet she cut off a lock of her own hair and a lock of the medium's and gave them to Florence Marryat. One was almost black, soft and silky, the other a coarse golden red.

Nandor Fodor in his *Encyclopedia of Psychic Science* lists several other cases of hair being cut from materialized forms:

> On another occasion she [Katie King] asked Florence Marryat to cut her hair with a pair of scissors as fast as she could. 'So I cut off curl after curl, and as fast as they fell to the ground the hair grew again upon her head.' The severed hair vanished. In some instances these souvenirs did not disappear.
>
> Crookes in a later writing speaks of a lock of Katie as still before him. Similarly the lock which Prof. Richet cut from the head of an Egyptian beauty remained. Prof. Richet said 'I have kept this lock; it is very fine, silky and undyed.'
>
> Microscopical examination shows it to be real hair; and I am informed that a wig of the same would cost a thousand francs.

Marthe's [the medium] hair is very dark and she wears her hair rather short.'

A mound of ectoplasm like a snow bank (Ethel Post-Parrish)

Rev. Lena Jefts, in her pamphlet, *Lo, I am with you always(13)*, relates the following:

> One of the most interesting formations of ectoplasm that I have seen in my years of experience occurred in a materialization séance. One of the group asked Silver Belle to tell her how she was able to build up the spirit people. Silver Belle, Ethel Post-Parrish's main control, replied "You would not understand if I told you." A few minutes later, she said "I want to do something."
>
> She then proceeded to call a lady from the group and asked her to hold back the cabinet curtain on one side and instructed me to hold back the other side. Silver Belle must have sensed that I was worried because she said "Don't worry; I have already protected my medium from the light."
>
> When we parted the curtains, we could plainly see Ethel Post-Parrish sitting in her chair apparently entranced. Silver Belle stood beside her fully materialized and in front of Silver Belle there was a mound of white about two and one-half feet high – it looked like a snow bank[6] but she told us that it was ectoplasm. She then proceeded to dip her hands into the mass and showed us how she was able to manipulate it in order to form the body and clothing of the manifesting Spirit.
>
> It was a most interesting demonstration and gave us some idea of what was going on in the cabinet during a materialization séance.

---

6. Hannen Swaffer describes ectoplasm likewise. In *My Greatest Story(224)*. He writes, "it appeared to be a living substance that I have seen perhaps 50 times, and in the case of [medium] Helen Duncan, it resembled 'living snow'.

Mr Perriman, husband of medium Mollie Perriman, describes a manifestation of ectoplasm as looking like 'snow' in his book, *Broadcasting from Beyond* (1952).

Materialized man brings entranced medium from cabinet in séance full of family reunions (Ethel Post-Parrish)

Before a mixed audience of twenty-five people seated in the materialization room Sunday evening, 8th August 1943, at Camp Silver Belle, Ephrata, Pennsylvania, medium Ethel Post-Parrish gave an 'involuntary test' séance never to be forgotten by those who witnessed it. The preliminary addresses by the Rev. Lena Jefts concluded, the large light in the centre of the room was extinguished and the sitters found themselves peering at those opposite them; the outline of each individual being plainly discernible by the illumination of the ruby-coloured light hanging in the corner of the room. After a verse and a chorus of one hymn, Silver Belle came out of the cabinet. In her best terpsichorean manner, she greeted old friends by their first names, introducing herself to newcomers as the medium's guide and cabinet worker.

"I am going to work hard tonight and try to get as many of your loved ones through as possible. Just be patient, won't you?" And with her infectious tinkling laugh, Silver Belle returned to the cabinet. Silver Belle kept her promise—she did work hard. Singularly five spirits came in, greeted their relatives and disappeared.

Silver Belle then called out from within the cabinet "Mi'lena." which is a pet name she has for Mrs Jefts. Acknowledging the call, Mrs Jefts said, "Yes, dear, what is it?" "Mi'lena, I said I was going to work hard tonight", Silver Belle continued, "And I am going to do something with my medium I have never done before." "What do you mean, dear?" There was a dubious tone in Mrs Jefts' voice. "My grandfather is here tonight and he is going to materialize for you and I am going to have him take the medium out of the cabinet so you all can see her in trance, and then I want some people to come into the cabinet to prove it is really empty." Everyone present was warned not to touch either Chief Baconrind, the Spirit Grandfather of Silver Belle, or her medium. Silver Belle preceded her grandfather and held the curtain on the left open while the two figures emerged!

Chief Baconrind, standing at least six feet three tall, supported the entranced body of Ethel Post-Parrish. Slowly very slowly, the Chief took the first step outside of the cabinet. The medium's right arm hung out rigidly from her body and as the two figures proceeded

182

toward the centre of the room, it reminded one of a puppeteer carrying a life-sized marionette whose strings had been broken. The locomotion of the medium as she was led to the centre of the room appeared to be that of an automaton. A faint glow from the ruby lamp cast a strange pallor on Mrs Parrish's face. The phenomenon was magnificent. Silver Belle waited for the figures to stop and then called some of the spectators into the cabinet. Five responded, including Mr and Mrs Max Klauser, Scarsdale, New York; Dr Julian Ortez, Wilmington, Delaware; Emily Fritch, Reading, Pennsylvania; and Wynn Ellis of New York City. After these people returned to their chairs, Chief Baconrind guided the inert medium back to her cabinet. As the curtains closed on these three principals of the scene, there was an audible sigh of relief from the sitters. To break the tension, Silver Belle laughed from within the cabinet and asked "How am I doing?"

In rapid succession, the following phenomena occurred:

Ella Carter and a Dr Baker, both in spirit, materialized for Joseph Graham, Bryn Mawr, Pennsylvania. These two held the floor simultaneously and for several minutes talked to Mr Graham. Ella Carter moved from the centre of the room to her right and stopped a few feet away from me. I could see that she was a very beautiful spirit. Pointing in our direction, she asked "Will you two gentlemen go and verify that the medium is in the cabinet?" Dr Ortez and I did. Ella Carter reached the cabinet before us and pulled aside one of the curtains to let us enter. Dr Ortez entered first and then myself. "Put your hand on the medium's head," the Spirit directed me. As I did, I could feel the moisture of perspiration on her hair caused by the heat in the tiny cabinet. Mr and Mrs Max Klauser of Scarsdale, New York, were greeted by Mr Klauser's sister, Martha, as she materialized and stepped through the curtains. A moment after the first greeting – and with Martha standing in the room talking to the Klausers, a verbal barrage emanated from the cabinet, much to everyone's amusement. The voice identified itself as 'Senta', Mrs Klauser's daughter. This was indeed an unusual and happy family reunion.

In conclusion, Silver Belle brought out three spirit forms: the mother, father, and grandfather of Mrs Emily Fritch of Reading, Pennsylvania. These three materialized Spirits walked from the cabinet to the front of the room passing Mrs Fritch who remained by her chair near the other end of the room. Then they returned to her and the four conversed together for a few minutes. The three spirits returned to the cabinet; the two men preceding Mrs Fritch's mother,who turned just before entering the cabinet to say a final 'Goodbye'. (*A Report printed in the Psychic Observer Oct 25, 1943*)

Doctor takes pulse of materialized spirit (Minnie Rose Harrison)

In *Visits By Our Friends From the 'Other Side'(14)*, Tom Harrison writes:

> When we were chatting over supper after a séance, Mr Brittain Jones, by now a regular member of the home circle, remarked that, being a Doctor, he would very much like to feel the pulse of Aunt Agg's materialized body sometime and we agreed to mention it during our sitting the following Saturday.
>
> Come the following Saturday evening, Aunt Agg materialized as usual. But before we had any time to say anything to her about Mr Jones' request, she turned directly towards him, held out her arm and said she had come that night with the express purpose of letting him feel her pulse!

In Tom's video (now a DVD) – '*Visitors from the Other Side*' he tells us:

> Aunt Agg said "I understand you would like to take my pulse." She held out her arm, lifted her robe and allowed Dr Jones to take the pulse on her wrist with his fingers. Mr Jones was delighted of course to have such an immediate response and there and then felt her pulse. He confirmed that it was quite normal and then added in his typically dry humorous manner "Thank you, Mrs Abbott, (which he always called my Aunt) you'll live." Aunt Agg chuckled and responded, "Thank you, Mr Jones, I am living and I'll continue to live."

It is thought that Mr Jones, a surgeon and in charge of the Middlesbrough Hospital, might have gained the idea of taking the pulse from reading Sir William Crookes' book *Researches in the Phenomena of Spiritualism* where he records that:

"One evening I timed Katie's pulse. It beat steadily at 75 whilst Miss Cook's [Florence Cook, the medium] pulse, a little time after, was going at its usual rate of 90."

On this same theme, Maurice Barbanell writes in the chapter titled "Flesh and Blood Materializations" in *Spiritualism Today* that at a few of Alec Harris' séances, a sitter, Dr Douglas Baker, was allowed to examine several of the spirit materializations with a stethoscope and said their hearts beat at 72 to the minute. In addition, Dr Baker said that they had weight, could be embraced, had pulse beats, breathed, had intelligence of their own and personalities.

Related to this is the pulse rate of the medium when under the control of different trance controls, Nandor Fodor writes in his *Encyclopedia of Psychic Science:* "Taking a careful record of medium John Tichnor, of New York, Conan Doyle found his pulse beat 100 when controlled by Colonel Lee, 118 when under the ontrol of Black Hawk and 82 when normal."

Materialized form displays how ectoplasm performs miracles by the power of thought (Alec Harris)

In *Alec Harris: The full story of his remarkable physical mediumship(225)*, Louie Harris tells us of Dr Laubscher, a trained psychiatrist, who also carried out a physical examination on one materialized spirit known as Black Feather[7].

The Red Indian Spirit was of striking personality, with a decided aquiline nose. He was much taller than Mr Harris and appeared to be a man in his thirties, whilst Mr Harris was 68 years old. The Spirit was known as Black Feather, and there was the black feather clearly visible sticking out of his headdress. Down the sides of his neck hung two distinct black plaits of long hair. He came up to Dr Williams and myself and asked us as medical men to examine him. He turned his face in every direction within the illumination of the red light so that we could study his strong chiselled features, most unlike that of Mr Harris. Then Dr Williams and I counted his pulse rate, felt his heart beat and his ribs and actually passed our hands

7. Account also published in Laubscher's book *In Quest of the Unseen.*

around his powerful naked chest. His abdominal muscles were taut and we could feel the hollow under his ribs as his chest billowed outwards. Having done physical culture and muscle control as a young man I was aware that such control of the abdominal muscles could not possibly have been exhibited by Mr Harris, a man of 68 years.

The Red Indian seemed an entirely different personality and informed me that all this was for my benefit. He displayed his majestic bearing and his warrior build, as well as his desire to prove to myself and my colleague that ectoplasm could be condensed until it was flesh and bone. This solid being with a clearly defined personality came to give Dr Williams and myself a demonstration of how ectoplasm could perform miracles by means of laws manipulated by thought. He stood there before us, and then melted away into the world which our physical senses could not penetrate.

Dematerializing spirit (Alec Harris)

Alec Harris was an exceptional materialization medium and his potential was foretold by another physical medium, Helen Duncan. In *Spiritualism Today*, Maurice Barbanell states that Mrs Harris was told in a private sitting with medium Helen Hughes that if she and her husband would start a home circle with regular sessions they would one-day obtain full-form materializations. The development of that mediumship is told in the book *Alec Harris: The full story of his remarkable physical mediumship*

In this dramatic personal account, George Cranley describes what can be termed as a 'joy guide' in an Alec Harris materialization séance:

> The most fascinating part for me was when a guide dressed in the most beautiful white robes walked out of the cabinet and said "The young man from Cape Town, come forward." I did...and found myself literally looking straight into his eyes. I asked who he was. "I am one of your guides." came the reply. He told me his name and the area he came from. I asked if I might touch his robes, but he said "Please don't, but I will show you something." He then fully extended his arms so I

could see the whole of the spirit drapery. Neither his face nor neck was covered with any sort of ectoplasm. I stood there thinking, 'How can I touch you?' so I said "May I touch your hands?" He said "Yes" and held them out. I took them in mine and we chatted for ten to fifteen minutes about my future spiritual work.

Much of what he said seemed impossible at the time, but a lot has been fulfilled. Suddenly he said "I have to go now." I thanked him for coming, but still held on to his hands. Something made me look down at his feet. As I did so I saw the bottom half of his body dissolving away, but his hands were still solid. Then his hands melted away between my fingers yet my hands were still closed. The last thing I saw was his head slowly sinking to the floor saying "I am going now." and disappearing under the curtains like a streak of light.

Spirit materializes to thank medium who proved his survival to his parents (Alec Harris)

In *Spiritualism Today(17)*, Maurice Barbanell writes this of an Alec Harris séance attended by both him and medium Helen Hughes:

For Helen Hughes, it was an outstanding occasion. One of the first to materialize was a young man, Douglas Hogg, a Battle of Britain pilot who had died on active service. He had since proved his survival to his parents through her mediumship. He showed his features distinctly and asked her to stand up so that he could talk to her face to face. It was touching when, after gripping her by the hands, he thanked Helen for making it possible for him to convince his parents of his continued existence.

I was moved to observe that almost with reverence he kissed her on the forehead. She had no difficulty in identifying him because clairvoyantly she had seen him on many occasions.

"Hit me on the chest" (Alec Harris)

In this dramatic account George Cranley describes how he was invited to touch one of the temporarily solid spirit forms:

One Friday morning, I received a telegram which simply said "Séance tomorrow night. Can you come?" I wired back that I was on my way, went down to the airport at Cape Town with my whole month's wages, bought a ticket and flew to Johannesburg. I arrived three hours later, stayed in an hotel overnight. Next day, my friend took me along to a modest house where I was introduced to the medium, Alec Harris, and his wife Louie. A small bedroom, part of which had been curtained off to provide a cabinet, was used as the séance room.

There were eight of us, four in the front row and four immediately behind. I was invited to sit next to the medium's wife, directly in front of the opening in the curtains. Louie led the singing, which went on for about twenty minutes. I was beginning to feel a bit restless when, all of a sudden, I heard a voice from behind the curtain. "That's Alec's guide, Christopher," said Louie, "he speaks with a lisp." The curtains parted as if drawn by unseen hands and there stood, what looked to me, a vague white outline next to the medium. There was more singing.

The curtains opened again revealing a more fully formed figure, but still not clear enough as far as I was concerned. ... The room was lit by a number of red bulbs. No dimmer switches were used, which made it very easy to distinguish everything quite clearly. Suddenly, after more singing, there appeared from the side, not the front, of the curtains, a Red Indian. He stood in front of my friend. "Greetings, Black Feather," she said. He was her guide and regularly materialized whenever she was present.

After exchanging a few words he turned towards me and said, "Will the young man from Cape Town come forward?" Before the séance, Louie told us not to touch the materializations unless invited to do so, as it could harm the medium. I stood up and walked over to him.

He was bare from the waist upwards, with one black feather in a band round the back of his head; the lower half of his body was just draped in ectoplasm. "Feel my skin," said the figure.

He was very tall, well over six feet. I had to stretch up to touch the side of his face. Copper-coloured, the skin had a leathery feel about it.

Then he said "Feel my chest." I did as requested and noted the chest was quite solid. "Hit me on the chest," he said. "Are you sure?" I asked. "Yes," he replied. I did. "Harder!" he said. Using the palm of my hand, I hit him on the chest. He never flinched and again said "Harder!" Summoning up all the energy I could muster I hit him on the chest. My hand just bounced off. The figure turned to me with a half-smile on his face and said "You may sit down now." I sat down absolutely staggered.

During the course of the séance, which lasted around three hours, about fourteen people materialized. At the very end of the séance the curtains parted. Christopher said "We have no more power left." As he spoke, from the medium's solar plexus came two great clouds of ectoplasm to the left and to the right. In the ectoplasm appeared literally hundreds of miniature faces. The guide said these were some of the people who had been present, but unable to get through.

Mother materializes and exhorts her daughter to do the work (Helen Duncan for Lilian Bailey)

In W. F. Neech's *Death is her Life(52)* we read this remarkable story of how the mother of medium Lilian Bailey materialized and spoke to her. Earlier in the same Helen Duncan séance Wootten had also materialized and pleaded with Lilian to 'be his medium':

> But Albert had another surprise for in store for Lilian. "There is a lady here for you now," he said. No sooner had the words left his lips and there flowed from the curtained recess the tall golden-haired figure of a beautiful vibrant woman.
>
> "It was the most wonderful moment of my life," testifies Lilian. "There was Mrs Duncan all of twenty stone, dark-haired and who spoke with a thick accent. And there beside her stood my mother, slim, fair as a angel, and saying in that perfectly phrased, silvery-toned diction of her "Oh Lily. Oh Lily! ...""
>
> "Here", she said, "stand beside me, my dearest child. I never died, Lily, I'm still alive."
>
> The mother looked into her eyes and told her "Do this work, Lily, do it, darling. Uplift those who are sunk in despair and in ignorance of what awaits them beyond death."

"I just felt I could do nothing worthwhile, Mother", Lilian replied, "but I've promised I will now, so ....."

"Do it now, Lily", said her mother softly, "it is a wonderful work you have been chosen to do. Good-bye for now, darling. We will meet again." Then, swiftly, as if she had no time to spare, she wagged her finger admonishingly and said, exactly as she did while she was on the earth plane, "Remember now, be careful how you cross the road." As she dropped her hand she seemed to dissolve through the floor until only her head was there, and then that melted away too.

Lilian said that there was nothing her mother could have done that was more characteristic of her than that wagging finger and telling her to be careful crossing the road, something she had done in life, even after Lilian had left school.

Feathers pulled from a materialized parrot (Isa Northage)

In *A Path Prepared* are many reports which had previously been printed in the *Two Worlds* magazine and were, with permission, included in the book. This is one, from 28th July 1939*(46)*:

> I recently attended a materialization and direct voice séance at the home of Mrs Northage at which some remarkable phenomena took place. First we had the materialized form of a parrot, which flew freely around the circle, finally resting upon my shoulder, flapping its wings against my cheek. Mrs Northage's child control stated that she would pull feathers from the parrot's tail, and after the séance we found a number of these feathers upon the floor.

> Signed D. M. Antliff, Secretary, Matlock Spiritualist Church

Two materialized people are later printed (William Eglinton)

In Paris in 1885, medium William Eglinton met artist James Joseph Jacques Tissot who sat with him and subsequently visited him in England. A remarkable materialization séance at which two figures were plainly seen, and one, a lady named Kate, was recognized as a relation, has been immortalized by Tissot in a mezzotint entitled *Apparition Medianimique*. This beautiful, artistic production shows the two figures illuminated by spirit lights which they are carrying in their hands *(see below).*

Materialized were Kate, Tissot's deceased fiancée, accompanied by Ernest, the guide of the medium. Sadly, Kate contracted tuberculosis and, unable to bear the pain inflicted upon Tissot by her declining health, she decided to end her own life in November of 1882 at the age of 28. It is said that Tissot remained by her coffin for 4 days and within a week left his home in St. John's Wood permanently. Tissot never fully recovered from his loss, and became very spiritual in the time after Kate's death.

Private and Investigative Sittings

Private and Investigative Sittings

My first impression was that Mrs Piper was either possessed of supernormal powers or knew the members of my wife's family by sight. My later knowledge of her sittings and personal acquaintance with her has led me to absolutely reject the latter explanation and to believe that she has supernormal powers.

William James, the Father of American Psychology

Many great moments of modern mediumship occur in private sittings. However, the private nature of the information received sometimes prevents their disclosure. Regardless of that ample incidences exist that are able to be known publically. These sittings could have been included in Automatic Writing or Trance Sittings but I felt they deserved a category of their own.

Cleric convinced of Bishop's return (Helen Hughes)

George Cranley records this Great Moment on his website:

A retired Congregational minister, Rev. George Sharp, who often shared Spiritualist platforms with Helen Hughes, told the remarkable story of how a Bishop's spirit return convinced him of survival.

During a private sitting with Helen, Sharp's grandfather communicated. He was followed by a man who said he had been the Bishop of Auckland and had met the grandfather in New Zealand.

"He never visited that country," was Sharp's retort. The 'dead' Bishop insisted they had met there. "I gave him a Bible," he added. "On the fly-leaf I wrote, 'To Robert, my friend, from the Bishop of Auckland'."

This began Sharp's quest to check the spirit's statement. Three close relatives denied Robert had been to New Zealand. Finally, Sharp asked his ninety-four year old grandmother. "Who told you?" she asked. Without disclosing the reason, Sharp pressed the question. Robert's widow then admitted that early in their marriage her husband went into exile to New Zealand after an unfortunate episode.

"He would never have come back to me," she added "had it not been for the man of your cloth." She told Sharp to fetch a parcel from an old chest in her bedroom. He opened it to find a Bible. On the fly-leaf was the exact inscription given through Helen's mediumship.

Molly Ross (Geraldine Cummins)

According to Michael Tymn one of the more interesting evidential private sittings was that of Molly Ross, who had several sittings with automatist Geraldine Cummins beginning in late 1928. From Geraldine Cummins' book, *They Survive* we read that Molly's sister Audrey had died in 1894 and another sister, Margaret, had died in 1925. When a third sister, Alice, died on 11th October 1928, Molly wired Cummins in Dublin, requesting that Astor, Cummins' control, find Audrey to let her know that Alice was now on her side and probably in need of help. Four days later, on 15th October, Molly received a letter from Cummins, postmarked 12th October, saying that Margaret had communicated and said that Alice was not alone when she was slipping out of her body…that Audrey and Mater (their mother) came to her.

Margaret also communicated that she had not yet approached Alice because she was not yet fit to draw near the newly dead. Besides, Margaret added, she would not have been received kindly by Alice as they constantly quarrelled when they were alive. This point was particularly evidential to Molly, since it was true that there was much friction between Margaret and Alice.

On 10th November 1928, Molly sat with Cummins and heard from both Margaret and Alice. Alice mentioned Molly being at her deathbed and said she regretted that her husband, John, and her son, Ronald, were not there when she left the body. Molly confirmed the deathbed scene as accurate and pointed out that John and Ronald arrived several hours after the death. These were facts also unknown to Cummins.

Alice said that she regretted not having treated her second son, who was living in East Africa, as an equal to Ronald. Molly confirmed that Ronald was the favourite son and noted that Ronald was favoured in Alice's will, another fact which Cummins could not have known.

194

As the writing became fainter, Margaret took the pencil and explained that Alice found it hard to write at the end as she didn't understand how to manage the words. However, she got through most of what she wanted to say. Margaret added that Alice also regretted treating her husband badly. Molly noted that this was also very evidential as Alice had bullied her husband dreadfully. Margaret then mentioned that Alice still resented the fact that Margaret cut her out of her will and left her share to Charles, their brother, who had no need of the money. This was another very evidential fact to Molly.

There was much phraseology that Molly identified with her sisters. In one sitting, Margaret said that Alice was 'blossoming out', a term she frequently used when alive. Margaret also said that she and Alice had had a 'fusillade', a word Margaret often used to describe their arguments when alive.

When Alice took the pencil, she referred to Charles as an 'odious man'. Molly clearly recalled Alice referring to their brother as an 'odious man' on numerous occasions when in the earth life. Alice mentioned having talked with their father (Pater) and his making reference to some 'numbskull' relatives. This was a word that Alice sometimes used when alive.

At another sitting, Alice informed Mollie that Margaret was giving her a hard time, saying "She is just as mulish as ever." Molly recalled Alice using that word many times in describing Margaret. Alice also told Molly that Audrey had taken her on a trip (in spirit) to the south of France. Molly noted that Alice, when alive, had longed to get away from England and spoke of getting away to the south of France.

Gibbes added that the writing did not bear any resemblance to Cummins' normal script and the phraseology was much different than that she used in her conscious state. Moreover, she concluded that the individuality of the spirit communicators made such theories as telepathy and universal memory highly unlikely.

Mrs Piper becomes William James' 'White Crow' (Leonora Piper)

American medium Leonora Piper's fame rose considerably when the mother-in-law of Harvard Professor William James, who later became the 'Father of American Psychology', came in for a reading. This was shortly after James's son had died. James' sister-in-law told him of Leonora Piper, who was unknown to them but who had been able to give details about the writer of an Italian letter simply by placing the letter on her forehead. James was skeptical but sufficiently curious and interested to go and see Mrs Piper for himself. At his first sitting, however, his former suspicious attitude was replaced by the conviction that Mrs Piper was producing genuine phenomena. In her trance, Piper was able to give detailed information regarding James's relatives, though none of these lived in the local neighbourhood. Some had settled in California, others in Maine, some were already dead.

Additionally, Piper knew that one of James's children was dead. "Your child," said the spirit which claimed to be talking through Mrs Piper to James, "has a playfellow here in our world, a boy named Robert Fr—." This name was found to be the actual name of a child who had died. James himself believed the information to be incorrect, and that the child referred to had been a little girl. Later, inquiries were made and it was shown that it was not the spirit which was wrong, but James – it was a boy. The medium made correct assertions about James – "You have just killed a grey-white cat by means of ether." Also, James's mother-in-law had lost a cheque book, but Piper immediately told him of its location.

For eighteen months, James controlled all séance arrangements with Mrs Piper[1]. In 1890, he wrote, "...taking everything that I know of Mrs Piper into account, the result is to make me feel as absolutely certain – as I am absolutely certain – that medium Leonora Piper knows things in her trances which she cannot possibly have heard in her waking state, and that the definite philosophy of her trances is yet to be found."

William James later famously said that Leonora Piper was his 'white crow' as per his famous quote relating to mediums being fraudulent, "If you wish to upset the law that all crows are black, you mustn't seek to show that no crows are; it is enough if you prove one single crow to be white." *(detail from www.survivalafterdeath.info)*

1. Mrs Piper took a small annual stipend from the researchers for the use of her time, but could have earned far more had she been interested in exploiting her talents for commercial gain. She sought no publicity and downplayed her abilities on the rare occasions when she consented to any media coverage.

77% of evidence true over 40 years of research (Leonora Piper)

Leonora Evelina Simonds Piper was the most tested medium in the history of psychical research. She drew the attention of several researchers and gave them sittings. Eventually, she was thoroughly studied for over 40 years by the American Society of Psychical Research and other groups. William James wrote:

> My impression after this first visit was Mrs Piper either possessed supernormal powers or knew the members of my wife's family by sight and had by some lucky coincidence become acquainted with such a multitude of their domestic circumstances as to produce the startling impression which she did. My later knowledge of her sittings and personal acquaintance with her has led me to absolutely reject the latter explanation and to believe that she has supernormal powers.

William James secured the rights to manage Leonora's sittings for two years, before turning over the investigation to Richard Hodgson who was a leading member of Britain's Society for Psychical Research. James then moved to Boston to become executive secretary of the American Society for Psychical Research.

Graham Jennings wrote in his article for *Two Worlds(4419)* that in 1888-89, James Hervey Hyslop, a Professor of Logic and Ethics, joined the investigation. After only twelve sittings, he declared:

> I have been talking with my father, my brother, my uncles. Whatever supernormal powers we may be pleased to attribute to Mrs Piper's secondary personalities; it would be difficult to make me believe that these secondary personalities could have thus completely reconstituted the mental personality of my dead relatives. To admit this would involve me in too many improbabilities. I prefer to believe that I have been talking to my dead relatives in person; it is simpler.

Hyslop eventually produced a table of all his sittings recorded by incidents. He defined an incident as being composed of several factors. For example, in the statement 'My aunt Susan visited my brother' there are four factors – my aunt, the name Susan, the visit and my brother. Out of 205 incidents 15 sittings, Hyslop made statistical calculations regarding the more important communications through Mrs Piper. He classed 152 as true, 37 as indeterminate and 16 as false. Of the 927 factors comprising these incidents, he classed 717 as true (making her accuracy 77% over 40 years of researched work), 167 as indeterminate and 43 as false. By this, he estimated her accuracy over her career.

Hodgson becomes so convinced that he can hardly wait to die (Leonora Piper)

According to Baird's book(1949), Hodgson explained "I had but one object, to discover fraud and trickery...of unmasking her." But about seven years into his investigation of Piper, he said:

> Today, I am prepared to say that I believe in the possibility of receiving messages from what is called the world of spirits. I entered the house profoundly materialistic, not believing in the continuance of life after death; today I say I believe. The truth has been given to me in such a way as to remove from me the possibility of a doubt.

Graham Jennings in his article for *Two Worlds* wrote: "Together, Richard Hodgson and William James satisfied themselves that Leonora's trance state was different from a hypnotic one by methods that seem outrageous. The medium's arm was severely pricked, ammonia applied to her nostrils and a lighted match to her arm, and an incision made in the wrist that scarred her for life."

Hodgson noted:

> I cannot profess to have any doubt that the communicators are veritably the personages that they claim to be, that they have survived the change we call death and that they have directly communicated with us whom we call living through Mrs Piper's entranced organism.

They also ruled out telepathy when they were able to verify information unknown to sitters at the time.

In a private sitting through the entranced medium Mrs Piper, Richard Hodgson's friend, George Pelham, reminded him of the varied details of their former philosophical conversations. Oesterreich writes "Pelham's parents were presented to him under assumed names, but he recognized them nevertheless and greeted all his old acquaintances."

All this made such a profound impression on Hodgson that he came to the conclusion that Leonora Piper was a genuine medium, truly communicating with George Pelham[2]. Hodgson's craving to learn more about life after death from his own experience became overwhelming, and he is reported to have said, shortly before his death, that he could hardly contain his impatience – "I can hardly wait to die."

A son gives the medium his family's names (Helen Hughes)

The following displays the evidential nature of Helen Hughes' mediumship. In a private consultation attended by Mr Hogg and his family, all of whom were perfect strangers to Helen, she pointed to Mr Hogg and said "There is a young Airman here, and you are his Dad." Turning to Mr Hogg's son-in-law, she said "This boy calls you Ian, and he calls himself Douglas." And to the two girls present, she said "and you two are sisters, Isobel and Mary." Each name and tie of relationship was perfectly correct.

This was the beginning of many communications from him and resulted in his materialization to thank Helen at an Alec Harris sitting –(see the section on Materialization).

Professor Hyslop is converted (Leonora Piper)

Dr James H. Hyslop's interest in psychical research was a result of his friendship with Professor William James of Harvard. Michael Tymn[3] writes in his article that Hyslop arranged for some anonymous sittings with medium Mrs Piper.

Hyslop recorded "When I entered the house I was introduced as 'Mr Smith'. I bowed in silence, did not shake hands, nor utter a word, and during the seventeen sittings published in my report Mrs

---

2. Pseudonym given by Hodgson to his friend George Pellew, an associate of the ASPR who died in 1892, aged 32 following a fall. A month later he began communicating with Hodgson and addressed many friends by their names and idiscussed events with them, thus convincing Hodgson of his reality.
3. Detail extracted from Michael Tymn's articles on Hyslop on ASCSI and AECES websites)

Piper did not hear my voice in her normal state, except twice when I changed it into an unnatural tone to utter a sentence, in one case only four words. My object was to conceal my identity, because I had been present at a sitting six years before and met Mrs Piper afterward. Since then, I had grown a full beard."

Although Mrs Piper was primarily then an automatic writing medium and Rector had replaced Dr Phinuit as her primary spirit control, she worked totally in trance. After Mrs Piper went into the trance state, Hyslop took his place behind and to the right of her, from where he could see the automatic writing. Dr Hodgson sat nearby and recorded the session.

The first part of the first sitting was full of confusion, Hyslop wrote. While several names and relationships were correctly given, he then received a series of names which meant nothing to him. Some days later, however, he discovered that all of the names and facts were pertinent to an acquaintance of his so this sitting had the initial appearance of a proxy sitting. However, toward the end of the session, the name Charles was spelled out with the claim that it was his brother who had died of typhoid fever after suffering a very bad throat. He further communicated that he had died in the winter when snow was covering the ground and then changed the cause of his death to scarlet fever, although it was initially diagnosed as typhoid. He also reported seeing their mother, who had died after him.

"My brother Charles died at four and a half years in 1864 of scarlet fever and measles, so diagnosed, with a very putrid sore throat of a diphtheritic character," Hyslop recorded. "It was in March and a heavy snow fell on the day before and on the morning of his death, a fact which I remember because I was sent on an errand that morning. My mother died five years after my brother Charles." In an attempt to trick Mrs Piper (or Rector), Hyslop asked Charles if he had seen their brother George. The fact was that George was still alive. The reply came through Mrs Piper's hand that George would not be over there 'for a while yet'.

At his second sitting with Mrs Piper, Hyslop was immediately addressed with "James, James, speak to me," by someone claiming to be his father. But the communicator was not able to write anything else before Charles communicated again confirming that it was their father, who had died some two years earlier. At the end of the sitting, as Mrs Piper was coming out of trance, she uttered "Hyslop," and then "Tell him I am his father."

At the third sitting, Hyslop's father came through more strongly, stating that he remembered the talks he had with his son about the afterlife and its conditions, including the ability of a spirit on that side to communicate. Hyslop clearly remembered the discussion.

At the next sitting, the senior Hyslop wrote through Mrs Piper "What do you remember, James, of our talks about Swedenborg? Do you remember of our talking one evening in the library about his description of the Bible?" The son also recalled that discussion. The father further communicated "Shut out the thought theory and do not let it trouble you." Hyslop interpreted this as a reference to a discussion he had had with his father about the possibility of thought transference, or mental telepathy, accounting for mediumistic communication.

Many other evidential facts were communicated by the father. He mentioned that his son's voice was the last he heard on his deathbed. He asked what happened to his old horse, giving the horse's name, Tom. He said that his old friend, Steele Perry, had moved west. He referred to another friend, Harper Crawford, being involved in a dispute over putting an organ in their church. The latter two facts were outside the scope of mental telepathy as Hyslop knew nothing about them, although he later checked with relatives and found them to be true.

Professor Hyslop continued to sit with Mrs Piper periodically over several years. There was much more in the way of evidence coming to him from deceased relatives. At one sitting, his uncle, James McClellan, communicated and mentioned that Hyslop was named after him, which Hyslop confirmed as correct. The uncle also said that he despised the (nick) name Jim, which Hyslop knew nothing about. However, when Hyslop checked with his cousin, one of the uncle's daughters, he was informed that his uncle did, in fact, dislike being called Jim.

There was confusion and difficulty with names at times, but Hyslop eventually came to accept the 'spiritistic' hypothesis, ruling out fraud, telepathy and teleoteropathy, which was the name then given to what is today called Super Psi or Super ESP. As Hyslop concluded, fraud was clearly excluded. Even if Mrs Piper knew he was coming to sit with her, and she didn't, she would have had to employ a private investigator to dig up obscure facts in a town nearly a thousand miles from where she lived, this at a time when travel and communications were slow and relatively expensive. She would have had to assume that none of Hyslop's relatives would mention that a private investigator was there asking about the names of horses, nicknames, church disputes, etc. and the investigator would have had to somehow have found out about private conversations Hyslop had with his father.

The fact that information unknown to Hyslop but later verified as true was communicated seemed to rule out simple person to person telepathy. As for a more cosmic telepathy – one in which the medium taps into minds and memories anywhere in the world or in some cosmic computer and then relays the information back to the sitter in a conversational manner – Hyslop felt that there was no adequate scientific evidence for such a theory and that it represented a process far more incredible than spirits. When Hyslop was criticized for his interest in psychical research, he asked "Why is it so noble and respectable to find whence man came, and so suspicious and dishonorable to ask and ascertain whither he goes?"

Proxy Sittings

Proxy Sittings

"If you wish to upset the law that all crows are black,
you mustn't seek to show that no crows are;
it is enough if you prove one single crow to be white. "
William James

Proxy sittings are sittings in which a third party goes to the medium in place of the person who desires evidence. The proxy sitter usually knows nothing about the person he represents or about the deceased who will be requested to communicate. In this way, telepathy is eliminated as the source of any information received at the sitting. Psychical researchers from the Society of Psychical Research and American Society of Psychical Research used proxy sittings and recorded their findings in its scientific journals. In addition, Nea Walker, who was Sir Oliver Lodge's secretary, wrote a book, *Through a Stranger's Hands*, on her experiences as a proxy sitter. Other books on proxy sittings include: *Beyond Normal Cognition*, by John Thomas; *An Outline of Survival Evidence,* by Gardner Murphy; and *Science and Psychical Phenomena, by G. N. M.* Tyrrell.

Husband communicates in German and provides evidence (Minnie Soule)

Michael Tymn in researching Case Files for the Evidence Room at www.ascsi.org reports on this intersting case.

Dr James Hyslop, Professor of Logic and Ethics at Columbia University, and one of the most distinguished American psychical researchers, reported the following incident. Hyslop received a letter from a woman in Germany, a stranger to him, asking for the name of a medium in Germany near her, as she wished to confirm that her recently deceased husband's spirit lived on. Hyslop responded that he was not familiar with the mediums in Germany, but if she would come to America he would arrange for sittings with someone he trusted. The widow replied that she could not make the trip, but she suggested that a sister of hers (whose name was different from her own) who lived in Boston and might take her place at a sitting.

Accordingly, Hyslop arranged for the sister to have a few sittings with Minnie Soule, who was using the pseudonym 'Mrs Chenoweth', a medium who was working with the American Society for Psychical Research. He took the safeguard of not telling the sister the name or location of the medium, not giving the medium any information about the sitter, and being sure that Soule was in trance before the sister entered the room. Because of these precautions, Hyslop was satisfied that the medium did not even know whether her visitor was a man or a woman.

Automatic writing by Soule's hand began almost immediately and indicated that a man was present who was anxious to make his existence known to his wife. Throughout the sittings (spread over a period of thirty-six hours) numerous statements identifying the husband came through, including:

1. He was a philosopher.

2. He was a friend of the late Professor William James of Harvard.

3. He was greatly impressed by some documents which James had lent to him.

4. His mother was dead.

5. He had a missing tooth at a particular location.

6. He was fond of fixing things, especially clocks.

7. He liked to annotate his books.

8. He used to carry a small bag containing his manuscripts and reading glass.

9. He had taken a long railway journey shortly before his death.

10. He had died with an intense pain in his head.

11. He was mentally confused when he died.

12. He was at home, but felt away from home when he died.

In attempting to give his name, the spirit first wrote the letter 'T' then the letter 'h'. Later, he wrote 'Taussh', 'Tauch' and 'Taush'; all of which are phonetically close to the actual name of the widow: 'Tausch'. Hyslop tried addressing the communicator in German (a language unfamiliar to Soule) and got replies in German, among them that the visitor was a 'Geschwister', (literally meaning sibling

– brother / sister) which was correct. In response to Hyslop's written queries, Tausch's widow confirmed every statement to be accurate.

The Case of Bobby Newlove (Gladys Osbourne Leonard)

In *She spoke to the dead: The Life of Gladys Osbourne Leonard* Suzy Smith records that in September 1932, Rev. Drayton Thomas received a letter from a stranger, a Mr Hatch, who wrote:

> For ten years my stepdaughter has lived with me and my wife, and her little boy has been the life and centre of our lives. He was particularly loving and loveable. A few weeks ago, he died of diphtheria, aged ten, Bobbie Newlove...
>
> Drayton Thomas said to Feda "I have a very earnest request for news from a little boy, Bobby Newlove."
>
> At the subsequent sitting the boy was said to be there, and because Drayton Thomas suspected that he might be too young to be a successful communicator, he asked his own father, whom Feda called 'Mr John', and his sister Etta to help the child. From then on things went well, a great deal of evidence being furnished. The boy told Feda it had been several months since he had died. When Drayton Thomas checked, it was actually three months, rather than the 'few weeks ago' that Mr Hatch had said in the letter.
>
> "He was very pleased at winning something not very long before he passed over," said the control. This, it was learned, was true. He had, in a competition, won a salt-sifter shaped like a dog that gave him much pleasure. "He played indoors with coloured marbles. It was something they did on a table," Feda said. (Yes, he played a game with coloured marbles and a card pattern on the table.) Then Feda asked "Is there a photograph of Bobbie in a rather peculiar position? I see him full face … with something in front of him, as if there is a board in front of him. It's as if he had been photographed sitting at the back of … a board or a tray or something ... He wore on his head something round ... if it was a cap it had no peak in it – Mr John is trying to draw a ring – Bobbie put it on. You'd better say something round that was new, to wear on his head, that he was pleased at having. It was as if he thought it was rather

important, putting this round thing on his head."

Mr Hatch replied "This is certainly remarkable. The last photograph we have of Bobbie is in fancy dress. He is the Jack-of-Hearts with boards back and front like a sandwich man. On his head is a crown as in a pack of cards. He was so fond of putting it on that his mother had to check him lest it should be worn out." Feda then asked "What does Bobbie want to say about his nose, his nose hurt?" the medium's hand rubbed her nose.

"Bobbie was learning to box," Mr Hatch responded "and on the last lesson his instructor, usually very gentle with him, gave him a blow on the nose which brought tears to his eyes. He complained afterwards that it hurt when he washed."

Feda said there was something that had weakened Bobbie's system and had put a strain on his heart had made him more susceptible to diphtheria and unable to fight it. Mr Hatch confirmed this. "Yes, the illness started with tonsillitis, turned to quinsy, and no doubt these weakened his heart."

"Nine weeks before he went over," said Feda, "there was something that might not have seemed important, but it was. Wait a bit – 'pipes, pipes' he says."

Mr Hatch could not recognize this at all. "There was a place where he went regularly ... where he introduced into his system this poisonous condition ... where he infected his system. At his place were animals you call cattle. Make a point of this. It was unsafe there. He went to this place with another boy ... It was up a hill past his house and past his school ... The animals will be the best clue ... His parents were not familiar with this place and did not know he went there." There was more of this nature from Freda.

The Hatches could make nothing of it, but when Drayton Thomas visited Nelson later, after the series of eleven sittings was over, he followed the clues one by one. They led him to a place called Marsden Heights. High up on the hills cows were grazing. While he and Mr Hatch stood there a woman approached. Thomas made some remark about the fine view and they entered into conversation. He asked if she knew whether children came there to play. She replied that they did and that they sometimes made mischief – among other misdeeds they had 'broken the pipe'.

Further inquiries elicited the information that there was a spring part way down the hill where water issued from a pipe. They walked down the slope to see the spring and found water coming from the hillside; by it, a displaced iron pipe several feet in length. Another pipe was found about three minutes' walk from the first one. The second pipe, tucked away at the end of a footpath, protruded over a kind of trough filled with water. So they had found the pipes on a hill where cows grazed. But could water coming out of the hillside in this way have been contaminated?

This they had to find out from an authoritative source. They contacted the Medical Officer of Health, who visited the two springs to investigate. He then wrote in confirmation;

"The water in both pools is obviously liable to contamination from surface water and is not fit for drinking purposes. Any person, child or adult, might develop a low or even acute infection from drinking such water. Water issuing from the pipes themselves is suitable for drinking, but not the pools into which the water fell."

If nothing else, the cows drank from these pools. Bobbie's friend Jack, when questioned, said that he and Bobbie had played in this water several times in the weeks before Bobbie's series of illnesses commenced. A child who played with water could scarcely avoid getting it into his mouth. Perhaps the little boy's spirit was right – this was where he caught his infection."

This case is discussed in detail in Fontana's book *Is there an Afterlife.*

208

Public Demonstrations of Mediumship

Public Demonstrations of Mediumship

*The boundaries between Life and Death are at best shadowy
and vague. Who shall say where one ends, and the other begins?*
Edgar Allan Poe

Public demonstrations of mediumship are an integral part of services of worship within the religion of Spiritualism. They were also used to build awareness of and promote Spiritualism in the United Kingdom[1] so that antiquated laws against mediumship could be repelled. Practicing mediumship, as a Spiritualist or even in the privacy of your own home, was technically illegal in the United Kingdom until 1951. Indeed, from Estelle Roberts' biography, *Fifty Years a Medium* we read that Hannen Swaffer, when on the public platform, challenged the Police, generally on duty at the rear of the Hall because of the large audiences, to arrest Estelle Roberts and she carried her own Solicitor's telephone number around with her should the necessity arise for him to bail her out of jail!

At about the same time (1950), there were, in Britain, around 500 Spiritualist churches under the auspices of the Spiritualists' National Union.

For many years before 1951, there had been efforts to publicize the movement of Spiritualism through lectures and public demonstrations of mediumship. These public demonstrations were very popular and well received all around the country, particularly during World War II. Many mediums took part but four women were at the forefront of these demonstrations. They were mediums Lilian Bailey OBE[2], Estelle Roberts, Helen Hughes, and Bertha Harris and not only do Spiritualists owe them a debt of gratitude for their work, but also today's mediums can emulate them due to the extraordinary level of their mediumship.

1. Today though, Spiritualism has emerged as Britain's eighth largest religious group according to figures published on the British Office of National Statistics' website. The figures show that in 2004 there were more Spiritualists in Great Britain than there were Roman Catholics.
2. Lilian Bailey was awarded the OBE for her service in the First World War. The OBE (Order of the British Empire), is an order of chivalry established in 1917 by King George V to honour the many thousands of people who had served in numerous non-combatant capacities during the First World War.

The archaic laws of the Witchcraft Act of 1735 and Section Four of the Vagrancy Act of 1824 were the legal basis to arrest, prosecute and jail anyone engaging in the practice of mediumship. These meant that mediums could be arrested and go to jail, and, in fact Helen Duncan and several others did. An article in *The Guardian* reports that: "Six months after Helen Duncan's trial, in September 1944, 72-year-old Jane Rebecca Yorke was also successfully prosecuted. Mrs Yorke was found guilty on seven counts and was bound over in the sum of £5 to be on good behavior for three years. The Witchcraft Act of 1735 was invoked as late as December 1944 when police warned Emily Johnson, the president of the Redhill Spiritualist Church, that if her activities continued she would be liable to prosecution."

On 12th December 1944, Emily Johnson was visited by police officers who warned her that 'trance speaking, trance healing, clairvoyance, and psychometry were offences', as they amounted to 'conjuration' that if these activities continued she was liable under the Witchcraft Act of 1735. She was induced to give an undertaking that trance, clairvoyance, and psychometry would be discontinued. The police insisted that this be a written undertaking. The Redhill Church felt that under these conditions it would be impossible to carry on and the church had to be closed. This was probably the most blatant example of religious intimidation.

The Witchcraft Act was repealed, The Fraudulent Mediums Act 1951 came into being and Spiritualism became a legally recognized religion. After the repeal of these laws, demonstrations of mediumship became perfectly legal and even more popular. According to Maurice Barbanell, in *This is Spiritualism*, in 1959, every Sunday night, a quarter of a million in Britain, according to his estimate, witness demonstrations of mediumship at one of the four thousand Spiritualist services that were held.

The repeal of these laws had been sought well before 1951 but during and for some time after World War II Private Member's Bills (Bills introduced by individual Members of the British Parliament) were suspended. It was not until 1950 that an opportunity emerged and Spiritualists through the agency of MP Thomas J. Brooks, himself a Spiritualist, instigated this change. Brooks' friend Walter Monslow won a spot in the annual ballot for Parliamentary Bills, and Brooks persuaded him to introduce a Bill to repeal the Witchcraft Act of 1735 and replace it with a law criminalizing deliberate deception. So with Brooks' guidance, the Fraudulent Mediums Act of 1951 was passed unanimously and Lord Hugh Dowding, a great supporter, helped steer the bill through the House of Lords. This act prohibited a person from claiming to be a psychic, a medium, or other spiritualist while attempting to deceive and make money from the deception (other than solely for the purpose of entertainment). It was in turn repealed on 26th May 2008 and replaced by new Consumer Protection from Unfair Trading Regulations following an EU directive targeting unfair sales and marketing practices.

Describing the public demonstrations of medium Estelle Roberts, Maurice Barbanell in *Power of the Spirit(108)* writes:

> When you witness a demonstration by Estelle you will see a dramatic, compelling personality who never loses her poise or equilibrium. Sometimes you see her bend her head to talk to spirit forms that are clearly visible to her but unseen by the audience. Occasionally, she strains to catch their messages and encourages them to repeat what was said when she is not sure that she hears it correctly. Estelle has had no lessons in public speaking, deportment or voice training. Yet she dominates the scene, whether the assembly is composed of thousands or of a small intimate audience.
>
> The two questions that she nearly always asks the recipient of her spirit messages are, 'Could I have known that?' and 'Have I ever met you before?' Estelle possesses a tenacity which is admirable to watch in action. .

When a medium takes to the platform at a large meeting he or she is in a very different position from any other public speaker. They have nothing prepared in advance – no notes, no idea of what they are to speak about, nor how long they might be speaking for. They must rely totally on the Spirit World. They are there to transmit the Other World's messages.

Estelle herself recalls that before a meeting she always suffers with 'nerves' – not that the spirit people would fail her but that would somehow fail them but then that would disappear.

When she took a large meeting, often in front of several thousand people, she found she could not recall a demonstration when there were not many more spirit messages than she could possibly give. She once asked her Guide, Red Cloud why this was so and he told her that just as people packed the hall here, because they knew and trusted her so did the spirit world. She was no less known and trusted by them.

Estelle explains that "The receiving and transmitting of messages is always a most exhilarating experience. I feel myself vibrating with the power of the spirit as I walk from side to side of the platform, pointing to people in all parts of the audience, even to the back of the gallery."

On the public demonstrations of medium Helen Hughes, Maurice Barbanell again in *Power of the Spirit(117)* writes:

> None can surpass her. Her method of giving spirit messages in public is in a category of its own. Everything is done at great speed, almost without pause. Frequently she breaks off in the middle of one spirit message to start another from a communicator who has suddenly made himself visible or audible to her. Then, knowing that the previous recipient will be disappointed at the thought that the message will not be completed, she provides reassurance by saying she will return to it when she has successfully transmitted this new message.
>
> All her vitality and energy are poured into a public demonstration that usually last about half an hour. Then she announces that the 'power' is waning and she has to stop. Despite that I have known her to stand up and continue, as, for example, when the audience applauds her. This applause, she says, has the effect of stimulating the power that has waned and enables her to continue.

Psychic News reported in 1944; "At this meeting Helen Hughes will demonstrate the superb mediumship that has made her famous all over the country.Throughout the land crowds flock to meetings when they see that Helen Hughes is announced to demonstrate her brilliant mediumship. She has earned her place in the front rank by the irrefutable evidence she gives at all her demonstrations."

And in *Two Worlds*: "In less than forty minutes she gave descriptions to over twenty people. Sixty-six names were given."

A Glasgow clergyman, on one occasion, after giving an address preceding her demonstration, said that her mediumship was a great ministry of helpfulness which had been 'the means of convincing the doubting, cheering the desolated and comforting the broken-hearted. If that is not a divine mission, what is it? It is a most God-like work.'

Sheer unflappable tenacity (Estelle Roberts)

Estelle Roberts' public mediumship was known for its tenacity and complete confidence in the spirit world even when the recipient repeatedly says the evidence is wrong. Maurice Barbanell, in *Power of the Spirit(110)*, gives us this example:

He has brought a Jim with him.

I can't place a Jim.

He's your mother's brother.

Yes, that's right.

He's met Aunt Jinny.

I don't remember her.

She's an in-law connected with your mother. Her name is Mary Anne Jane.

Oh, yes!

They have brought Mary with them.

Mary? I can't recall her.

Well, I must help you. She is your father's sister.

Oh yes!

On another occasion, the medium began her communication by saying, "I will find her if I can." – obviously speaking to the spirit who was with her.

She scanned the audience and pointed to one woman. "There is a young airman who wants to talk to you," she said. "You are his mother. Before this meeting, you went to his portrait and asked him to get through tonight, if he could." "Yes," admitted the woman. Estelle then gave the boy's age and asked, "Who is Ken?"

"A friend," was the reply. Quickly Estelle added, "Ken belongs to the lady sitting next to you." She then went on pass messages from both boys.

She told them that Ken said, he knew that his Mum had asked him 'to get a look-in if he could'. The two boys – victims of the war – were laughing and joking and this she passed on to their mothers, adding significantly, "If these are the dead…" Estelle smiled as she announced that the boys were addressing her as "Auntie."

Ken described how he had watched his mother go to a drawer and take out his 'wings'. He referred to his 'old writing book' which had at the end, 'a figure of an airman with a hat that is cock-eyed.' All of this was accepted by his mother, who was overjoyed when Estelle said that Ken was showing himself doing his favourite trick of pushing his hat off his head until it came on to his nose. This 'trivial' incident, was excellent evidence for the mother.

Barbanell makes the comment that some people say they do not care for Estelle Roberts' platform manner and her self-assurance. "What they fail to realize is that these qualities enable her to give successful demonstrations of clairvoyance under difficult conditions. Yet, when you meet her off the platform, there seems to be no trace of that dynamic personality revealed in her public demonstrations. The explanation, I am sure, is that years of close co-operation with her guide have resulted in the development of this vitalized personality which emerges when she exhibits her mediumship in public."

Advancing single file up the aisle (E. A. Cannock)

According to the paper *Light* in 1919[3], Mrs E. A. Cannock, a well-known London clairvoyant, described at a Spiritualist meeting how a number of deceased soldiers during the First World War adopted a novel and convincing method of making known their identity. The soldiers (as seen in her clairvoyant vision) advanced in single file up the aisle, led by a young lieutenant. Each man bore on his chest what appeared to be a large placard on which was written his name and the place where he had lived on earth. Mrs Cannock was able to read these names and descriptions, and they were all

3. From *History of Spiritualism* vol 2 by Sir Arthur Conan Doyle

identified by various members of the audience. A curious feature was that as each name was recognized the spirit form faded away, thus making way for the one who was following.

Rotten Park Road (Tom Tyrell)

According to Barbanell one of the greatest clairvoyants that England produced was Tom Tyrell. In *Power of the Spirit(127)* he writes:

> His demonstrations were so astounding that when I heard them for the first time I could not believe it was a genuine performance. As a young man, I went, while on holiday, to a Spiritualist church in Paignton, and Tom was giving demonstrations. He specialized in reading memorial cards. His recital included the full name of the communicator, the address where he had lived on earth, complete with the number of the house, the street or road, the district or town, the age when he passed on and the date, and a word-by-word recital of the memorial card. Yet it was all perfectly genuine.

When Tyrell was developing his clairvoyant gift he was determined to take his ability to the highest he could achieve. He made a pact with his guide that he would only transmit a message from spirit if he, Tom, could read the communicator's own memorial card, as it was held in his hand.

Once at a demonstration in Birmingham he saw on one card. Rotten Park Road. He asked if there was such a place and was told indeed there was.

Seemingly nonsensical or fragmentary information can seem frustrating, but the great mediums dealt with them with complete trust in the spirit world.

Illustrating this, Paul Beard writes in I*nner Eye, Listening Ear: An Exploration into Mediumship(22):*

> If information only comes in a fragmentary way, it is especially difficult for the medium to find the right context in which to put it. Medium Bertha Harris once received such a fragment – one of redness and from a male communicator.

She first said he had a red beard, but then went on to say "No, he lived at Redhill." This was correct.

When a medium hears something apparently nonsensical she will want to suppress it as obviously wrong. She has to have the courage to speak out.

Medium Annie Brittain once heard, "A lawn made of turnip seeds." She summoned her courage and relayed it and it turned out that this correctly described a practical joke the communicator had once played on the recipient, his brother, to whom he had purposely supplied the wrong seeds to lay a new lawn.

Also, medium Estelle Roberts, on the platform, said she had heard the word 'lie', and wondered if she was being asked to lie down. She went on to recognize that the reference was to a village [Lye], the name of which was spelt differently, but is pronounced as she had heard it.

Mediumship blindfolded with billets (Thomas John 'Jack' Kelly)

As previously mentioned Billet reading can be purely psychic in nature, but when it brings in a spirit communicator can be considered mediumship. In *Power of the Spirit(165)*, Maurice Barbanell describes the billet reading of medium T. John Kelly as follows:

> The first time I witnessed Kelly's ballot-reading ability was at Lily Dale, America's largest Spiritualist camp. The medium removed his spectacles and invited a man from the audience to tie three handkerchiefs over his eyes. They were tied so tightly that I expected the medium to cry out from the pain. After being entranced. Kelly stood up. Though he was blindfolded, he moved with unerring accuracy up and down the platform, never bumping into a table on which were placed vases of flowers. Neither did he collide with anybody when he descended some steps to walk among the audience.
>
> Hundreds of sealed envelopes containing the written questions littered the table. As he dealt with each one, the medium threw it into a nearby waste paper basket and he hardly ever missed. In every case, he read the identification code written on the sealed envelope and the questions on the folded paper inside. His dead father relayed the spirit replies. So

accurate was the information transmitted that unusual names presented no difficulty. When a spirit communicator gave a message, the town in which he had lived was often given. Frequently, the place where the questioner was residing was also stated, as were occupations, dates of passing and of birthdays. I noted one instance when a woman was told her birthday and even the time when she was born.

The spirit guide deprecated questions of a fortune-telling nature. When he read one sealed envelope and said it contained these words "What does the future hold for me?" he answered "Exactly what you make it." I took complete notes of Kelly's spirit messages, which lasted almost an hour. In one case, a questioner asked for communications from four dead relatives, her sister, brother, father and mother. The reply was not only to give the messages, but to supply the names of all these relatives. It was really amazing to hear the guide say, for example, "The envelope with number 958518 on it, with the yellow paper inside..."

The next time I witnessed a demonstration by Kelly was on board the S.S. Washington when we were in mid-Atlantic on our way to Britain. During an on-board demonstration, Kelly pointed to an individual and said "You, the man with the grey hair and with your hand to your mouth. Your mother is standing by your side. You have asked for a message from her, although I have not yet come to your ballot." Details of the mother's passing followed. The passenger was amazed, as he later admitted to me. This, he had to confess, was undoubtedly a spirit message from his mother.

On other occasions, he [Kelly] would say "I am going to tear all round the question, but leave it intact." Then, when he had read some of the questions, even without opening the envelope, he would ask a member of the audience to verify that he was correct. One man received a striking message. Not only was his ballot read, but he was told the presence of five spirit relatives, all correctly named, even to one whose name was Ann Farley!

The correct grave, socks and a baby mitten (Helen Hughes)

Helen Hughes' public mediumship can only be described as selfless and touching. She was known to give public demonstrations on seven successive nights. When she was on such an intensive tour, she did not normally give private sittings during the day, but this rule was repeatedly broken for those whose bereavement made them otherwise inconsolable. Her demonstrations had a dramatic quality as recipients frequently shed tears at the sheer poignancy of the communication. In *Power of the Spirit(120)*, Barbanell writes:

> I recall a mother who wept freely when Helen gave spirit messages from her son whose earthly career ended while serving with the R.A.F. The medium told how the mother frequently examined a postcard photograph of several graves and wondered which one contained her son's physical remains. Helen solved the mystery saying "The third is his grave, but the number of it has changed twice. But he is not there," she added "he is with you tonight." Equally as touching was the case of the war victim who cheered his mother by declaring through Helen's mediumship, "When mothers give way, how do they expect boys to keep going?'
>
> Another miniature drama concerned the spirit return of a sailor whose wife was told something she would never forget – how he always carried in his pocket the mitten of the baby who survived him.
>
> Then I remember the woman whose two sons, both killed on war service, were described by Helen. After transmitting the messages, she moved along the row to where a young man sat. Pointing to him, she said "You are their brother." He acknowledged this to be accurate and smilingly assured the medium that she was right when she added that he was now wearing socks which belonged to the older of the two war victims!

Fabled demonstration within the British parliament (Estelle Roberts and Helen Hughes)

Within Spiritualist literature, there is the often repeated but never sourced, fabled story of Estelle Roberts' and Helen Hughes' demonstration of mediumship within the halls of the British Parliament. On 16th July 1951, Helen Hughes was invited to speak after a dinner by the Spiritualist Parliamentary Committee of the House of Commons and from Estelle Roberts' autobiography, *Fifty Years a Medium(90)* we read:

> For hundreds of years, witchcraft was the subject of dire punishment according to English law. The story is told of King James I sailing to meet his bride, Ann of Denmark, in 1589. The sea was rough and His Majesty was very seasick. The King believed firmly in demonology and declared that his discomfort was brought about by evil spirits invoked by witches working in league with his enemies. Determined to outlaw any recurrence of such misfortune, he set about the Passing of an Act making witchcraft a punishable offence. By 1735, however, public opinion in the efficacy of witchcraft had become considerably modified so that a new Act was drafted changing the offence to 'pretending to conjure up spirits'.
>
> In 1824 the Vagrancy Act became the law of the land. This was designed to protect gullible people from 'rogues and vagabonds' like itinerant gypsies who told fortunes. Although the Vagrancy and Witchcraft Acts became law before modern Spiritualism began, they were successfully used to prosecute mediums. Winston Churchill, as Prime Minister, spoke strongly against this practice when, in the midst of the war, the Witchcraft Act was invoked to prosecute a medium who was imprisoned. These two Acts, which had the effect of making séances illegal and denying religious freedom to Spiritualists, were still on the State Book at the end of the Second World War.
>
> A campaign to repeal the sections which affected mediums began to gather momentum, and a vigorous attempt was made to end this archaic legislation. A Spiritualist Member of Parliament, Mr T. J. Brooks, invited me to attend the first of a series of all-party dinners in the House of Commons, the purpose of the gatherings being to enlist the cooperation of M.Ps in redressing our grievances. This function was attended by a large number of well-known men and women from political and social spheres.
>
> After coffee had been served I was called upon to recount

some of my psychic experiences. I did so and followed my words by a practical demonstration of some of the things I had been talking about.

One man, a skeptical Scotsman seated next to Maurice Barbanell, was vocally unconvinced by my opening preamble, and sat back to receive my demonstration of clairvoyance in the same skeptical frame of mind. A few minutes later, however, I unwittingly gave him more food for thought in this direction than he had believed possible. Among the spirit messages I transmitted came one for the Scotsman – from his son. The boy had ended his earthly life in a burning aircraft and this I told the father, together with the words of comfort that the son offered. I am sure that he left the dinner table in a far less skeptical frame of mind than when he had arrived.

Mrs Helen Hughes was the guest-medium at another dinner, and I was present at a third. It is impossible to estimate to what extent the minds of the M.P.s who came were influenced by these demonstrations, though something may be read into the fact that several of them attended more than once. The fact remains that not long afterwards Parliament amended the Witchcraft and Vagrancy Acts replacing them by the Fraudulent Mediums' Act of 1951.

A son who didn't forget his birthday and a mother who greets both her daughter and son (Cecil Cook at Carnegie Hall)

This great moment is mentioned in Cecil Cook's autobiography, *The Voice Triumphant(93)*. It shows the evidential nature and versatility of Cecil's mediumship. Cecil's spirit guide, 'Pink Rose', was especially adept at dealing with the public as she spread the message that there is no death. From *The Voice Triumphant* we read:

Several times I [Cecil Cook] have held open meetings in Carnegie Hall in New York City, giving the opportunity to Pink Rose to do the work she loves. She delivered beautiful lectures each time and at the conclusion gave messages to strangers in the audience. Most of the hundreds of people present were strangers, and many were skeptics having no knowledge of Spiritualism. Conditions thus were extremely hard, but Pink

Rose enjoys overcoming this difficulty and proving to many at one time the knowledge and power of those on the Other Side.

Singling out a woman at one meeting, she [Pink Rose] said: "Lady, you never have been to anything like this before and do not understand it. I wish to give you a message, however, and am sure you will appreciate it. You have a beautiful son, by the name of Harry, on our side of life. Today is his birthday and he would be twenty-four years old if still with you."

"Why, that is right", exclaimed the woman, "he was young when he passed and I had forgotten him." "Yes", said Pink Rose, "he was only six years old, but he never has forgotten his birthday or his mother, and helps you all the time."

Among the many present at another meeting was an Irish woman who happened to be passing Carnegie Hall and, seeing the crowd of people, stepped in out of curiosity to find out what was going on. Unknown to her, a brother had done the same thing and was seated on the opposite side of the hall.

After delivering her lecture Pink Rose began giving messages. Finally she pointed to this woman and said:

"Lady, your name is Mary and you never have been in a place like this before. Your mother is with us. This is Saturday and your mother has been here [in the Spirit World] since last Sunday, just one week. She is very happy and finds everything more glorious than she imagined it could be. She loved God and the reward of Spirit beauty is hers."

The woman wept a little and said everything was true.

Pointing then to a man on the opposite side of the room, Pink Rose said to him: "Your name is Jim and you are the brother of the lady to whom I gave this message." Brother and sister, standing up, recognized each other with surprise, neither having any intimation that the other was present, although the man had been startled at the message he heard Pink Rose giving.

Pink Rose continued "Your mother wishes me to say that she guided both of you here. She says also that she now is with Henrietta and met her first when she passed over." It seems that just before this mother passed, she opened her eyes and, gazing intently, seemed to see someone invisible to the others about the bed, and said "Henrietta!" the name of a girlhood chum who had preceded her to the Spirit World. Now the brother and sister realized what had happened.

Twenty appearances at the Royal Albert Hall (Estelle Roberts)

In the first half of the 20th century, medium Estelle Roberts unselfishly made twenty appearances at the Royal Albert Hall in London where attendance routinely reached 7,000. So popular was she that all her appearances were sold out very quickly. It is understood no other medium has had so many appearances at this famous and prestigious venue.

As a medium, Estelle Roberts is truly in a league of her own. Her mediumship was truly phenomenal and she is held in the highest regard as not only one of the finest but also one of the most versatile medium ever. Normally withdrawn and unassuming, this tiny lady, once on the platform before packed halls of thousands of people, spoke with exceptional authority, conviction, and accuracy. We read from Stashower's *Teller of Tales: The Life of Arthur Conan Doyle*:

> Five days after his death, on 8th July 1930, over 6,000 people crammed into the Royal Albert Hall in the hope that the famous author would communicate with them from beyond the grave. On the only empty chair in the hall was a card that read 'Sir Arthur Conan Doyle'. The medium Estelle Roberts, an old associate of Conan Doyle, took the stage and embarked on a long, inspired monologue.
>
> The audience sat in rapt attention as she related tales of whole families reunited in the spirit world, and then pointed out their loved ones in the crowd. "There was something uncanny", one journalist noted, "in the sight of ten thousand people sitting in the Albert Hall, half afraid, yet half hoping that they might be singled out."
>
> "There is a gentleman over there with hardly any hair," said Mrs Roberts, pointing to a man in the gallery. "Yes, there! That's right. I see standing there in front of you, a spirit form of a young soldier." She peered into the lights, as if for a better view. "He looks to be about twenty-four. In khaki uniform. Upright. Well-built. Mouth droops a little at the corners. He

223

passed suddenly." Mrs Roberts angled her head, as though listening to a soft voice. "He gives me 1916 as the year of passing. He distinctly calls you 'Uncle', 'Uncle Fred'." The man in the gallery stiffened, and nodded that the details were correct. "He speaks of a brother Charles," she continued. "Is that correct? He wants to know if you have Aunty Lillian with you. Do you understand?"

From his seat, the man nodded more vigorously. "The boy tells me that there is a little anxiety going on, and wants me to tell you he is helping you. He—" Abruptly, as if pushed by unseen hands, Mrs Roberts broke off her discourse and took a few lurching steps across the stage. She turned to an empty space on the platform behind her. "All right!" she said, as though addressing a large and unruly knot of people. "All right." She turned back to the audience and pointed to a woman seated in one of the boxes.

"There is gentleman here, John Martin. He says he is looking for his daughter Jane. Correct?" The woman in the box confirmed that her name was Jane, and that her late father's name had been John Martin. Mrs Roberts continued "He has got her mother, Mary Martin, with him. Little Willie is with them. Also your sister Mary. Your sister-in-law Elizabeth is with him. You understand?" Mrs Roberts opened her mouth to continue, and then pitched forward as though shoved by invisible hands. "All right!" she said, glaring at the empty space behind her. "Just a minute!" She turned to the front of the platform, gathered herself, and carried on.

Fannie Higginson's mother makes contact only an hour after her passing (Annie Brittain)

From Longton Spiritualist Church's website we learn of this Great Moment. In 1902 at the tender age of fourteen, Fanny was introduced to Spiritualism when she visited a Spiritualist Church with her aunt. During the service, Fanny was given a message by medium Annie Brittain which would change her life. The medium told Fanny that her future spiritual development lay in trance mediumship and that she would have a son who would become a world famous platform medium. Also during the message, Fanny was told that there was a spirit lady with her on the platform who was also named Fanny and was in fact the 14 year-old's mother. Stating that this was impossible as she had left her mother only one hour previously, the medium advised Fanny to return home. On her arrival home, Fanny was devastated to know that her mother had indeed passed away earlier that day.

This message through Annie Brittain became a milestone in the history of Spiritualism proving that prophetic evidence can be valid. Fanny Higginson served Longton Spiritualist Church for seventy years as a gifted trance medium, giving over one thousand private sittings. Recipients described the evidence given as 'life changing'. In fact a famous mining company would not dig test bores without consulting her, so accurate was her advice. In addition, Fanny bore a son, Gordon, and the prophecy was fulfilled when he became a world famous platform medium.

Names, names, names on 100th anniversary of the Hydesville rappings (Helen Hughes and Estelle Roberts at the Royal Albert Hall)

A demonstration of mediumship was given before a capacity crowd at Royal Albert Hall in London on 31st March 1948, on the 100th anniversary of the rapping manifestations at the Fox cottage which heralded the advent of Modern Spiritualism. Here follows an account of part of this demonstration as retold by George Cranley on his website. Firstly by the medium Helen Hughes:

> Mrs Hughes began her demonstration by asking for someone named Mrs Wilcox. After a lady had responded, she described to her a boy named Tony. This was accepted. The name Hobbes was given as the surname, with the request that birthday greetings should be conveyed to his family.
>
> To a person in the hall Mrs Hughes described an old gentleman, and with him Jimmy Brown. "I've got to tell you," said the medium "that he has found out all about George who, when in the body, was a bit of a mystery. He was at your home on Sunday and heard all the good things you were saying about him, (Yes) but he says he was not as good as all that."

"He wouldn't change places with any of you. I get the name Alma." (That is my name). "Do you know Doris?" (My sister) "Have you been laying down the law to Arnold?" (Yes) "He says you had a dickens of a time, but don't be so dogmatic; Arnold will come to it eventually. Have you been trying to convince him?"(Yes, rather) "Arnold will come to an understanding shortly, take your time." "I have a boy here named Ian Moore," said the medium to a lady in another part of the hall. (Accepted.) "He has never communicated before? Has he?" (No.) "Do you know Digby, a young boy, he's with David?" (Yes.) "Reginald has come with Mrs Rankin," said Mrs Hughes pointing to a lady in the hall. "This young man was shot through the hip." This was not immediately accepted. Then Mrs Hughes said, "Have you lived in India?" (Yes.) "Mary Rankin knows you, she is talking about India." (Yes, I can place her.) "You have always studied the occult." (Yes.) "Mary Rankin met you in India. Did you stay in Calcutta?" (Yes.) "Well she is here with you now in London."

To another recipient, Mrs Hughes gave the name Duke which was recognized. "Michael is with him." (My son.) "They are both RAF boys who have come together." (Yes.) "There is a boy with Michael named John, he knows you, he crashed over Essen, Germany; he is now saluting and saying "All is well with the boys you loved."

"I would like to come to the gentleman with his hands over his face," Helen said as she pointed to one of the galleries. "I have to give you the name Tony, a boy killed in the American Army." (Accepted.) "He is so glad to see you here, Mary is here too. She is of the Catholic faith." (Yes, that's right.) "She tells me she will help you until you meet again."

Further messages were given and accepted.

Now part of the demonstration given by medium Estelle Roberts that same evening:

Turning to a lady in the galleries to the immediate right hand of the stage, Estelle gave the name Taylor. She made a very fruitful contact and was able to convey a considerable amount of acceptable evidence of spirit return. "Do you know the name George?" (Yes.) "William?" (Mother's brother.) "Jimmy? (Yes)

"He speaks of Emily?" (Yes, my mother-in-law)."Elizabeth?" (Yes.) "Anne?" (Yes.) "Fred?" (Yes.) Jane, Jenny, cousin of mother?" (Yes.) "Arthur is with them." (Arthur who?) "Just a minute, I will ask him for his surname – Arthur Mitchell." (Yes.) "He reminds you of an anniversary just now." (Yes, my wedding.) "I now get Flora Annie Williams, you called her Aunt Flossie when a young girl." (Correct.) "I now receive the name of gentleman, Geoffrey Scott, you used to call him Scottie. He had auburn hair and a freckled face; you have a photo of him with Teddie; they are leaning over their motorcycles."

Mrs Roberts then gave several anniversary dates. "There is one on April 12th," she said. (Yes, my sister.) "She hasn't forgotten. June 14th?" (Mother's birthday.) "October 16th?" (Anniversary of my father's passing.) "December 2nd?" (Father's birthday.) "All convey their love to you." "I don't know you, do I?" (No, not at all.)

"I want someone named Mrs Andrew," said Mrs Roberts facing the body of the hall. A lady responded. "Your husband is here, and is calling you Mary." (Yes, that's my name.) "He on the platform and I have never seen anyone so excited before. Has he recently, passed over, about four or five months ago?" (Yes, only six weeks) "He has met John – known as Jack." (Yes.) "He says that the pain that he endured in the physical body has all gone, he can now walk about everywhere. 'Give my love to the boys', he calls. He will be with you on the anniversary in June." (Yes.) "As soon as it is possible he will help to adjust your physical condition especially your arms, legs, and feet." (That's true) "I do not know you, do I?" (No.)

Edith Proctor and Mrs Black, double recipients (Helen Hughes)

In *This is Spiritualism(42)* by Maurice Barbanell, we read:

Sometimes, in a very large and crowded hall, the communicators will show themselves to Helen Hughes on the platform, give evidential details about themselves, but offer no indication where the persons they want to reach are seated.

Once, this tactic on the part of a spirit figure had a remarkable sequel. The scene was the Caird Hall, Dundee, which seats nearly three thousand people. It was a crowded meeting. Mrs Hughes, in the course of her demonstration which followed my address, gave a detailed description of a girl whose name, she said, was Edith Proctor. Before the medium could transmit the spirit message, a woman seated in the balcony said she knew Edith Proctor. As the medium narrated evidential details concerning the girl, the recipient volunteered that she understood every one of them. She also acknowledged the accuracy of the medium's statement that Edith's father was with her in the spirit world. Helen Hughes hesitated for a few seconds and then pointed to another woman seated in the middle of the hall. "You know Edith Proctor, too," she said. "Yes," came the reply. After another pause, Helen told the second woman, "You are her mother." This relationship was confirmed. Again the medium paused, and then said, "I hope you won't be embarrassed if I ask you a question." The woman smiled, and Helen continued, "I get the word 'Black'. Does that mean anything to you?" "Yes," was the answer. One more pause and the medium finally said, "Are you now, Mrs Black?" The woman admitted that she was. The medium added that the daughter sent her congratulations on the re-marriage.

Helen Hughes returned to the first person who had acknowledged the message, and said "This girl comes back to you. You must have known her very well." The reply was, "Yes." "Do you live outside of Dundee?" Again confirmation came. "Well, this girl did not live very far from you." That statement produced the recipient's final "Yes."

A brother returns (Estelle Roberts as told by Ivy Northage)

This great moment is a retelling of when medium Ivy Northage attended one of Estelle Roberts' public demonstrations. Taken from *While I Remember* by Ivy Northage, it changes Ivy's indifference toward her mediumship into a genuine dedication.

When Chan [Ivy's spirit guide] told me I should go and hear Estelle Roberts – the foremost medium of that day – and see exactly how she demonstrated, it proved to be a watershed for me. What is now the Spiritualist Association of Great Britain was then the Marylebone Spiritualist Association based in Bloomsbury and they used to hire a large hall in Southampton Row. On Sundays, coming home from a walk with the children we used to see crowds queuing outside the entrance. Occasionally, we would see Estelle Roberts arriving, a distinguished figure in the beautiful velvet cloak that she always wore.

At the time Chan told me to go and watch her demonstration she had left the Marylebone Spiritualist Association and was working independently. She had taken the Odeon Hall in Bond Street above Chappells, the piano people, a very beautiful room, reached by a side door from a flight of steps that by-passed the shop.

My mother and I arrived early, knowing that for an Estelle Roberts demonstration one might not otherwise get in. The stairs were carpeted and we had sat down on the upper step to wait for the doors to open when we were joined by a very ordinary-looking woman in a navy blue costume with a very large hat. Sitting on the step immediately below us she looked up timidly and asked, very hesitantly, if we had been there before. I replied that we had not seen Mrs Roberts demonstrate but that we knew her and about what she did. As this lady then told us that her brother, a vicar, had just died, she burst into tears. "I'm so ashamed," she said "here I am, the sister of a vicar. I have supported him all these years and now that he has died I have no belief, no comfort. I have nothing I can hold onto, and I am so ashamed." Here she wiped some fresh tears away and murmured, as if to herself, "If only he could tell me that he is still around somewhere! Then I feel I could face life without him."

She went on to tell us that he had only suffered a brief illness. It was still the custom then to bring the dead home and the night before he was to be buried she had entered the room where his coffin was placed in the centre. She went up to the open coffin, took hold of his hand and held it, and said "Oh, Charles, if there is anything – anything at all – that you can tell me that will assure me that you have not gone, please, please, try!" Then she told us "for some reason I went across the room to where I had put a vase of roses. I took one, I snapped off the stem and I uncurled his fingers and placed it between his fingers and the palm of his hand, and closed them again." She went on "I don't know how I heard of this lady but somehow her name was given to me, and the address of this place. I don't really know why I am here, it may be very wicked of me, but I must know. I must know one way or the other."

My mother and I felt terribly sorry for this woman. Our hearts went out to her and when the doors opened she came in and sat beside us. In due course Estelle Roberts entered, her appearance and her somewhat regal bearing just as I had observed from the street when passing by. After greeting the audience she launched confidently into her demonstration giving message after message that, judging from the way in which they were received, were remarkable in the accuracy of their detail. This went on until the end, when she said "I want to come to the lady sitting near the back. The lady in navy with a very large hat." I nudged her and told her just to answer 'Yes'. She lifted her head and murmured assent.

"Your brother is here," announced Estelle Roberts from the platform. "He has asked me to say that he heard exactly what you were asking of him and that yes, of course he is still with you and of course he will continue in his love and protection of you. He is telling me that you did this –." She turned and marched across the platform to a vase of flowers, took one out and snapped the stem. "You brought it back," she went on "you uncurled his hand, you placed the flower within his fingers and you put it back on his chest. He knew, he is saying 'I knew. I was there and I will always be there'." That was the last message of the afternoon. The lady's tears after that were of joy and for the very first time I realized what a wonderful gift of mediumship could be.

Exact names and other evidence (Helen Hughes)

Helen Hughes was a modest medium, who worked tirelessly as an ambassador for the Spiritualists' National Union. According to the *Psychic News,* she was one of the most beloved mediums that

Spiritualism had ever produced and was dubbed, 'Helen the Beloved'. George Cranley tells us that in one of her many public demonstrations, she pointed to a woman in the auditorium and said "Is your name Nellie?" (Yes.) "Well, then you know Mr Bramwell and I have to tell you that he is here and he's brought Harry and Mrs Wilson. She says she's all right now and thanks you for what you did for her. She suffered from a weak heart. She tells me that your name is Boynton." (Correct.)

For another recipient, Helen Hughes received a message from "someone called Eva, who was a musician." She then singled out a woman from the crowd and added, "You are Eva's mother. She played the piano and had a companion, Elsie, who has also passed over. Her full name is Eva Huxley." (Yes.)

Helen continued, "There is a Mrs Richardson in the gallery. I get the name Jimmie Richardson. He worked in an office by himself. He brings Robert and Lizzie, and also Mary Bewick. He tells me your godmother was Mary McIntyre, and that she was in some way connected with an off-licence for the sale of beer when you were fourteen to seventeen years old." (Quite right.)

The following four Great Moments are included with permission from George Cranley.

Return of an abducted boy (Mona van der Watt)

Mona van der Watt was a little known but extraordinary medium who lived in South Africa. One of the most moving examples of how helpful Mona van der Watt's mediumship could be was illustrated in the dramatic account, front-paged in the *Psychic News*, of how her guide located a missing boy. The parent – *Psychic News* did not reveal her identity – had a heart-breaking story to tell.

While living in the then Belgian Congo, this lady was legally separated from her husband and was given the custody of their four-year-old boy. Soon after the separation, her husband's brother stole the boy from the front door of her house. With a false passport, the father took his son to the USA. The wife was frantic because she could not get news of her child. She even made the journey of thousands of miles to the USA where she searched without success for two years. Then she returned to her family in Cape Town. Every possible channel for help was tried. In turn, the mother consulted lawyers, clergymen, and officials responsible for the administration of the Congo. Alas, because of internal troubles there, all official avenues of help were closed. Moreover, none of her legal papers could be traced.

At this stage, almost at the end of her tether, this woman was taken to see a demonstration by Mona. Mona's guide gave the mother a message which indicated that the spirit world was aware of her plight. He said, guardedly in a public demonstration, that she had lost something that was very dear to her, but this would be found. On no account was she to give up hope. The message also stated that her problem was linked with the USA.

After the service, the mother asked for a private sitting with Mona. Mona's guide then discussed her troubles fully, saying he knew that she was looking for a child. This woman would be helped by the spirit world, he added. The guide forecast that she would return to the USA. At the right time, guidance would be provided. During the next 18 months, the mother visited a Spiritualist church at regular intervals and was always given similar encouragement. At a later private sitting, she asked the guide if she should leave South Africa and go to Israel to try and make a new life for herself without her son. She explained that the strain was proving too much. "No, you must not go to Israel," said the guide "You will find your child. Just hold on a little longer."

At the next séance the guide volunteered "Now is the time that you must write, as a mother, to Mrs Kennedy because she is the first lady of the land, and ask for her help." He stated again that she would return to the USA and find the boy. The mother complied with the spirit request and wrote to Mrs Kennedy. Later, she received a letter from the American Consul in Cape Town asking her to call at his office. This official explained that the letter she had sent to Mrs Kennedy had been handed to the FBI.

The Consul disclosed that, at the time she wrote to Mrs Kennedy, her husband had applied for a permit to practise as a dentist in America. Once more she consulted the medium, who advised her to go to the USA, which she did with the Consul's help. Meantime, her husband was questioned by the American authorities.

Realising that something was amiss, he fled again with the boy. When his wife arrived in America it was a bitter disappointment because she could find no trace of either of them. Now strained to the uttermost, she wrote to Mona for help. The guide replied counselling her to stay in America. He insisted that she should continue with her quest and not return to Cape Town. Once more he repeated his assurance she would find her child.

The mother then decided to employ a private agency, but alas with no results. Once more she asked for spirit help. The reply was that she should write to Mrs Kennedy again and this would lead to co-operation with the FBI. At the time Mrs Kennedy was the President's wife. The medium heard nothing for a while. Then one day her telephone rang. It was the woman's mother to say that she had received a cable from her daughter. She particularly wanted Mona to know that after four years her little boy had been found. The FBI did co-operate, as was foretold. They succeeded in tracing the husband in Canada. Because all her legal papers had vanished in the Congo troubles, the mother had to go through the ordeal of another court case in Canada before obtaining full custody of her boy.

When she saw Mona she said to this medium "You gave back my God, peace and hope – and then you gave me back my little son." Those of us in the church who knew of the case were delighted when the lady brought her little boy to say 'Thank you' for all the prayers that had been offered for his safe return.

Public demonstration in trance (Mona van der Watt)

The reporter from the *Psychic News* told readers that a high-pitched voice emanated from Mona's left shoulder. At times, the voice would travel across the audience and speak to people from just above their heads, but that was exceptional. Usually the voice addressed the guide, who then repeated the communication through the entranced medium. The controlled Mona 'walked around the hall without faltering. Her eyes were shut, but the guide knew who was before him'. Occasionally when demonstrating mediumship [via trance] before an international audience, such as at the International Spiritualist Federation Conferences, she would wear a throat microphone so that all could hear the spirit voice which relayed communications to her. During the demonstration, everyone had a good opportunity of hearing the voice mediumship. On one occasion when he obtained permission to place a microphone as close to her left shoulder as possible the spirit voices which manifested sounded like a record being played at very fast speed. The guide then relayed what was being said. To his astonishment, when playing the tape back, he clearly heard his grandmother's voice as well as a guide who had frequently been described to him. Both relayed very evidential messages.

What he particularly noticed was that though the gist of the communication was relayed by the guide it was not necessarily word for word as said by the spirit contact. Her guide often used African words which when roughly translated meant 'I'm sorry I didn't quite catch that' or 'Give it to me again' which illustrates the difficulty communicators have of getting an accurate message across. The reporter said he was often amused when he heard alleged mediums saying with absolute confidence 'they are telling me this or telling me that' when he knew how difficult it was to get one sentence over with any degree of accuracy.

Blindfold Public Demonstration with billets (Keith Rhinehart)

Keith Rhinehart was noteworthy in that he gave very evidential public demonstrations of mediumship, but he frequently also did them blindfolded.

One Sunday a man who admitted that it was only his second time at the billet services was asked to stand up. He was then told by Keith Rhinehart who was on the stage, blindfolded, that Anna, his wife, was asking for Steve and, that she loved him. She was reported to say that a candle must be lighted for her at the table on Christmas, because she would be there.

Then Dr Kensington, Keith's control, began to describe a dress, with red flowers and green leaves and dashes of yellow in it. The man by this time was standing there shedding tears, for he was told that he had very recently had this dress out because it was a favourite of his wife's, and that he had been sitting and holding it and crying.

After the service, this man was asked about his message. He showed the billet that had been returned to him. It read "To Anna, please talk to me, I love you." It was signed merely "Steve." He said that his wife had died just a few weeks earlier, and that the night before he had taken out his favourite dress of hers (which answered the medium's description) and had sat and held it and cried over it. Needless to say, he had not told anyone of this.

Billet reading with spirit art (Keith Rhinehart)

Although not generally recognized as a Spiritual Psychic Artist, nonetheless, Keith Milton Rhinehart produced some of the most remarkable demonstrations of the phenomenon known as Spiritual Psychic Art because of his adept physical and trance mediumship.

No medium in history has produced more scientific evidence regarding psychic phenomena than Keith Rhinehart brought forth during his career. During a séance in Israel on one of Rhinehart's world tours he produced Spiritual Psychic Art under the strictest test conditions.

After being entranced by his spirit guide Dr Robert John Kensington, Dr Kensington instructed each participant to write questions on their billet card and place the card into a sealed envelope. Once all the envelopes had been collected, Dr Kensington through Rhinehart's mediumship answered all the questions on the billet cards without ever opening the envelopes. Then he returned the billet card back to each participant. When each person opened their envelope there on the back of the billet card was a drawing of the person's Spirit Guide.

Spirit Lights

Spirit Lights

May I reach That purest Heaven — be to other souls
The cup of strength in some great agony,
Enkindle generous ardour — feed pure love,
Beget the smiles that have no cruelty —
So shall I join the choir invisible,
Whose music is the gladness of the world.

George Eliot

During a séance, lights may be seen by all the sitters which are physical phenomena caused by the spirit world. They may glow dimly or brightly and move about or remain stationary. Mr Perriman in *Broadcasting from Beyond* describes spirit lights as "Huge patches of lights twinkling like stars in the heavens." In fact, the illumination was so great that he and his wife, Mollie, despite sitting in a room without any normal light, could see each other.

According to Raymond Buckland, author of *The Spirit Book*:

Spirit lights are frequently seen when a physical medium is operating, though they can occasionally be observed apparently independently of any person. They are often dancing globules or sparks of light that seem to fill the air, indicating that there is spirit presence in the room. Such psychic lights may represent an initial stage of materialization.

Spirit light from the ectoplasm of a cat (Mina 'Margery' Crandon)

According to Nandor Fodor in his *Encyclopedia of Psychic Science*:

On the question whether ectoplasm is a purely human contribution or animals might also have a share in it, interesting light was thrown in a séance with Margery. She took a cat with her into the cabinet. As told by F. Bligh Bond in *Psychic Research, 1929*: ...."presently we all observed a luminous appearance over the table, like a tall pale flame. This seemed to move slightly and vary in height. Then came Walter's voice, 'Here, someone take this animal out; it's croaking.' The sitter on Margery's left, bent over and took up the cat from her lap.

It was quite comatose and stiffened ... Walter then explained that he had borrowed the cat's ectoplasm and that was what we had seen as a flame on the table."

Medium's wife illuminates a lost handkerchief (John Sloan)

John Sloan's wife Agnes had been a regular sitter in the physical circle, and she continued to visit it after she had 'died'. John missed her terribly and was always wishing that he could join her. The Sloans affectionately referred to each other as 'Mammy and Daddy Sloan'. During one sitting when John dropped his handkerchief in the darkened room and couldn't find it, his 'dead' wife's voice immediately spoke from the Other Side, saying "Never mind, Daddy. I will let you see it." A beautiful light then appeared and hovered and spread about the floor for a while, after which the handkerchief was lifted up and placed in Mr Sloan's hands by someone on the Other Side. Mrs Sloan's voice said "There it is, Daddy." and John was so touched by the experience that he replied through his tears, "You are just the dearest wee lassie that ever was."

Solid luminous light upon his moustache (Ada Besinnet)

The mediumship of Ada Besinnet was known for spirit lights. Arthur Conan Doyle, Admiral Moore, and Hewat McKenzie all noted the production of very brilliant lights. These appeared to be small solid luminous objects. Arthur Canon Doyle had, on one occasion, the curious experience of having one upon his moustache. He stated that had a large firefly settled there the effect would have been much the same. *(see Evan Powell on www.psychictruth.info)*

One inch spirit lights (Minnie Harrison)

Tom Harrison writes in *Visits by Our Friends From the 'Other Side'(27)*:

My notes for sitting No.26 on 26th October 1946 show that we had four Spirit Lights at about one minute intervals, each lasting for two or three seconds, before the trumpet phenomena began. They were about one inch in diameter and appeared in the area in front of the fireplace. As we developed we had many more instances of such type of lights much brighter than the first four. Often two or three would be seen at the same time and they would remain for eight or nine seconds. We were told that they were in fact the incandescent ends of ectoplasmic rods which were emanating from the medium.

About a year later, on the 22nd November 1947, we were startled by a number of very bright flashes of spirit lights – completely different from the earlier type which had ceased some months before. Each flash lit up the whole room, very similar to a camera flashlight – but I can assure you there was no such equipment in that room. A few came before the trumpet phenomena with more coming from behind the cabinet curtain during the Materialization. They were of such intensity that even with only the 15 inch gap at the top the entire room was illuminated. We were told that Gladys' brother in Spirit, Douglas, was the 'technician' responsible for these particular Spirit lights.

Four weeks later on 20th December, as Aunt Agg was drawing back the cabinet curtain to step into the room for her weekly chat, her face was lit up by two bright lights from behind the curtain. From this you will understand that these lights were under the complete control of our Spirit helpers and therefore not dangerous to the medium – unlike any unexpected bright light used by anyone sitting in the Circle, which is extremely dangerous.

In Tom's later book *Life After Death: Living Proof (194)* he tells us how at a Christmas Party séance in 1954 they had bright twinkling lights actually on the Christmas tree and on a later occasion they had coloured lights on the tree.

Lights like stars and a comet (Franek Kluski, pseudonym of Teofil Modrzejewski)

Nandor Fodor reports in his *Encyclopedia of Psychic Science* that French psychical researcher Dr Gustave Geley conducted a séance with the Polish medium Franek Kluski on 15th May 1921.

Dr Geley stated:

A large luminous trail like a nebulous comet, and about half a metre long, formed behind Kluski about a metre above his head and seemingly about the same distance behind him. This nebula was constituted of tiny bright grains broadcast, among which there were some especially bright points. This nebula oscillated quickly from right to left and left to right and rose and fell. It lasted about a minute, disappeared and reappeared several times. After the sitting I found that the medium, who had been naked for an hour, was very warm. He was perspiring on the back and at the armpits; he was much exhausted.[1]

Geley and DeBrath, in *Clairvoyance and Materialization: A Record of Experiments* report:

Then in weak light, slightly phosphorescent vapour floats round the medium, especially above his head, like light smoke, and in it there are gleams like foci of condensation. These lights were usually many, tenuous, and ephemeral, but sometimes they were larger and more lasting, and then gave the impression of being luminous parts of organs otherwise invisible, especially finger-ends or parts of faces. The lights usually floated around the medium, but at times went some distance from him. Lights like stars appeared here and there, moving above the medium to the right and to the left. They shone and moved and vanished in the half-dark. They looked like will-o-the-wisps. Some were more diffuse and spread out to form nebulous discs of various sizes.

---

1. Found in Gale's *Encyclopedia of Occultism and Parapsychology* 2001: on www.encyclopedia.com

Spiritual Healing

Spiritual Healing

Healing is the highest form of mediumship.
Harry Edwards
The affections suffered by the body the soul sees with shut eyes.
Hippocrates

Spiritual healing is a form of mediumship in which the medium becomes a link between healing intelligences in the spirit world and the patient. For example, Harry Edwards in *The Power of Healing* said he felt that spirit guides assisted him as he did his laying-on-of-hands with forty to one hundred people a day. He placed his hands on each person for several minutes, usually in silence, while others waited their turns. However, physical contact is not necessary as the patient can be near to the healer or in another location. Additionally, the patient's faith in spiritual healing is not a requirement and the patient does not even need to know healing is given to them (see the section titled 'Absent Healing').

The ectoplasmic humerus (William Lilley)

Spiritual healer William Lilley was born into a Spiritualist family in 1914 and owes much of his early training to his mother who had been a practicing medium. After a remarkable career in the UK, in 1949, he went to South Africa with his wife and son, David, where he continued his spiritual healing. William Lilley's life and ministry would be truly remarkable up until this point, but there is still one absolutely phenomenal moment in modern mediumship yet to be told – that of the 'ectoplasmic humerus'.

Before a large crowd of witnesses, many of whom wrote sworn statements to what they saw, an entranced William Lilley used his finger to cut open a patient, then removed a diseased humerus bone (the bone in the upper arm), replaced it with ectoplasm which materialized into a new bone, and then closed the wound with his finger. Yet, this act of selfless service to his fellow man landed Lilley in court as he was charged with the offence of conducting medicine without a licence! The prosecutors actually used the diseased bone

Lilley extracted as evidence against him. William's son, Dr David Lilley, writes:

Desmond Jackson was the young man from whom the humerus was removed. The disease was tubercular osteomyelitis not cancer. The bone was indeed replaced by ectoplasm and was completely functional, enabling Desmond to participate in sports. The bone which was removed has been preserved and is still in my possession. Desmond and his mother appeared in defence of my father in the second of his court cases and testified in court regarding the remarkable healing. The records of the court proceedings are available. The case was reported in *The Pretoria News* and *The Star*. The *Psychic News* carried a full page account of the healing in 1953.

Doctor demands to know what was done to his patient (Olga Worrall)

Ambrose and Olga Worrall in 1985 wrote in *The Gift of Healing: A Personal Story of Spiritual Therapy(140)*:

A case of considerable importance involved a high official of one of the major league ball clubs who had a growth on his throat which had been diagnosed as cancerous. When he came to the altar for healing, Olga placed her hands on his neck, her left hand on the front part of his throat, the right hand on his back. She held her fingers in this position for a few moments, and felt what she described later as a tingling sensation go through her hands. At the same moment, the man himself looked up and said "I feel terrific heat going into my throat."

The following Wednesday the baseball executive returned and asked Olga if she would place her hands on his neck again as she had done the previous week, because his throat felt so much better and he believed further therapy of this nature was indicated. He said also that he had an appointment after the service with a cancer specialist. Olga placed her hands again on his throat as she had at the previous session and again the man experienced intense heat passing from her fingers into his throat. (This heat had nothing to do with actual physical

243

pressure.) Olga's fingers were not exerting any pressure but were held lightly against the skin. That night there was an evening service at the church. Dr Day was in his office just prior to this service when a man barged into the office, thoroughly distraught. "What have you done with my patient?" Dr Day was frightened. He did not know what had happened. Further, this doctor, a Johns Hopkins specialist, was a member of the board of the Mt. Vernon Place Methodist Church.

He then proceeded to tell Dr Day that the patient had come to him following a session of the New Life Clinic and that the cancer which had been the size of a half dollar was gone and all that remained was a scar about as thin as a thread. The growth did not return. The baseball man at the last report we had was retired and living happily in Florida.

A healing that built a Temple (Thomas John 'Jack' Kelly)

The Healing Temple, at Lily Dale Assembly [America's largest and longest running Spiritualist summer camp], had its origins in a remarkable healing in the summer of 1953. After completing a ballot [billet] reading message service while blindfolded at the Lily Dale Auditorium, Rev. Jack Kelly was walking out the back door with his wife, Mrs Kelly, by his side. A lady, wearing dark sunglasses and using a cane while holding the arm of the man beside her, approached them and addressed Mr Kelly. "Oh, Mr Kelly, I did so want a message today but did not receive one." He replied "My apologies ma'am, but the service is over." As he spoke he heard his spirit teacher say "Have her sit down; we want to work on her eyes." So, she was seated and spiritual healing was given.

A crowd, which included Louis Vosburgh, gathered to watch. The lady said "Why, the doctors said that my optic nerve was irreparably severed after my head hit the windshield during a car crash. But, my sight…It's returning! My sight is returning!" Louis Vosburgh was so impressed he said "Why, there should be a place, a special place, no, a TEMPLE here at Lily Dale set aside only for Spiritual Healing for it is the truly highest form of mediumship. I will fund it myself if need be." So, while Louis Vosburgh started making plans for the erection of the Healing Temple, Rev. Kelly started to hold healing services at the Auditorium on Sunday evenings during the summer season of 1953 and 1954. Meanwhile, Mr Vosburgh acted as his own contractor and spent almost $ 30,000 of his own money [in 1953] to build the Lily Dale Assembly Healing Temple. It was erected for Rev. Kelly's exclusive use as a Healing Temple and dedicated on 3rd July 1955 in a ceremony attended the famous Hollywood actress, Mae West.

An account of this healing was reported in the *The Dunkirk Observer* (3rd August 1952)

> Mrs Donna Ball, of Gulf Avenue, Pittsford, NY, who has been attending the Lily Dale Assembly at Lily Dale, has reported that she has regained the sight of both eyes, which were injured in an auto accident March 14th, at Pittsford, and that her right hand, which was paralyzed, has also become strengthened. Mrs Ball attributes this healing entirely to the spiritual powers of Rev. Thomas J. Kelly of Buffalo … On July 13th she reports that Rev. Kelly gave her a 'healing by laying on of hands' in the Lily Dale Auditorium, which was witnessed by approx. 40 persons and that she immediately regained sight in both eyes.

A skeptic assists in a public demonstration of spiritual healing (Harry Edwards)

In one of Harry Edwards' early public demonstrations, after Maurice Barbanell had given a short address, Edwards told the assembled throng that he was the medium for a spirit power which was able to help sufferers. He then asked for volunteers for healing – particularly those that the doctors could not help.

In *Power of the Spirit* Barbanell tells us "There was no attempt to induce religious fervor, mass hysteria or emotionalism of any kind. No lights were lowered; no spotlights were used; no hymns were sung. Yet in every case he was able to show an improvement that was both dramatic and remarkable."

Edwards then asked if there was anyone in the audience who was skeptical about the healing. A young man responded and was asked to join Edwards on the platform, who then told the surprised skeptic. "Well then, you are going to help me to heal this woman."

This was a severe case of curvature of the spine and Edwards placed the young man's hands on the spine to feel the displacement. When he had satisfied himself about the extent of the curvature of the patient's spine, Edwards placed one hand over the skeptic's hands and his other arm around the patient and in a few seconds the spine was straightened.

Edwards then asked the skeptic, "Are you satisfied there is no more curvature?" The skeptic replied that he was and Edwards told him that, he too could be a healer.

Barbanell says that the young man later told him that he had gone to the demonstration out of curiosity but he was going to strive to develop that healing gift so he could help others.

Message of health confirmed at 6:45 pm (Margaret Lyon)

In *Power of the Spirit(33)* we read this account of a healing through Margaret Lyon who set about developing her healing gift after the death of her young son:

> A doctor was badgered by his mother, who was interested in Spiritualism, to consult Kahesdee [Lyon's spirit doctor]. He had already sought a specialist's advice and was told he was suffering from tuberculosis. Because the doctor was very ill, Mrs Lyon visited him at home. Kahesdee disagreed with the diagnosis and stated that all she could see was a septic abscess on the left lung. She announced that she could not permit it to be drained, as it had been suggested, because it could be cured by psychic healing. The doctor refuted all she said because of the specialist's diagnosis. "We will argue about that after a pathological examination of the sputum has been made," Kahesdee replied.
>
> A sputum test was made twenty four hours later. The verdict was, 'Non-tubercular'. Even then the doctor had his fears. He believed that he might have latent tuberculosis. Kahesdee was equal to the situation. She advised the guinea-pig test, which is considered to be the final in these matters. After six weeks, the animals were alive and well. In connection with this case, there is a fascinating story to be told. While Kahesdee was giving her diagnosis, she described the spirit presence of the

246

doctor's father, saying that she could see him, for the purpose of identification, holding a hypodermic syringe filled with yellow liquid. "Did he specialize in vaccines?" she asked. "Yes," was the doctor's answer, as he admitted the accuracy of his father's description.

The communicator announced that he was pleased because his son was in good health, and added that he would acquaint his wife with that fact. "Note the time," were his parting words to his son, "because this message will be confirmed." The doctor looked at his watch. It was 6:45 pm. All this took place in Glasgow. The doctor's mother, in London, did not know that her son was receiving spirit healing.

It was a Sunday and, worrying about her son's health, she wondered if she could obtain comfort at a Spiritualist meeting. She went to the nearest church, where a medium happened to be giving clairvoyance. The mother received the first spirit message. The medium described the presence of her husband, who once again showed himself holding a hypodermic syringe. And he repeated, almost word for word, the message he had given through Kahesdee. The spirit message from the medium was received at about 6:45 pm. The two letters crossed – one from the son to his mother describing the Glasgow end of the story and the other from the mother to the son telling of the London sequel.

Unconditional exemption from wartime service (William Lilley)

This great moment in modern mediumship is not great because it was awesome phenomena, but rather because it was a milestone in recognizing the legitimacy of this form of mediumship. At a time when Spiritualists were arrested and jailed, a court in the United Kingdom officially recognized the legitimacy and value of spiritual healing.

In 1940, Great Britain was at war and every able-bodied man between the ages of 18 and 41 stood to be pressed into military service. William Lilley, born into a Spiritualist family and having attended his first circle at the age of ten, was already an established spiritual healer with a thriving practice. Years earlier, he had quit a factory job and was supported in starting his first healing sanctuary in Leeds by a wealthy former patient whom he had cured and who was now a fellow healer who worked at his side. Faced with immediate conscription, Lilley appealed and was accepted for non-combatant roles, but then requested unconditional exemption from service. Dr Letari, Lilley's main spiritual guide, promised that when the appeal was heard he would control Lilley and address the tribunal.

Arthur Desmond, in *The Gift of Healing: The Story of William Lilley the Healer(32)* recounts what followed:

> The appeal was heard at City Library, Manchester, on 13th April 1941, before a judge, Sir Miles Mitchell and a third member. The evidence extracted provided them with a first-hand insight into spiritual healing.
>
> Q. You have people coming in to see you and you deal with people according to their letters received by post?
>
> A. Yes.
>
> Q. From long distances?
>
> A. Letters received from all parts of the world.
>
> Q. You practice your gift of healing with people from all over the world?
>
> A. By absent healing.
>
> Q. How do you give them this personal healing when letters are received by post? How do you send it? Is it telepathy?
>
> A. It is transmitted by prayer to patients wherever they may be, and who are relaxed and connected by prayer at specific times each day.
>
> Q. Is it something which passes between you and the patient even over the ocean?
>
> The tribunal then sought a definition of the word 'Sanctuary'.
>
> Q. How many people work with you in these Sanctuaries?
>
> A. There are three healers excluding myself.
>
> All three, Lilley explained in answer to further questions, possessed the same power to heal, but lacked the gift of diagnosis. A member of the tribunal asked if the Sanctuaries worked for profit.
>
> A. Oh No.

Q. What charges do you make?

A. We charge only for herbs, and then only a nominal sum introduced three months ago.

The tribunal was plainly perplexed how the applicant could diagnose a case, and prescribe herbs, when he had never seen the patient. Lilley's reply was succinct and enlightening:

"A patient in America or India will send me a handkerchief, giving no indication of the illness, and from the handkerchief, I would obtain a diagnosis and then prescribe the necessary treatment."

Q. Why should you require herbs when you are a spiritual healer?

A. We are definitely spiritual healers, but the herbs of the field are God's gift, and we must make use of them.

Arthur Richards, Lilley's wealthy benefactor, a former patient of his and now a fellow healer, revealed to the tribunal that 200 people visited the Leeds Sanctuary each week for treatment. Over 90 percent of them had been given up as incurable by material means. In healing them, Lilley had no thought of personal reward, and Richards counted it 'a great privilege to have supported him with all my heart, soul and pocket'.

"Do you think," Richards was asked "that Lilley should continue with his present work in the national interests? You regard it of national importance?"

A. It is of world importance, replied Richards.

A member of the tribunal: "Oh yes, but let us deal with this country first."

When Lilley was recalled, he was overshadowed, as promised, by Dr Letari. The question – very properly was a leading one. – "Could you not render this service if you were in the army?"

Dr Letari "No. While we know that the German cause all this destruction, we cannot blind ourselves to the fact that such destruction was taking place in man's heart years ago, and this war is the manifestation of those conditions. We must therefore look at it from an entirely different angle. There are men and women all over the world who have been suffering, not because of war, but because of some condition of disease – diseases not only of the body, but also of the mind. To those who suffer from them, I can bring a light, I can bring the understanding that this life does not end here."

He continued with a lucid and scholarly exposition of spirit visitation, emphasizing his conviction of the continuity of life beyond the grave – and then the 'dead' who are partaking in that life, who know better? He frankly admitted that even the spiritual healer did not achieve a 'possible' in his cures. He said "We visit children, many possibly suffering from tubercular and other 'incurable' diseases. We go into the highways and by-ways of life to find these children who have been suffering for many years before the war, and will continue to do so until light is given to them. We cannot always heal the body or the mind in this material life, but if we do not, we at least have the satisfaction that comes of giving them an understanding of spiritual existence.

"I know that we pass to another life – a spirit life. This material existence is but an experience to give us a realization of the future. Therefore I help out not only those who visit the Sanctuary, but those at a distance who have been cast aside as seemingly forgotten, with nothing to look forward to, nothing to live for. Those are the people to whom I can give a realization of the after-life."

Dr Letari's eloquence moved many of his hearers. They were unaware; however, they had been addressed by a guide.

The tribunal retired to consider its verdict. It reached it within two minutes. It granted Lilley unconditional exemption. His healing ministry would go forward uninterrupted. For the first time in its eventful history, the national importance of unorthodox healing – the healing that the Cancer Act was at pains to stigmatize, the healing that the medical mandarins would incontinently snuff out – had received official recognition. To fight disease, it had been decided, came before fighting man.

William Lilley combined trance healing and psychometry. After Dr Letari assumed control of him, he would diagnose the patient often by handling an object sent to him. Lilley would receive the diagnosis clairaudiently before healing was given. Because the diagnosis came through clairaudience, it was unnecessary for Lilley to take on the physical conditions of the patient. Lilley stated that if he had to take on these conditions, he would soon be broken down in health. He stated:

> A part of my work is diagnosis. By handling a handkerchief or some similar piece of clothing or article from the person who is ill, I can feel a vibration running up my arms, and clairaudiently I hear the voice of the spirit doctor telling me what to say.
>
> Everyone, without exception, radiates vibrations of varying intensities and of sensitivity that is peculiar to them. These are absorbed by any article of clothing or other object continually close to them. A handkerchief, for example, sent with a request for diagnosis, retains the vibrations of the user, and it is from these that the patient is spiritually in immediate contact with, the vibrations being received as colours. Each physical organism radiates its own colours in a psychic aura, the shades denoting whether the part is in health or disease.

So many diagnoses that stenographers worked in shifts (William Lilley)

As the work progressed between William Lilley and Dr Letari he had so many diagnoses to give that stenographers had to be employed in shifts to cope with the work. Later Dr Letari found he could dispense with psychometry and just began to use the name of the patient. There were even incidences in which the patient was anonymous with no name, age, gender, or location given. These were listed as 'Friend of Mrs—' or 'Relative of Mr—'. When using just the name of the patient, the names and addresses of the patients by post were tabulated, and each allotted a serial number, with space remaining in a ledger for the symbols for the diagnosis to be recorded by the stenographer to Lilley's clairaudient dictation. The secretary called out the number, and the medium repeated from clairaudience the diagnosis which was written into symbols apposite to that person's condition. According to Lilley in *The Gift of healing(91)*, a diagnosis took about 20 to 30 seconds to dictate. If Lilley were in trance for two and a half hours, employing stenographers in rotation, he could give as many as ninety-eight separate diagnoses in a single session! A remarkable feat in trance healing!

Lilley avoided naming the illness in his diagnoses. For example, from handling a pen-knife, he reported:

> There was a fall six to eight years ago caused by a street accident. Slight pus in lower intestine due to catarrh of stomach. Also creating nervous debility. Treat the stomach and the condition of the kidneys will adjust itself. No condition of growth but rheumatoid is present. No risk of mental disorder. No abnormality.

When compared against diagnoses given by conventional doctors, Lilley's diagnoses not only matched up with those of the earth doctors; they frequently exceeded them. They frequently gave data – in particular, pathological findings – not contained in the reports of the orthodox practitioners. Concurrent with the diagnosis, Lilley clairaudiently heard the nature of the treatment to be extended and he dictated a prescription after each diagnosis, either with herbal or homeopathic medicine. These remedies could be sent to postal patients at a nominal charge. Both the diagnosis and prescription were mailed to the patient along with a letter which affirmed Lilley's great privilege in sharing freely with the patient his spiritual gift and informing the patient that absent healing has begun on their behalf.

Lilley recorded all patient records in a ledger and invited patients to report at two-week intervals on reactions and progress noted. Each week, Lilley reviewed any follow up letters to repeat or change a prescription according to the conditions they revealed.

Six whiskies for six days (Ted Fricker)

Ted Fricker was noted for his instantaneous cures and the following story is from his autobiography, *God is My Witness(41)*.

Early in his healing career, four men from the local press visited Fricker to see what his healing was all about. They stated that as a test one of them was the patient and if Fricker cured him they would give him a wonderful write-up in the newspaper, but if not, then they'd say it was just a load of rubbish. Fricker agreed, and he immediately heard a voice which guided him from spirit "Don't worry, you must make this one of the fastest cures you've ever done. The man between the two on the sofa is the patient and he has an ulcer. Count the third button up on his vest, and when we tell you, put your hand across and touch him there and tell him he's cured."

Fricker looked straight at the man telling him he was the patient and he had an ulcer. Without getting out of his chair, Fricker then reached across with one hand and touched him at the spot while putting the other hand on his side saying "Right, you're cured then." The man said that was ridiculous but Fricker then suggested to have an X-Ray taken to prove it. The man's friends objected and said they had another way to check if he was cured – to take him to a restaurant, give him six whiskies followed by a huge steak and fried chips which he had not been able to have in years! The same treatment was meted out for six consecutive days and then the newspaper had a banner headline about a 'miracle' cure.

250 healings on a Saturday morning (Ted Fricker)

As stated in the previous 'Great Moment', Ted Fricker was known for the quickness of his spiritual healing. Patients reported healing in a matter of seconds to two minutes with five minutes being the maximum length of time he would regularly give to a patient. It was said "If you want it quicker, go to Fricker." He would routinely give 250 healings on a Saturday morning.

The queue of people waiting outside Ted Fricker's house on a Saturday morning routinely stretched around the block and throughout the neighborhood. Assuming he worked 8 am to 12 noon continually, that averaged out to less than a minute of healing per patient and 250 patients – all on a Saturday morning!

He swallowed a safety pin and advice was ignored (Margaret Lyon)

In *Power of the Spirit(37)*, Barbanell writes:

It was the medium who told a sad story of what happened when Kahesdee's [the medium's spirit doctor] advice had been ignored. Margaret Lyon had been invited to visit a child in its home. The grandmother was interested in Spiritualism, but the parents were not.

The doctors had asked that the child, a weakly lad of three, should be sent into the country. Kahesdee diagnosed pulmonary tuberculosis and advised against the baby's removal. The doctors had said nothing about the child being consumptive. The skeptical father, who refused to accept Kahesdee's opinion, said to the spirit doctor "Seeing you are so clever, perhaps you can tell me what happened to the wee one this morning," pointing to another child about eighteen months old.

Kashedee replied "If you mean that the child swallowed a safety pin, do not worry about it; it was closed. It will be passed through the bowel tomorrow." This happened the next day. Kahesdee repeated her warning that the boy was not to be taken into the country, saying that if he were his body would be brought back in a coffin in less than a week. The spirit warning was rejected. Within seven days, the child's body was returned in a coffin.

Child cured of polio at a public demonstration but doctors disbelieve (Harry Edwards)

As reported by Ramus Branch, in *Harry Edwards: The Life Story of the Great Healer(139)*, it was after World War II that Harry Edwards' healing career as a spiritual healer really took off. His public demonstrations of contact healing at venues ranged from the humblest local Spiritualist Church to the Royal Albert Hall. During these public demonstrations of healing, Edwards would usually ask for those suffering from conditions that he had found to respond most rapidly to contact healing, but he was always careful to point out that, in most cases, patients would require further treatment and that a complete cure was not always to be expected. Even so, he began to experience foretastes of the treatment he would receive later at the hands of the medical members of the Archbishops' Commission.

One such case was reported in the *Cambridge Daily News* in 1948. At a demonstration at Cambridge Guild Hall, Edwards had given healing to four-year-old Phillip Goodliff who, being crippled by polio had to be carried onto the platform by his mother. A minute after receiving healing, the child, after discarding his leg-iron, was 'romping' around the front of the hall and creating such a disturbance that his mother had to remove his shoes. However, the orthopedic surgeon who had treated the boy, Mr Noel Smith, despite the fact that the child could now walk, declared that the treatment for infantile paralysis should be on 'scientific and proved lines'.

Spirit doctor materializes, touches, and heals patient (Isa Northage)

Allan MacDonald writes in *A Path Prepared: The Story of Isa Northage(89)* of a testimonial by a Mr W. Molson, January 26, 1959 on the healing given to her via the mediumship of Isa Northage. Mrs Northage's spirit doctor, Dr Reynolds, frequently materialized and performed healing . This is one of those cases:

> Firstly Sambo, the coloured guide, welcomed us all, and during the course of his short conversation with us the medium became deeply entranced. As soon as this state was complete her main guide and helper, Dr Reynolds, appeared, fully materialized. He was particularly concerned with my own health condition at that time and chatted with me just as any doctor would chat with a patient in his consulting room, taking my head in his materialized hands and examining it. The touch of those fingers was as normal and natural as the touch of any human hand, and after he had made the kindly inquiry: "Nervous, Molson?" he proceeded to adjust a splintered bone in my head which had caused trouble for many years following a serious accident. As a result of the brief manipulation which he performed I was completely free of all ill-effects which had troubled me as a result of that particular injury for a period of over three years.

The Light that heals (Alec Harris)

In *Alec Harris: The full story of his remarkable mediumship(220)* Louie tells us that on many occasions their Healing Guide would materialize during a séance. This is just one of those occasions:

At the very beginning of a circle the Guide, whom we called the 'Healing Scientist', would emerge from the cabinet fully materialized, draped in his gossamer fine ectoplasmic white robe. Almost immediately a strange light, an unearthly blue-white luminosity, appeared in the region of his solar plexus, glowing with a pulsating energy, increasing and decreasing gently in strength. At the peak of its brilliance the whole body of the Spirit was illuminated by a sort of inner radiance. In fact, one evening when the Spirit Scientist was bending over me his robes parted and it seemed to me that the light was situated deep inside his body making the whole figure luminous. It was a breathtaking sight. I cannot find words to describe the beauty of this shining vision, or the effect of contact with the Healing Light.

"This is the light that heals," explained the Scientist. "When a medium gives healing this is the power that flows to the sick. Although you cannot see it in the healing circle, it is always there and brings great relief." …

At a circle in South Africa there were present Major and Mrs Chisham. It transpired that the Major had been 'stone deaf' for twenty years. His wife explained that she had brought him with her to the séance as he was very anxious to witness Spirit materialization and would be content only to see the Spirits even if he was unable to hear them.

During the circle the Healing Scientist made his appearance, and pointing to Mrs Chisham said "Bring your husband here to me. We may be able to help him tonight." Major Chisham left his chair and stood in front of the Scientist. The Spirit raised his arm and seemed to draw ectoplasm from out of the air. Shaking it slightly so that it billowed out, he proceeded to lay it over Major Chisham's head, placing the ends of it in each of that gentleman's ears. It glowed with the same unearthly blue-white light; it had a phosphorescent quality. The two figures stood motionless for a few minutes, illuminated by the glowing ectoplasm pulsating gently. Then this strange substance was withdrawn, and it disappeared as mysteriously as it had materialized. Major Chisham then returned to his seat and the circle continued.

The next morning my phone rang and an excited Mrs Chisham

on the other end of the line exclaimed "Oh, Mrs Harris, I can't believe that this has really happened. My husband can hear perfectly, even the faintest whisper." Her voice shook with emotion. "After all these years! It's a miracle! Really a miracle!" As I replaced the phone I once again said a mental 'thank you' to our wonderful Spirit Healers.

The 'Miracle Girl' continued (George Chapman)

We now continue the account of healing on Dorothy James after the absent healing, given by George Chapman, which saved her life. The treatment now goes forward with contact and trance healing.

More than two months after the accident, Dorothy James was finally allowed to leave the hospital. By then the staff knew her as 'The Miracle Girl', because she had not only survived but had partially recovered. She was still in bad shape and faced the prospect of many more operations and a difficult road ahead, with no prospect of full recovery in sight.

George Chapman came to see Mrs James immediately after Boxing Day during his off-duty time at the Aylesbury Fire Brigade. He talked with her for a little while about her accident and about the hospital but, while he was still talking; she fell into a deep sleep. Only when she woke up after a long and refreshing slumber did she find out from her mother, who had been in the bedroom that George Chapman had gone into trance, and that Mr Lang had performed a number of spirit operations and had then ordered that the patient was not to be wakened, but allowed to sleep on. When she awoke she asked her mother "Where's the gentleman gone?"

Mrs James continued:

Instead of telling me, my mother said "Don't try to pull yourself up in bed, you'll hurt yourself!" I told her "No, don't touch me, I can do it myself." I remember putting my right arm down – the arm that I couldn't use or feel before – and I cried out "I can lean on my arm!" And oh! There can be only one explanation – the gentleman must have done it ...

The next morning Mr Chapman came again – straight from the fire service and still in his uniform. He hadn't been home to have his breakfast. He wanted to see what progress, if any, I had made since the previous day ...

On this occasion I saw Mr Chapman go into trance. He took off his wrist-watch and put it on the side-table, and then went over to the corner and muttered a prayer. I watched him and noticed that his body went down a little bit. I thought that my eyes must be playing tricks on me again, and I felt upset because since his first visit the previous day I had had no eye trouble at all. When he spoke to me a few moments later, Mr Chapman's voice had changed completely. It was not Mr Chapman's quiet voice, it was a deep husky voice and it seemed to me as though the words were sort of blurred. He came over to me, moving his hands and flicking his fingers and I had the impression he was talking to doctors and nurses, asking for instruments and things.

He never touched me, but was obviously working on my head and I felt a strange sensation. Then he started working on my shoulders. My arms had been pulled out from my shoulders during the accident, and the right one hadn't been set back properly. Again he didn't really touch me, but I could feel the bone moving inside the socket. It didn't hurt; it went sort of numb ...

During that afternoon and the following day I improved rapidly. I felt so much better – my speech was better, I could move my arm much more easily and my vision was so much clearer. For the first time since my accident I really started feeling on top of the world. When Mr Chapman came again – that was on the day before I was due to go back to hospital – I saw him go into trance the second time, exactly in the way he had done so on the previous occasion.

We talked for a little while and out of the blue ['Dr Lang'] said "You do believe that I am going to make you better?" I assured him that I did, but I told him that I had to go back to the hospital next day. "I've no intention of staying there," I said. "No, you won't have to, young lady," he said "I shall see you again next week – here in this house."...

Here's where our story gets really interesting. J. Bernard Hutton in *Healing Hands* reports:

Mrs James was taken back to the hospital the following day but she was convinced that she would not be requested to stay. When the doctors examined her it was to find an improvement in her condition that was beyond their capacity to explain. They agreed to her request that she should be allowed to return home, because, they said, they believed the home atmosphere might be beneficial....

She continues with her story:

When they took the plaster off at the hospital, my right leg was three-quarters of an inch shorter than the left, and they said that I would have to have a special surgical shoe built, Well, I didn't want to have this, and I fervently hoped that Dr Lang could do something. So I told him about it when he came again through Mr Chapman, and of my dread. I could see he understood my feelings. While he was operating on me that day, I suddenly had this funny feeling, as if someone was lifting my leg and putting weights on the end of it....When I returned three days later to the hospital, the doctors were flabbergasted when they measured my legs and found that they were both the same length!

There was another remarkable thing. When they set the ankle and put pins in my bones they set the ankle-bone too far forward. When they took the plaster off and discovered it, they made arrangements for me to be operated on in April 1955 so that they could try and correct it. I told Mr Chapman about it when he came the next time...

While we were talking, he changed in his chair and Dr Lang came through. Almost immediately he started operating on my ankle, moving his hands and fingers and talking, and truly I could feel things being done. As soon as he finished, I could see that the ankle-bone had been moved into its proper place. Before he left, he told Jeff to phone the hospital in four days time and tell them that the proposed operation was no longer necessary. Well, Jeff did as Dr Lang had asked, but the hospital didn't take much notice of what he had said. They insisted that I come in for the operation, but when they examined my ankle they were speechless. They said they just couldn't understand how my ankle-bone could have gone back into its right position without an operation or treatment. And they said that they wouldn't need to have me in to do anything on my ankle at all.

When the Aston Martin tore into Mrs James and did its grisly job on her body, it did not neglect her face. Her features were ripped and crosshatched by scars. When she was strong enough she was sent to the famous Stoke Mandeville Hospital for plastic surgery. This is what she said about that episode in her life:

> Having had all those operations at the Buckinghamshire Hospital, I was frightened of what lay in store for me again, and the next time Mr Chapman came I told him about it. To cut a very long story short, Dr Lang performed a plastic surgery operation on my face. When he finished he wanted to know exactly when I had to go to hospital, and I told him that it was to be in a fortnight's time.
>
> He then said "Oh, by then it'll be cleared up. Don't forget to bring that to the doctor's notice, and ask whether you can have your name taken off the list." Well, I did, because my face became as it is now – with powder on you can't see a thing – and when the lady doctor from the Stoke Mandeville Hospital examined me she was stunned. She couldn't understand it. She said there was no need for plastic surgery now. Once again Dr Lang had performed a miracle.

Teleportation

Teleportation

*The increased employment of scientific methods promote exact
observation and greater love of truth among inquirers,
and will produce a race of observers who will drive the worthless
residuum of spiritualism hence into the unknown limbo of
magic and necromancy.*

Sir William Crookes

The teleportation of human bodies through closed doors or over
a distance is a rare but still a documented occurrence. The Gale
Encyclopedia of Occultism and Parapsychology defines it as a
composite phenomenon fitting between levitation and apports and
is a form of telekinesis, the movement of material objects without
human contact. However, teleportation is reported in the Bible as
shown in the following verses:

Ezek. 11:1, Moreover the spirit lifted me up, and brought me
unto the East gate of the Lord's house which looketh eastward.

Elijah, walking with Elisha, was carried away by a
whirlwind.

Habakkuk was carried from Judea to Babylon to bring food
to Daniel in the lion's den, and then carried back to Judea
through the air.

In the *Acts of the Apostles* 5:23, the warders of St. Peter's
prison testify: "The prison house we found shut in all safety
and the keepers standing before the doors; but when we opened
we found no man within."

When St. Philip baptized the Ethiopian, the author of the *Acts
of the Apostles* notes (8:39-40), "And when they were come up
out of the water, the spirit of the Lord caught away Philip that
the eunuch saw him no more... But Philip was found at
Azotus." The distance between Gaza, the scene of the baptism,
and Azotus was 30 miles.

Teleportation in the modern era is difficult to verify as several of
the famous purported occurrences of teleportation involved mediums
who were later exposed as fraudulent.

Accounts of teleportation (Agnes Guppy, Charles Williams and Frank Herne)

In the Gale Encyclopedia we read the following: "In England, accounts of teleportation were published in the Spiritualist press between 1871 and 1874 of several mediums including Agnes Guppy, Charles Williams and Frank Herne (*Spiritual Magazine,* July 1871) and Lottie Fowler (*The Spiritualist,* March 15, 1872)."

Thomas Blyton writes in his reminiscences in *Light* (April 11, 1931):

> I was present on one occasion at a private home séance at Hackney in London, when without warning or preparation, in total darkness, Mr Frank Herne was suddenly placed in the midst of the sitters; and after recovering from our surprise and resuming the séance, Mr Herne's overcoat, hat and umbrella were dropped on the table. John King, speaking in the direct voice, explained that his band of spirit people had found an unexpected opportunity to transport Mr Herne from where he had been with friends, witnessing a theatrical play that evening; on his appearance at Hackney he was in a semi-conscious condition.

Grave suspicion surrounds some of the phenomena in the mediumship of Guppy, Herne and Williams but the incidences of teleportation given here were either through the mediumship of other physical mediums or witnessed by reputable sitters."

In her morning gown and bedroom slippers (Agnes Guppy with Frank Herne & Charles Williams)

Gale *Encyclopedia of Occultism and Parapsychology* gives us this on Agnes Guppy's famous teleportation which occurred on 3rd June 1871. There were ten witnesses and eight sitters. Mrs Guppy was teleported from her home in Highbury (North London) to the house of Williams on Lamb's Conduit Street (West Central London), a distance of over three miles. The case was the occasion of much facetious comment in the daily press. *The Echo* printed a serious report. The story was summed up on the basis of the sitters' written testimony by Abraham Wallace in *Light* (1918) as follows:

Neither door nor window could have been opened without the admission of light. After various phenomena usual in dark séances had taken place someone asked Katie King, one of the controls, to bring something. Another member of the circle observed, in a joking sort of way "I wish you would bring Mrs Guppy." Upon which a third remarked "Good gracious, I hope not, she is one of the biggest women in London."

Katie's voice at once said "I will, I will, I will." Then John [King's] voice was heard to exclaim "Keep still, can't you?" In an instant somebody called out "Good God, there is something on my head," simultaneously with a heavy bump on the table and one or two screams. A match was struck, and there was Mrs Guppy on the table with the whole of the sitters seated round it closely packed together as they sat at the commencement. Mrs Guppy appeared to be in a trance, and was perfectly motionless. Great fears were entertained that the shock would be injurious to her. She had one arm over her eyes, and was arrayed in a loose morning gown with a pair of bedroom slippers on, and in a more or less décolleté condition.

When telling me the story, Mrs Guppy very naturally said how much she disliked having been brought in such a state into the presence of strangers. There was a pen in one hand, which was down by her side. From the first mention of bringing her to the time she was on the table three minutes did not elapse. It seems that Mrs Guppy had a pen in one hand and an account book in the other. She had been making up her weekly accounts and had just written the word 'onions', the ink still being wet on the page.

After Mrs Guppy had shaken off the effect of the shock, the séance was continued with her presence. During this part of the séance, her boots, hat, and clothes arrived from her home, as well as lots of flowers. After the séance one Mr Harrison, editor of *The Spiritualist,* together with three of the sitters, offered to escort Agnes Guppy to her home. There their inquiries convinced them that Guppy was really sitting in the room with Miss Neyland, writing her accounts at the time that one of the séance sitters wished her to be brought. Her husband also bore testimony to the fact that his wife shortly before her disappearance, had been up to the billiard room where he was playing billiards with a friend. This visitor corroborated his statement.

Regarding this translocation of Mrs Guppy, Frank Podmore states in his book *Modern Spiritualism* (1902):

> They there learnt from Miss Neyland, a friend of Mrs Guppy's, who had come out as a medium under her auspices, that an hour or two previously she had been sitting with Mrs Guppy near the fire making up accounts when suddenly looking up she found that her companion had disappeared, leaving a slight haze near the ceiling.

Disappeared from the séance room (Mr Henderson)

In another case of teleportation from the Gale *Encyclopedia*, the authenticity of which is difficult to establish, the subject of teleportation was a sitter in Guppy's house. His name was Mr Henderson. Ten sitters held the séance on 2nd November 1873. Suddenly it was discovered that Henderson had broken the séance chain and disappeared. The doors and windows of the room were locked. About the same moment of his disappearance, he was discovered at a distance of a mile and a half in the backyard of the house of his friend, Mr Stoke. Nine people noticed his sudden arrival. The night was wet. His boots and clothes were 'almost' dry.

Teleportation from a séance room (Mr C. V. Miller)

A report of Willi Reichel's experiences with Mr C. V. Miller, the California materialization medium, as given in *Psychische Studien* (January-February 1906) states:

> 'Betsy', the principal control of Mr Miller, called Herr Reichel first into the cabinet in order that he might assure himself of the presence of the medium there asleep. He examined all again and considers it impossible that the medium could have quitted the cabinet in a normal way; in front of the curtains were seated the twenty-seven persons who formed the circle on that evening, and the windows looked out on a much frequented street. The weather, moreover, was very windy and

wet, and it would have been impossible, he says, to open a window without causing a current of air to be felt at once. After about four minutes 'Betsy' told him to go with three other persons to the first floor and Mr Miller's housekeeper gave them the keys. They found the medium breathing heavily on a chair; they brought him back into the séance room, where he awoke, and remembering nothing.

Two incidences of teleportation (Carlos Mirabelli)

On the basis of the original Portuguese documents, psychical researcher E. J. Dingwall, in *Psychic Research* (July 1930), now in the Gale *Encyclopedia of Occultism and Parapsychology,* recounts:

> The teleportation of the medium [Carlos Mirabelli] from the railway station at Luz [São Paolo] to the town of S. Vincente, a distance of some 90 kilometers. The report states that at the time the medium was at the station at Luz in company with a number of people and was intending to travel to Santos. Shortly before the train started he suddenly disappeared to the astonishment of everybody. His presence in S. Vincente being ascertained 15 minutes later by telephone, it being proved that he was met in the town exactly two minutes after his disappearance....
>
> On another occasion, when the medium had been secured in his armchair by means of various ligatures, he vanished utterly from his position, the doors and windows remaining both locked and firmly secured. Five sitters remained in the séance room whilst the rest went in search of the missing man. He was soon discovered in a side room lying in an easy chair and singing to himself.

Disappeared from a locked and sealed room (Franek Kluski, pseudonym of Teofil Modrzejewski)

F. W. Pawlowski, Professor of Aeronautical Engineering, in 'The Mediumship of Franek Kluski of Warsaw', *Journal of the American Society for Psychical Research(19)* (1925) provided a detailed account of his observations of medium Franek Kluski, confirming the strict controls, while pointing out that when no ladies were present Kluski was entirely naked. Doors were locked and sealed and strips of waxed paper bearing secret marks and signed by those present were passed over the crevices. Secret trap doors were ruled out before the sittings.

On one occasion, Pawlowski reported, Kluski disappeared from the locked and sealed room, and was later found sound asleep in another room of the apartment. He apparently had been dematerialized and then rematerialized in this teleportation.

Transported medium asks "Haven't you finished yet?" (Alec Harris

Teleportation and dematerialization happened a number of times with Alec Harris but this first time was quite unexpected as Louie tells us in the book, *Alec Harris:the full story of his remarkable physical mediumship(95)*:

> In 1940 we heard the dreadful news of the fall of Dunkirk, and were saddened by the tragic loss of so many young lives. Sitting with us at that time was a Mrs P, who had two daughters whose husbands, Jack and Arthur, were in the Military Police, and were serving with units engaged in the relief of Dunkirk. One of the daughters, who also sat with us, begged the Guides to take care of 'the boys'.
>
> At the following voice circle we were sitting as usual linked by our hands, with the sitter at the end of each row sitting close to and touching the wall, so that nobody could possibly pass. We were all singing lustily to keep up the power, when we were told, unexpectedly, not to sing but to keep very quiet. This was most unusual. Singing was considered to be absolutely necessary to raise the vibrations and maintain them. However, we did as we had been instructed, and waited in silence for what seemed a very long time for something to happen.
>
> I began to experience a peculiar sensation; one that I could not explain or understand. I felt a kind of strange emptiness. I remarked to the others that I had a feeling that none of the Guides was present.

Then an unfamiliar voice spoke from the cabinet offering a most unusual suggestion "Wouldn't you all like to go downstairs and have a cup of tea?"I was flabbergasted! What a ridiculous remark to make.

Then there came a knocking at the door, which was always kept locked during a séance. And Alec's muffled voice filtered through from the other side of the door, coming from the direction of the landing outside, saying "Haven't you finished yet?"

There was a prickling at the nape of my neck, and my hair felt as if it were standing on end. Alec, I knew, should be inside the cabinet, securely bound to his chair, in the room, not outside, with the door bolted from the inside. How could he possibly have got out. I was really frightened. I feared that my husband would come to harm if he could be moved about by Spirits like this.

I sprang to the door, and opened it. There stood Alec, well and in good spirits, and fully conscious. We all plied him with the questions; Why? How? When? To everything he could only answer that, in some inexplicable way, he had found himself out on the landing, with Chang beside him. He could offer no explanation as to how he got there. It was 1 am and so quiet that any one of us would have heard the slightest movement had there been any.

I was troubled about this incident. Chang, perceiving this, spoke to me later, when Alec and I were alone after the circle in our bedroom. Taking Alec in trance, he spoke through him saying "You asked us to look after the boys, Jack and Arthur. They were in grave danger tonight. You will find out that what I am saying is true. They had need of us, and we were being kept back from assisting them by your thoughts and desires for the circle. So we took the medium out of the room, knowing that you would then close the circle, and leave us free to aid them."

He then administered a gentle reprimand "You must have confidence in us, and not worry about the medium, for we have promised to look after him."

Temperature changes

Temperature changes

Seek the friendships and companionships which evoke within your heart a gentleness, a peacefulness of lovingness, who can exchange with your thoughts their own wise wisdom and blend their auras with yours that your mediumship [soul] may be strengthened and enhanced.

Ramadahn, Spirit Guide to Medium Ursula Roberts

Frequently during séances, changes in temperature will occur with sitters reporting a noticeable reduction in temperature, followed with a rise back to normal temperatures at the end of the séance. But it was not until séance rooms were equipped with scientific devices that changes in temperature could be verified.

Nandor Fodor wrote in his *Encyclopedia of Psychic Science* that Walter, the control of Margery Crandon, said that the cold breezes and the drop in temperature is a result of the sitters and the medium. In Margery's séances, a maximum-and-minimum thermometer was employed to measure the temperature. In one case the initial temperature dropped from 68F to 42F, a difference of 26 degrees. After the breezes had been blowing for a while Margery often complained of feeling as though cobwebs were on her face. Prof. Henslow describes the sensations of the sitters for Dr Hooper of Birmingham as of that of 'an intensely cold dew or mist' and when apports were being produced 'the sitters felt as if they were sitting up to their knees in cold water'. Sir William Crookes wrote in *Researches into the Phenomena of Spiritualism* that phenomena, are generally preceded by a peculiar cold air and on some occasions, the cold was so intense that he could only compare it to that felt when the hand has been within a few inches of frozen mercury. Concerning the experiments at the Castle of Millesimo with Marquis Centurione Scotto, Nandor Fodor wrote in his *Encyclopedia of Psychic Science* that Ernesto Bozzano recorded:

> On the evening of 7th July 1928, the heat was very oppressive. We happened to mention this disadvantage. Almost immediately blasts of unusually strong, icy air, were felt by all of us. There was a continual change in the direction

from which these air currents came; sometimes they descended from the ceiling, then we felt them in front of us, or at our sides, or blowing from behind us; sometimes they were like small whirlwinds. It felt as though several electric fans were working in the center, outside and above the circle. In the next séances the phenomenon was repeated and perfected.

Almost immediately we felt strong blasts of icy air which rapidly increased in force, giving one the impression of a powerful supernormal electric fan which periodically wafted its pleasant, cooling currents of air over the sitters... These currents were so strong that our hair waved in the wind, and men's coats, and the lace on the ladies' dresses were blown about. Ernesto Bozzano adds that the breezes sometimes brought down the temperature of the séances room by as much as 20 degrees.

According to Maurice Barbanell in *This is Spiritualism*, the drop in temperature is unmistakable and necessary, as he writes:

A few minutes after the séance began; the four other visitors and I felt the cold psychic breezes which always accompany the production of these phenomena. Just as the cabinet, we are told, is used to store and condense the spirit power necessary to produce materializations, so the cold breezes are said to indicate part of the process used by the invisible operators to obtain their results. The drop in temperature is unmistakable.

Additionally, Professor F. W. Pawlowski reports in 'The Mediumship of Franek Kluski of Warsaw', *Journal of the American Society for Psychical Research (1925)(19)* that tests demonstrated there was a dramatic reduction of temperature in the séance rooms with medium Franek Kluski present and that compass needles would move about violently when he was nearby.

Temperature changes during séances (Dorothy Stella Cranshaw Deacon or Stella C.)

Harry Price, the psychical researcher established a definite connection between phenomena and the drop of temperature. In his experiments with Stella C. at the National Laboratory of Psychical

Research he noticed a maximum drop of 20.5° Fahrenheit. At the close of the séances the temperature was again normal. But often the drop in the temperature of the room was permanent. The medium's temperature was always higher at the end of the sitting but she herself always complained of feeling cold. The rapidity of her pulse beats was always accompanied in the trance by a pronounced coldness in the extremities. Below is an excerpt from Harry Price's *Fifty Years of Psychical Research*:

With the advent of Stella in 1923, I determined thoroughly to test the possibility of recording these alleged thermal changes, and installed a delicate recording thermometer. The results of our observations were startling. As I have already mentioned, at the first séance the mercury fell no fewer than 11° Fahrenheit, accompanied by violent telekinetic movements of the séance table.

At nearly all of the séances in this series, the instrument measured a fall in temperature. The sudden changes appeared to synchronize with violent telekinetic displacements. The thermometric records of eleven séances are tabulated below:

No.	Date of sitting	Time of start of sitting am.	Temp at Start	Time of Finish pm	Temp at Finish	Minimum (Intermediate)	Fall	Rise
1	Mar 22	11.32	60°	12.35	62°	49°	11°	13°
2	Mar 29	11.38	61°	12.47	65°	49.5°	11.5°	15.5°
3	April 5	11.20	64.5°	12.43	65°	57°	7.5°	8°
4	April 12	11.20	62°	1.30	66°	58°	4°	8°
5	April 19	11.18	63.5°	1.15	64.5°	43°	20.5°	21.5°
6	May 3	11.40	67°	1.45	74°	no fall		7°
7	May 10	11.5	58.5°	12.25	64°	57°	1.5°	7°
8	May 17	11.0	57.5°	12.55	64°	57°	0.5°	7°
9	May 24	11.15	59°	12.55	65°	58°	1°	7°
10	June 7	11.6	62.5°	12.55	68.5°	61.75°	0.75°	6.75°
11	June 21	11.15	63.5°	12.45	68.5°	62.5°	1°	6°

Trance Sittings

Trance Sittings

*When I see now for myself the extraordinary difficulties in
getting messages through from this side, I marvel not that we
got so little but that we got as much as we did .
For it is you, your conditions which make
the barrier to communication.*

A message from W. T. Stead in Julia's Bureau on 2nd June 1912

It is unusual today for mental mediums to routinely go into trance for their private sittings. However, many of the great mediums of the past were known for their sittings conducted in trance. These types of sittings could offer the sitter as direct a link as possible in mental mediumship to their loved one in spirit. However, they might also be a link to spirit controls that had a unique perspective on their lives and desire to share spiritual truths relevant to the sitter. As reported in Paul Beard's *Inner Eye, Listening Ear: An Exploration of Mediumship* "At a private session, Mrs Sharplin, a well-known medium, would say, 'We will speak to you, since you wish it, about your relatives, but first allow us to speak of spiritual things'."

An interesting phenomena related to trance sittings is reported in *"Margery": The Medium*, after a séance in which medium Margery Crandon was in trance, her cheeks and chin were wet with what the sitters thought to be neither tears nor perspiration, but perhaps the remnants of ectoplasm.

188 facts given at two consecutive sittings to Arthur Findlay (Bertha Harris and Mrs Agnes Abbott)

In his autobiography *Looking Back(333)* Arthur Findlay recounts that just six and nine days after his mother died, he had two sittings, one in Glasgow and one in London. No mistake was made, some statements being unknown to him were found later to be correct. In both cases the mediums could not have made any enquiries beforehand, and neither of them knew that his mother had died. Taking the sittings with the two mediums together, 188 facts were given which all were correct. There was no guessing. Nothing was vague. Everything said was correct and clearly stated.

Sitting with Bertha Harris, in Glasgow, on 9th February 1936 contained the following noteworthy facts:

You seem to bring an atmosphere of sorrow with you today. Someone has passed on within the past week. A lady, small, stooping, old. I should say about eighty years of age. Very closely connected with you. The lady mentions Mary and Elizabeth. She sends them both her love and gratitude. She has mentioned them in her will, giving them recognition. It is a money recognition. 'I always like to pay my debts,' she says. 'I have tried to repay them for all their kindness to me.' Her last conscious remembrance on earth was Mary and Elizabeth standing beside her.

Your Mother speaks of a red rose which was placed on her robe in her coffin on her breast! She says "Red is my favorite colour, but why did you not put the rose in my hand?"

Your Mother had very small hands and feet; she was proud of her small feet, she took size two in shoes! Your Mother mentions various small gifts she has left, for people with cards attached bearing messages and names. Arthur's daughter's gift is a necklace!

Your Mother mentions something in her bedroom with a small single drawer in it containing papers which will interest you. [When] I said I did not know of such a thing, she mentioned a bunch of keys and I said I did not know anything about this bunch of keys [but when] I returned home I looked round her room and saw her dressing-case, which was a mahogany box about 18 inches by 15 inches. I could not open it as it was locked and asked for the key. This was on, a bunch of keys. The dressing-case was opened, and after examining the inside we found a spring which released a single drawer in which we found quite a number of papers of interest. If I had not been told about this drawer it is unlikely I would ever have found these papers.)

Sitting with Mrs Abbott in London on 12th February 1936 contained these facts:

An elderly lady was present, from seventy-five to eighty years who had recently passed over. Among those who were waiting for her was a clergyman, who, when on earth, thought Spiritualism was the work of the Devil. He was an ardent minister, and used to wear a red hood, but he has now given up the foolish ideas which he preached.

Your Father and Mother are both in the spirit world, and they send you their love. All is well with your Mother. Your Father is very happy having her with him. Your Father can never thank you enough for all you did for your Mother. It will be repaid in the years to come.

You have many years in front of you, and he is glad that people look up to you. He approves of your books. Then reference was made to her furniture, and 'she hoped that the big furniture would not be sold.' (This was her wish on earth.)

Reference was next made to old family papers and to old family photographs. 'They are not old rubbish and, though you are not interested in them, you should keep them. (Correct.) She knew I was not especially interested in these, and she had made this remark, in these words, when on earth, to me.)

She then referred to a visit of recent years to Bournemouth which I had forgotten, and said so, but she said this was correct, and I now remember that a few years before she died, my wife and I did stay with her at a hotel in Bournemouth for a few days. She then referred to the pretty nurse who looked after her. She said she liked her very much indeed. She also liked drinking the powdered stuff just before passing, as it made her mouth feel clean and relieved discomfort.

Ninety-six facts were given at the sitting on 9th February 1936, and ninety-two facts were given at the sitting on 12th February 1936, making one hundred and eighty eight in all. Not one of the statements made was incorrect or even doubtful.

On the first occasion, with Mrs Harris, no appointment was made before Findlay and his brother called on her so she could not have known to expect them. Then in London an appointment was made through the International Institute for Psychical Research but no name was given in making the appointment so Mrs Abbott did not know who to expect and neither medium could have made previous enquiries to gain information about their sitter, which is a charge frequently made about mediums.

Communicators use humorous code (Evan Powell)

Maurice Barbanell, in *Power of the Spirit(99)*, writes:

> One of the most striking proofs – it was also very humorous – that I received through trance mediumship came through Evan Powell, a former miner who became the mayor of his town. In his heyday, he was a splendid materialization medium.
>
> On one of his infrequent visits to London, we met for a chat. He broke off to mention that he could see two spirit figures, a middle-aged woman and a younger man. Then he said that someone wished to communicate and proposed an impromptu sitting. What followed was one of the most subtle spirit messages I have received. I cannot give it in its entirety because it refers to a matter that is too private for publication. The middle-aged woman, I was told, wanted me to write something which would recall her to me. It began as follows, "My auspicious representation got everyone roaring....your clue" The rest I am compelled to delete. The message from the young man was, "We all like to elucidate riddles." Having written these words, I said that I still could not recall the communicators and added that the message was meaningless. I was told to take the first letter of each word of the message. These are M-A-R-G-E-R-Y-C and W-A-L-T-E-R. Of course, identification was easy with that clue. The communicators were Margery Crandon, the world-famous medium, and her brother, Walter, who acted as her spirit guide and was always full of fun at her séances.
>
> When I visited America, I was Margery's house guest in Boston. One day, Margery gave us a humorous imitation of a public figure that we all knew and her performance created roars of laughter. Evan Powell could certainly have not known about this happening. It was not only splendid evidence from Margery and her brother, but it revealed that after death are still possessed of a sense of humour.

The R-101 disaster (Eileen Garrett)

On Sunday 5th October 1930, the airship R101 under the command of Flight-Lieutenant H. C. Irwin crashed and burned, killing forty-six of the fifty-four passengers and crew of the R101. Two days later, on Tuesday, 7th October 1930, at 3 p.m., a séance was held at the National Laboratory of Psychical Research. On the AECES Top 40 Survival Cases website Malcolm Allen gives this report:

Joining psychic researcher Harry Price for the afternoon séance were Ethel Beenbarn, Price's secretary and stenographer; journalist Ian Coster, who had requested the session in the hope of contacting the spirit of Sir Arthur Conan Doyle; and Eileen Garrett, a medium of growing renown in England. This was Garrett's first visit to Price's laboratory; she did not know Coster nor had she been told the purpose of the session.

Garrett went immediately into trance and her control, Uvani, began to speak. He spoke not of the recently passed-on Doyle, however, but of a man named 'Irwin' who was apologizing for interfering but who insisted on speaking. Then, as Price reports 'the voice of the medium again changed and an entity announced that he was Flight-Lieutenant H. Carmichael Irwin, captain of the R101. He gave the listeners a detailed and apparently highly technical account of how the R101 crashed.[1]

Coster was at first miffed that he wasn't getting an interview with Doyle, but he quickly realized he was witnessing a historic event. He put the story out at once, and newspapers across England and around the world carried it, often with banner headlines. Transcriptions of the session were requested and carefully studied by experts investigating the crash.

Several of Irwin's statements — such as the ship being too heavy for its engines — were public assumptions or could be reasonably guessed. But many were technical, confidential, or simply unknown to anyone at the time. For example:

• Irwin said "Load too great for long flight. Same with SL-8. Tell Eckener."

---

1. The full story of the R101, and Eileen Garrett's part in it, is found in Fuller's book *The Airmen who would not die.*

278

No one at the séance knew the meaning of 'SL-8' or recognized the name 'Eckener'. The British experts who reviewed transcripts of the session knew that Dr Eckener was the designer of the Graf Zeppelin, but even they had to search through their records of German airships to discover that 'SL-8' was the identifier for another dirigible.

- Irwin said "Starboard strakes started."

'Strakes', a term foreign to all at the session, was originally a naval expression that was adopted by airship designers. Strakes are parallel layers of longitudinal plates that form the sides of a ship. Irwin was formerly a navy man, so it is a term that he would be likely to use.

- Irwin said "Impossible to rise. Cannot trim. Almost scraped the roofs of Achy. Kept to railway."

Achy, a French village, was on the R101's route. Achy was shown on the type of large-scale air-ordnance map carried by the R101, but the village was so small that it did not appear on any normal ordnance or road map. Neither did it rate mentioning in Baedeker's or Michelin's guidebooks. Witnesses near the town testified later that the airship had passed over extremely low.

When Will Charlton, the chief supply officer of the R101, after a long investigation told Harry Price that he was convinced that the only possible explantion was that Captain Irwin had communicated after his physical death, in spite of Price's tendency to remain non-committal, he replied "That in my opinion is the perfect answer."

Secret Royal trance sitting while blindfolded (Lilian Bailey)

Lilian Bailey gave trance sittings to many notable personalities in the 20th century. Kings and princes consulted her because of her remarkable gift as a trance medium. Further, Lilian Bailey was one of a handful of gifted 20th century British mediums who were responsible for Spiritualism becoming a State-recognized religion, owing to the impression that the stunning quality of her survival evidence made on all who witnessed it. Gordon Adams, Lilian Bailey's son-in-law, confided to Roy Stemman (Assistant Editor to Maurice Barbanell at the *Psychic News* for eight years) that a remarkable trance sitting had taken place in 1953. Stemman was sworn to secrecy. It was not until Lilian Bailey's death in October

1971 that he and others who knew the story were free to discuss it and he has included this report in his book *Spirit Communication*.

Lilian Bailey knew there were people who required her to perform under the strictest test conditions before they would be prepared to accept the evidence of their own eyes and ears, and she always did her best to satisfy those demands, within reason. So when she received a request from a stranger to give a séance at a house in Kensington, she agreed. A limousine took her to a well-appointed property; then she was taken on to another address. She was required to put on a blindfold during the journey so that there were no visual clues about the person or people she would be meeting. Again, she agreed.

She was eventually led into a room, where she sensed others were gathered, and was asked to conduct the sitting still wearing the blindfold. This was not a great hindrance, since she often worked in a trance. Puzzled but philosophical about the lengths to which people went to test her mediumship, she eased herself into a chair and soon felt herself drifting off into a trance, allowing her main spirit helper Bill Wootton, and others in the next world, to take over her body and speak through her lips.

In what seemed to her like no time at all, she returned to normal consciousness and was told she could remove the blindfold. As her eyes grew accustomed to the light she surveyed the sitters. Sitting in a circle on gilt chairs were the Queen Mother, the Queen, Prince Philip, Princess Margaret, Princess Alexandra and the Duke of Kent.

This astonishing experience, which happened a year after the death of King George VI, had clearly been arranged in the hope of receiving a communication from the dead monarch, and it was almost certainly successful. However, since she was in trance, Lilian Bailey knew nothing of the conversations that took place between members of the British royal family and those from the spirit world who wished to speak to them.Unsurprisingly, none of those who participated has ever commented directly on the secret séance.

Royal biographer and *Daily Telegraph* court correspondent Ann Morrow included this story in her book, *The Queen Mother*. She had asked Gordon Adams if Lilian Bailey was unnerved when she removed her blindfold. He replied: 'My mother-in-law had dealings with all sorts of people, such as the Chinese leader Chiang Kai-shek and the King of Greece. So she did not feel intimidated by royalty; it was all in a day's work for her.' The Queen Mother is reported to have continued to phone Lilian Bailey for some time after the sitting and further private sittings took place. Eventually, when she came to terms with her loss and was clearly satisfied that the dead king continued to watch over her from the spirit world, she asked the medium to come to Clarence House one last time. Removing a piece of costume jewellery [a gold brooch] from the dress she was wearing, the Queen Mother pinned it on Lilian Bailey's shoulder, saying: 'You know we do not have many possessions, but I would like you to have this.' It expressed her gratitude for the comfort she received. Almost immediately, she returned to public life.

Since the royal family have not confirmed the story, can we be sure that this remarkable event actually took place? Those who knew Lilian Bailey – who was awarded an OBE (Order of the British Empire) for services in France during the First World War, when she served with the Queen Mary's Army Auxiliary Corps – are adamant that she would not have invented such a story to boost her reputation. She was already famous and, since the story was never published during her lifetime, it did not affect her standing among Spiritualists or the public. That may not satisfy skeptics.

When writing her book, Ann Morrow received assistance from the Queen Mother and her private secretary, Sir Martin Gilliat. They saw proofs of the book and raised no objection to the inclusion of the report on the royal séance. The story was repeated, again without objection, in Ann Morrow's *Without Equal: Her Majesty Queen Elizabeth, the Queen Mother*, published in July 2000 to mark her centenary.

King George VI, of course, knew all about mediums when he was alive. When his speech therapist, Lionel Logue, had told him that he had visited mediums to seek evidence of his wife's survival after death, the King was not shocked – in fact he was quite supportive and remarked, "My family are no strangers to Spiritualism."

John, the monk, returns to Arnold Clare (medium unknown)

In *The Mediumship of Arnold Clare*, by Harry Edwards we read that the awakening of the mediumship of Arnold Clare can be linked to John, a monk whom he had met in 1917 at Mount Athos. Arnold, while serving as a member of the Navy, spent many hours listening to the wise old man, remembered that on leaving, John simply said that the two of them would meet again. Arnold hardly realized at the time what the circumstances would be when this happened. Later, during his naval service, he became acquainted with a Russian captain who invited him to his own home where circles were held with his wife as the medium. After attending a number of these, the medium began to speak 'with an intonation unmistakably John's and reproducing his natural inflexions'. During this occasion, the communicator reminded Arnold of what he had predicted: 'I told you, my son, we should meet again'. He continued to speak as he had done at Mount Athos, and advised Arnold that he was being trained for work.

'Faunus' message for Oliver Lodge (Leonora Piper)

Normally, When Mrs Piper was in trance controlled by certain personalities, she often gave specific information concerning the name, character and past of those present as well of others known to them, either alive or dead. These details were always quite uninteresting: the description of some one's cane, what sort of cuff-links he wore, and from whom he had received them as a present, etc. She made a point of reminding those present of various little details of their past, of which she was quite unlikely to have heard.

However in 1915, she gave the famous 'Faunus' message which was not her usual specific evidence, but rather a classical allusion from the spirit of Frederic William Henry (or F. W. H.) Myers that predicted the death of Sir Oliver Lodge's son, Raymond, in World War I.

In Part II Chapter 2 of *Raymond*[1], Sir Oliver Lodge, a distinguished British physicist, writes that the first intimation that he had that anything might be going wrong was a message from Myers communicated by Richard Hodgson (R. H.) through

1. First published by Methuen in 1916.

Mrs Piper in New Hampshire, America. This was during a sitting for a Miss Robbins (MISS R.) on 8th August 1915.

The information was sent to Lodge by the medium's daughter, together with the original script. Here follows an extract:

> R. H. - Now Lodge, while we are not here as of old, i.e. not quite, we are here enough to take and give messages. Myers says you take the part of the poet, and he will act as Faunus.
>
> MISS R. - Faunus?
>
> R. H. - Yes. Myers. *Protect.* He will understand. (A.L.P.[2] writes here that he is evidently referring to Lodge.) What have you to say, Lodge? Good work. Ask Verrall, she will also understand. Arthur says so. (According to Lodge, this is a reference to the deceased Dr Arthur W. Verrall whom Lodge knew.)
>
> MISS R. - Do you mean Arthur Tennyson?
>
> R. H. - *No. Myers* knows. You got it mixed (speaking to Miss R.) but Myers is straight about Poet and Faunus.

In order to interpret this message, therefore, Lodge wrote to Mrs Verrall as he was instructed, asking her "Does *The Poet and Faunus* mean anything to you? Did one 'protect' the other?"

She replied at once (8th September 1915) referring him to literature from the poet Horace, and wrote "The reference is to Horace's account of his narrow escape from death, from a falling tree[3], which he ascribes to the intervention of Faunus, the guardian of poets."

Lodge perceived therefore, from this interpretation of the 'Myers' message to him, that the meaning was that some blow was going to fall, or was likely to fall, and that Myers would intervene, apparently to protect him from it.

The above message reached Lodge at the beginning of September in Scotland. Lodge's son, Raymond, was killed near Ypres on 14th September 1915, and Lodge got the news by telegram from the War Office on 17th September.

---

2. (A. L. P.) the initials of Mrs Piper's daughter, Miss Alta Piper.
3. Interestingly, a fallen or falling tree is a frequently used symbol for death; perhaps through a misinterpretation of Biblical verse, Eccl. xi, 3.

Soon after the event, Lodge informed the Rev. M. A. Bayfield of the incident (saying at the same time that Myers had not been able to 'ward off' the blow). Bayfield replied "Horace says Faunus lightened the blow. As bearing on your terrible loss, the meaning seems to be that the blow would be 'lightened' by the assurance, conveyed afresh to you by a special message from Myers, that your boy still lives."

Sir Oliver Lodge accepted that the appropriate translation was 'lighten'. The bough fell and struck the poet (Lodge himself), but 'the blow' (his son's death) was 'lightened' by Lodge's knowledge of survival and Afterlife communication; then through the action of 'Faunus' (Myers) helping Raymond, Sir Oliver and his family were able to communicate with his son.

Raymond provides ample evidence of his survival (Gladys Osborne Leonard and Alfred Vout Peters)

Michael Tymn, in his article on the ASCSI website about Raymond's communication with his parents, writes this:

On 14th September 1915, Second Lieutenant Raymond Lodge, the youngest of six sons of Sir Oliver Lodge, was killed in action in Flanders. Eleven days later, on 25th September, Raymond began communicating with Sir Oliver and Lady Lodge through the mediumship of Gladys Osborne Leonard and Alfred Vout Peters. His initial message was that Frederic Myers, who had become Sir Oliver's good friend before his death in 1901, was assisting him in adapting to his new environment in the spirit world.

On 27th September Lady Lodge sat with Peters and was told by Moonstone, Peters' spirit control, that Raymond was referencing a photo of himself with a group of other men – one in which he was holding a walking stick. Lady Lodge had no recollection of such a photo (and so telepathy by the medium from the mind of the sitter was ruled out as a possibility).

It was not until two months later, when the mother of one of Raymond's fellow officers sent a condolence letter and mentioned a group photo, taken twenty-one days before Raymond's death that the message began to make sense. Lady Lodge immediately responded and requested a copy of the photo. Before the photo arrived, however, Sir Oliver sat with Mrs Leonard and asked Raymond about it. Raymond replied, through Feda, Leonard's control, that it was taken outdoors and that he was sitting while others were standing. He further recalled someone leaning on him.

Several days later, the photo arrived in the mail. It showed three rows of officers, the back row standing, the second row sitting on a bench, and the front row sitting on the ground, a military walking stick over Raymond's crossed legs and the arm of the officer behind him resting on his shoulder. Sir Oliver concluded that this evidence went beyond fraud, coincidence and telepathy and saw it as sort of a cross-correspondence in that messages about the photo came through two different mediums.

However before the photo was received, on 28th September, Sir Oliver and Lady Lodge again sat with Mrs Leonard; but instead of messages coming through her voice while she was in a trance, as was the usual method with her, the communications came by means of a tilting table. The sitters would place their hands lightly on the table and then recite the alphabet. At the correct letter, the table would tilt. For questions that could be answered with a 'yes' or a 'no', three tilts indicated an affirmative response and one tilt a negative. Sir Oliver explained that even though this method was much slower than the trance voice method, it was carried out as an experiment. Moreover, he felt that it might provide messages untainted by Mrs Leonard's mind, as he had come to recognize that certain communications were distorted as they had to be filtered through her mind.

After about four minutes, the table began to tilt and Raymond identified himself by his nickname, Pat. As a further test of identity, Sir Oliver asked him to name of one of his five brothers. The table spelled out N-O-R-M-A- before Sir Oliver interrupted and commented that Raymond was confused. He told him to begin again. The name N-O-E-L was then spelled out, which was one of Raymond's brothers. It was not until Sir Oliver later discussed this with his other sons that it began to make sense. "It appears that 'Norman' was a kind of general nickname," Sir Oliver explained "and especially when the boys played hockey together, which they often did in the field here, by way of getting concentrated exercise, Raymond, who was especially adept at this game, had a habit of shouting out 'Now then, Norman', or other words of encouragement, to any of his older brothers whom he wished to stimulate ... That is what I am now told, and I can easily realize the manner of it. But I can testify that I was not aware that a name like this was used, nor was Lady Lodge, we two being the only members of the family present at the Leonard table sitting where the name 'Norman' was given."

Here again, Lodge saw this as evidence against telepathy, as well as an indication that Raymond, who had discussed psychical research with his father when he was alive, was attempting to provide veridical information by giving a name unknown to his father.

Sir Oliver also asked Raymond to name an officer in his regiment. The board spelled out M-I-T-C-H-E-L-L. The name meant nothing to Sir Oliver or Lady Lodge, but Sir Oliver later checked with the War Office and discovered that Second Lieutenant E. H. Mitchell had been in Raymond's unit.

Between tests, Raymond talked about his new environment and activities in the afterlife, all of which Sir Oliver presented in the book. However, scientist that he was, Sir Oliver was constantly testing the medium. As something of a word association test, he asked his other sons to provide him with some names, words, or questions by which Raymond might further prove his identity. At another table sitting with Mrs Leonard, Sir Oliver asked Raymond the name of the man to whom Raymond had given his dog. The table responded with 'Stallard', which was correct and clearly something Mrs Leonard would not have known. However, Sir Oliver knew the name and therefore this did not rule out telepathy.

Passing on another question from his other sons, Sir Oliver asked Raymond if he remembered anything about the Argonauts. Three tilts came from the table, indicating that he did remember. Sir Oliver then asked him what he remembered. The word came T-E-L-E-G-R-A-M. Sir Oliver did not understand the connection, and his other sons were a bit puzzled until they remembered that while the brothers were on a motoring trip a few years earlier Raymond went into a post office and sent a telegram home to say they were all right, signing it 'Argonauts'.

Alec Lodge, one of Raymond's older brothers, sat with Mrs Leonard on 21st December 1915, but, in spite of what his parents had told him, was still skeptical. As a test of his own, Alec asked Raymond about his favourite music. Alec noted that he then heard Feda questioning Raymond, asking him *sotto voce* (whispering) "An orange lady?" Still confused, Feda then told Alec that "He says something about an orange lady." Alec felt that this was very evidential as '*My Orange Girl*' was the last song Raymond bought when 'alive'. Raymond, through Feda, also mentioned '*Irish Eyes*', another of his favourites. By the time Sir Oliver sat with Mrs Leonard on 3rd March 1916, he was convinced that she was not a charlatan, but he still felt a need to test her in still additional ways. Thus, at a sitting with her that day, he asked Raymond if he knew about 'Mr Jackson'. Feda struggled with understanding Raymond's response, but she communicated "Fine bird...put him on a pedestal." This was especially evidential as Sir Oliver was certain that Mrs Leonard did not know that 'Mr Jackson' was the name of Lady Lodge's pet peacock, nor that he had died a week earlier and was in the process of being stuffed and mounted on a wooden pedestal.

On 26th May 1916, Lionel Lodge and his sister, Norah, drove from the Lodge home, near Birmingham, to London for a sitting. Knowing that his brother and sister were scheduled to meet with Leonard at noon, Alec Lodge asked two other sisters, Honor and Rosalynde, to sit with him in the drawing room and focus on asking Raymond to get the word 'Honolulu' through to Lionel and Norah during their sitting with Leonard. Lionel and Norah knew nothing of this request. When Sir Oliver later read Lionel's notes of the sitting, he saw that Raymond said something about Norah playing music. Norah replied that she could not. Feda (through Mrs Leonard's voice box) then whispered to the invisible Raymond (attention directed away from Lionel and Norah), "She can't do what?" Upon getting a response from Raymond, Feda than said "He wanted to know whether you could play Hula – Honolulu. Well, can't you try to? He is rolling with laughter."

By the end of April 1916, a huge amount of evidence which Raymond had communicated to them had been accumulated by the Lodge family. "The number of more or less convincing proofs which we have obtained is by this time very great," Sir Oliver wrote, adding that some of them appeal more to one person, some to another; but taking them all together every possible ground of suspicion or doubt seemed to the family to be removed. "I am as convinced of continued existence on the other side of death as I am of existence here," Sir Oliver continued. "It may be said, you cannot be as sure as you are of sensory experience. I say I can. A physicist is never limited to direct sensory impressions; he has to deal with a multitude of conceptions and things for which he has no physical organ – the dynamical theory of heat, for instance, and of gases, the theories of electricity, of magnetism, of chemical affinity, of cohesion, aye, and his apprehension of the ether itself, lead him into regions where sight and hearing and touch are impotent as direct witnesses, where they are no longer efficient guides."

His book *Raymond or Life and Death* was first published in November 1916 and three further editions were published before the end of that year – a work of great detail and observation.

Medium's hand marked with communicator's bullet wound (Isa Northage)

From a report sent to *Two Worlds*, 9th December 1938 and reprinted in *A Path Prepared(45)* we read:

> The Spiritualist Brotherhood Church, Pontypridd, reports very successful meetings and transfiguration séances with Mrs Northage, of Nottingham, which were remarkable for an unusual phenomenon. Mr J. C. Flye says, "A young soldier who passed over in the war took control of Mrs Northage, spoke to me, related a number of incidents pertaining to his earthly life, told me the cause of his passing over, and gave a resume of his experiences in the Great Beyond.
>
> One of the peculiarities of his passing was that he was wounded by a bullet in the hand. On the medium recovering consciousness, we were astonished to find that the bullet wounds had produced clear marks on the hand of the medium in the exact place where my friend was struck. This was demonstrated before a large company. The phenomenon of stigmata has, of course, historical sanction, but this is the first case we have heard of where a deceased person controlling a medium has reproduced evidence of his wounds.

Bishop James Albert Pike and his son Jim (Ena Twigg)

On 2nd March 1966, Pike, his secretary Maren Bergrud, and Canon Pearce-Higgins had a trance sitting with Ena Twigg. Using his son, Jim's passport as a psychometric link, she said that Jim had been trying to contact his father and was asking for forgiveness for the suicide, which he said was because of 'too many pills'. She then relayed that Jim was pleased about his ashes being scattered at the Golden Gate Bridge which was correct.

He urged his father to continue fighting the church officials who opposed Pike's controversial beliefs. Ena Twigg went on to say that Jim was accompanied by a German intellectual to whom Pike had dedicated his new book. The book was still at the printer. It was called *What Is This Treasure?* and was indeed dedicated to Paul Tillich, a liberal theologian and godfather to Jim. Tillich also urged Pike to fight those church officials who wanted to charge him with heresy.

Twelve days later, just before leaving England to return to the United States, Pike again sat with Twigg. She went into trance and Jim spoke through her. He prophesied Pike's movements in the near future (which came true) and also told his father to contact the Spiritual Frontiers Fellowship, and a Father William V. Rauscher, an Episcopal priest, when he got back to America. Twigg apparently herself knew nothing of either Father Rauscher or of the Spiritual Frontiers Fellowship.

In the fall of 1967, Pike was again shaken when his secretary Maren Bergrud committed suicide. He tried to contact her through mediums but without success. Pike agreed to sit for a televised séance on CTV in Toronto, with medium Rev. Arthur Ford. This took place on Sunday, 3rd September. Allen Spraggett, religion editor of the *Toronto Star*, had arranged the program and acted as moderator. He first talked with Ford about mediumship and then with Pike, asking if the Bishop had any personal experience of communicating through a trance medium. Ford then put himself into a trance and his spirit guide, Fletcher, came through.

Soon Jim, Pike's son, came through and gave evidential details. On 20th December 1968, Pike married Diane Kennedy, who had taken over Maren Bergrud's position as director of the New Focus

Foundation (started by Pike the previous year). Pike left the Church and formed the Foundation for Religious Transition in April 1969.

A few months later, Pike and his new wife took a trip to the Holy Land. On 1st September they became lost in the desert. Diane had to leave her husband to go for help and could not locate him again afterward. When Ena Twigg heard of Pike being missing, she had a sitting with her husband Harry and Canon Peace-Higgins. They received a communication from Pike himself, giving directions to where his body could be found. It was found there, on a cliff in the Judean desert near the Dead Sea, on 7th September.

Verification of Spirit Guides

Verification of Spirit Guides

A son reported that his mother, in the moments immediately before
she died, looked upward and said: "Oh, it's so beautiful!"
Adventures in Immortality
George Gallup, Jr. and William Proctor

Mediumship requires the involvement of intelligences from the spirit world. However, verifying any life on earth the spirit guides had is a complex problem. They mostly claim a distant and inconspicuous life which defies verification. A few, such as D. D. Home's control who always spoke in plural and never gave his name, are hard to identify. The notion that spirit guides are entities separate from the medium has been thoroughly investigated. There have been incidences when spirit guides have been verified as such and even confirmed to have lived an earthly life sometimes with no apparent relationship to the medium. These great moments involve the verification of spirit guides as entities separate from the medium and in some cases of having verifiable lives on earth.

The appearance of Sambo (Ted Fricker)

Although this has already included in this book in Absent Healing it is worth another airing in this section as the verification of the separate identity of the spirit guide

As chronicled in Ted Fricker's autobiography, *God is My Witness (136)* Sambo was a spiritual guide and doctor who was always close to Fricker. A former African slave, he was clairvoyantly seen to be nearly seven feet tall and had black skin. His existence was not known outside the Fricker family.

On one occasion, a woman rang up Fricker's healing sanctuary asking for absent healing for her sister in America. Fricker instructed that she just think of Fricker by name and he would give absent healing. Two days later, an urgent telegram came from America stating to stop all absent healing. Apparently, the sister had done what was instructed when suddenly she felt the presence of someone in front of her. "I looked up", said the sister, "and there, standing in

292

front of me, I saw a black man about seven feet tall. I got the fright of my life. Then he spoke to me and said, 'Don't worry, gel, we'll fix you up!' Then I must have fainted, but in the morning when I woke up, I was completely cured!"

This great moment gives us an independent verification of role of spiritual doctors in Absent Healing and confirmed the existence of Sambo.

Spirit guide tells of book written about him (Evan Powell)

At one sitting, Black Hawk insisted that a book had been written about him. No one knew of it, so a friend of Evan Powell commissioned a book agent to find it. In 1932 a book was found which was titled *Life of Ma-Ka-Tai-Me-She-Kia-Kiak or Black Hawk*, dictated by himself. It had been published in Boston in 1834. A copy of the book was obtained and presented to Powell. Black Hawk also insisted that there was a memorial to him in Illinois.

The return of Dr William Lang (George Chapman)

According to Roy Stemman in the book *Surgeon from Another World*, George Chapman was a renowned trance healer whose spirit doctor was Dr William Lang.

William Lang (1852-1937) had been an eye specialist at London's Middlesex Hospital up until 1914. People who had known Dr Lang in life reported that Chapman, in trance, perfectly captured Lang's personality and mannerisms. Moreover, Dr Lang recognized his former patients without an introduction, and knew things about them that only he and they could know.

Joe Fisher in an account of his interview with Dr Lang, through George Chapman, included this detailed 'Note':

Dr Lang's daughter, Marie Lyndon Lang, was naturally skeptical when she heard in 1947 that her father had returned to inhabit, at intervals, the body of George Chapman. But after hearing his voice, observing his mannerisms and asking personal questions concerning events which only she and her father knew about, she made this declaration "The person who speaks through George Chapman and claims to be William Lang is, without a doubt, my father."

For thirty-one years until her death at the age of ninety-four in May 1977, Marie Lyndon spoke regularly with her deceased father. At her request, however, both her intimate connection to the increasingly popular Dr Lang and her consultations with him were kept secret until her passing.

Vowing "I am going to put this quack to confusion," Dr Lang's granddaughter, Mrs Susan Fairclough, reacted with angry derision when she heard that a healer was 'pretending' to be her grandfather. But after meeting George Chapman and Dr Lang, Mrs Fairclough had this to say "To my great horror, or rather, stupefaction, the man who was in this room was indisputably my grandfather. It was not him physically, but it was his voice, his behaviour. It was unquestionable. He spoke to me and evoked precise events of my childhood. And I was so impressed that all I could say was 'Yes, grandpapa' or 'No, grandpapa'."

Testimonials to Dr Lang's competence as a doctor has been furnished by a host of living doctors, few of whom wished to be named for fear of professional censure. After meeting Dr Lang for the first time in December 1969, Dr Robert Laidlaw of New York told how he discussed in a professional manner certain ophthalmological conditions and techniques, and added "I fully believed them, and I believe now, that I was conversing with the surviving spirit of a doctor who had died some thirty years ago." George Chapman's trance mediumship met the following criteria of evidence:

- The spirit communicator spoke as near as possible to the way he spoke on earth;
- He used the same phrases and mannerisms;
- He manifested other personal characteristics;
- He was able to give dates, names and details of his earthly experiences that can be verified; and
- He was able to discuss intimate matters with relatives and colleagues still on earth.

Only nineteen but she became a spirit guide (Isa Northage)

Isa Northage's main healing guide, Dr Reynolds, was seen many times, materialized and separate from his medium, but his records of having worked in Ireland 150 years before could not be traced. However another of Isa's guides, Ellen Dawes, was recognized by her own mother. Ellen became one of the guides who introduced proceedings at a séance and helped translate when foreign languages were spoken. In *A Path Prepared* Isa relates that:

> Ellen made herself known at one of the early experimental sittings when a sweet voice whispered through the trumpet "Mother, speak to me, it is Ellen." The feelings of that mother upon hearing her daughter's voice again cannot be expressed in words. It was the voice of Ellen Dawes, who was also aged only nineteen when she passed into spirit and said she was helping the Negro (Sambo) and would be with him all the time he was attached to me in my work.

"My son was an officer and a gentleman. He never dabbled in Spiritualism." (Lilian Bailey)

History has no record of William Hedley Wootton's involvement with Spiritualism when he walked the earth. But after his passing from a gunshot above his eye in World War I, he more than 'dabbled in Spiritualism' – he was a guide to one of the finest mediums of the 20th century, Lilian Bailey. Together, they did more than comfort the bereaved (among those they comforted was Elizabeth, the Queen Mother), they helped legitimize Spiritualism as a state recognized religion in the United Kingdom. When William Wootten lived, he was not a physician or a holy man; he was an Army officer with no known connection to Lilian.

However, William Hedley Wootton is verified to have lived through several highly evidential incidents. To begin, Lilian Bailey was twenty-six in 1921 and not yet involved in Spiritualism. She went to a library where she lived and borrowed a book, *Raymond or Life and Death*, by Sir Oliver Lodge. The book was named after Lodge's son who was killed in war and documented his spirit return. Reading this book enticed Lilian to borrow other similar books, and in one of these books, a reference was made to a man called William Hope, a psychic photographer who lived in Crewe, the same town as Lilian. Lilian wondered if he could get a photograph of her dead mother.

When she went to William Hope, she thought she would get a psychic extra of her mother, who had passed on shortly before but she did not get a picture of her mother. Instead on her photograph there appeared an extra of a coloured girl and a young man with a deep dark mark over one eye, both quite unknown to her.

Lilian's skeptical husband had tentatively suggested that Wootton, whose voice was heard via Lilian's mediumship in their home circle, was a figment of her imagination so to try to prove otherwise, Lilian had mentally asked Wootton to provide proof of his separate identity. Later, after being invited to attend a Helen Duncan materialization séance she had the joy of seeing her mother materialize. William Wootton also appeared showing himself as he was pictured on the spirit photograph. He gave his full name, William Hedley Wootton, and told Lilian that he was an ex-Grenadier Guards' captain, that he had been shot over one eye and killed instantly in France during World War I.

Anxious to acquaint his family with the news of his survival, Lilian asked him for their whereabouts. Warning her that it would serve no purpose, Wootton gave his mother's full address in Boston, USA. Lilian was able to confirm the service particulars Wootton had given her by comparing them with War Office records.

Then she wrote to his mother to check the rest of the facts. The address had been correctly given by Wootton, for there was a reply, but it was hardly what Lilian could have bargained for! Instead of being amazed at Lilian's extraordinary communication and eager to know more, the mother replied:

"My son was an officer and a gentleman and gave his life for his country. He never dabbled in Spiritualism."

Though this incident impressed Lilian's husband, he still would not admit that the facts given concerning Wootton necessarily proved his survival. Lilian, he argued, could have heard about Wootton when she was serving the army and might possibly have retained knowledge of his parents' whereabouts and other facts in her subconscious mind. But Lillian referred to Billy Hope's mediumship. How did he explain Wootton's face appearing on the same photograph as herself?

"Nursing Barbara's doll." (Lilian Bailey)

Researchers have long questioned the notion that spirit guides are separate entities from the medium and not a part of their subconscious mind. This great moment shows a spirit guide to be separate from the medium. Besides William Wootton, the other guide of medium Lilian Bailey was a girl named Poppet. She first manifested in a spirit photograph taken by William Hope, but at that time Lilian did not know who she was. As Lilian's mediumship developed and she sat in home circles, other members of the circle were astonished one night to hear, instead of the deep masculine tones of Bill Wootton, a quaint shrill foreign voice squeaking and chattering and shaking the medium's head in desperation because it could not make itself understood.

In *Death is her Life*(77) Neech records that Lilian, still immature as a medium, could not understand how such a personality could possibly be of service to the bereaved. She had no wish to encourage this unknown control to continue to manifest through her. "I disliked intensely," she confessed "being an instrument for some gibberish nobody could understand. A fight ensued; I was refusing to allow this to go on and mentally striving to force it away, all to no purpose. Much to my annoyance, this childish; voice persisted, demanding attention."

While Lilian was entranced, the voice persisted. One sitter who was an accomplished linguist told the medium afterwards that the voice addressed him in perfect Hindustani. The little girl, who could not speak a word of English, was drawn to the medium's daughter Dorothy, and in time a relationship was sealed between her daughter and the young girl. Until Lilian retired from her mediumship Poppet was never able to speak fluent English but she did work closely with Lilian. It was reported she was born in Ceylon several hundred years ago, was a cripple and an outcast and died at the age of four.

Poppet proved to Lilian's skeptical husband that she was a real person and not a creation of the medium's mind. The child materialized at one of Helen Duncan's séances, but still Lilian's husband would not accept her. She challenged him to name any test that would prove to him she had a separate existence from his wife. "I shall be in London in a few days' time," he said. "Take notice of what I do at seven o'clock that evening, and then tell me afterwards what it was."

The guide accepted the test.

When Bailey was in London, he was invited by a friend to go to his home for dinner. He arrived shortly before seven o'clock, just as his friend's child was going to bed. He did not know the name of the child – she was called 'Baby' by the family.

The child kissed her father 'Goodnight' and then, just as the clock struck seven came over to Bailey and placed her doll in his hands. The striking of the clock reminded Bailey of the spirit test.

"What did I do at seven o'clock that night?" he asked the guide, later.

"You were nursing Barbara's doll," was the reply.

"Who is Barbara?"

"That is the name of the little girl where you went for dinner," the guide said.

This turned out to be a much better test than Bailey had intended, for he did not know the name of the child.

He wrote to his friend in London, asking the name of his daughter, and the friend replied "Barbara."

Weight change during phenomena

Weight change during phenomena

It is easier for the spirits of the dead to communicate with
the dog than with man, even when man is represented by
the parents of the departed one.
Capt. A. H. Trapman in 'The Dog: Man's Best Friend'

During the early 20th century, mediums readily agreed to 'test conditions' imposed by psychical researchers. As phenomena were observed in one medium, it could be tested in another medium. This is what occurred with mediums Kathleen Goliger and Ethel Post-Parrish. Weight was found to be lost or gained during different phenomena . Researchers could confirm this when it was observed multiple times with various mediums. Research has shown that the change in weight is linked to medium's ectoplasm. According to Hannen Swaffer in *My Greatest Story*, Dr W. J. Crawford, of Queen's University, Belfast, had weighed it, traced its flow – and even certified that one medium, while exuding it, lost 54½ lbs. of weight!

Weight loss recorded after séance (Mina 'Margery' Crandon)

J. Malcolm Bird reports in *"Margery": The Medium* that both sitters and the medium lost between a quarter to a half a pound during a séance. This can be explained because of the possible ectoplasm used to produce phenomena.

Weight loss measured during séance (Ethel Post-Parrish)

According to Peggy Barnes(Jefts) in her pamphlet *Lo, I am with you always*, Ethel Post-Parrish gave a test séance (which meant it was under test conditions) in 1928. Two medical doctors, one from Birmingham, Alabama and the other from New York City, had asked Mrs Parrish that they might try an experiment. As they did not wish their names used, they were referred to as 'Doctor X' and 'Doctor Z'. Before the séance two weighing machines had been placed in the séance room. A large scale was placed in the cabinet and the medium's chair was placed on it. The second was a small bathroom scale and it was placed about ten feet from the cabinet.

After several of the spirit teachers had manifested, a beautiful spirit came from the cabinet and identified herself as the sister of Doctor X. As she walked from the cabinet she showed the cord of ectoplasm connecting her body to that of the medium. The cord looked like a fleecy rope and seemed to be connected at the back of the ectoplasmic body between the shoulders and ran along the floor through the curtains of the cabinet, presumably to the body of the medium. After exchanging greetings with his sister, Doctor X asked her if she would assist him in an experiment. She replied that she would be glad to do so if he was sure that it would not harm the medium. Silver Belle spoke from the cabinet and assured her that the medium was protected.

The doctor then asked his sister to come and step upon the scale that he might see how much she weighed. She complied with the request and with the aid of a little phosphorous light he was able to see the scale. "My goodness," he exclaimed "you weigh 35 pounds. I did not expect that." He then proceeded to take the pulse of the spirit and the respiration. He remarked that the pulse was very strong. While this was going on Doctor Z had been permitted to enter the cabinet with the entranced medium and we heard him say "Silver Belle, where are you? I can hear you but I cannot see." Silver Belle assured him that she was there but had dematerialized as all the psychic force was needed for the experiment.

Directed by Silver Belle, Doctor Z proceeded to take the weight of the medium and found that it had decreased nearly 37 pounds from her original weight taken before the séance. He then took her pulse and respiration and with the aid of a tiny flash light wrote them down upon a slip of paper. After this was over and the spirit form back in the cabinet, Silver Belle said in a tone of authority "That's all now. My medium cannot stand anymore."

After the séance was over the doctors compared notes and found that the pulse and respiration of the spirit were entirely different from those of the medium. When the medium came from the cabinet she was quite pale and complained of being weak and tired. The spirit controls tell us that the use of psychic force or energy is a drain upon the vitality of the medium. This is especially true when there are negative vibrations in the room. Later I asked Dr Banks why the medium had lost 37 pounds when the spirit only weighed 35 and he said that the other two pounds were in the cord of ectoplasm connecting the spirit form to that of the medium.

Weight loss after apports (Thomas Lynn)

According to Nandor Fodor, in his *Encyclopedia of Psychic Science*, striking experiments were carried out at the British College of Psychic Science in 1929 with Mr Thomas Lynn. He was searched, stripped and put in a bag and his hands were tied to his knees with tapes. Many small objects, a cheap pearl necklace, a small reel of cotton, a button, a shell and a screw nail were apported and photographed at the moment of their arrival. During the sitting, the medium lost 10-12 ounces in weight. Additionally, *Psychic Science* (Vol. 8, no. 2, July 1929) outlines the experiments on his mediumship by James McKenzie and Major C. Mowbray on Thomas Lynn. Observations include extrusions of ectoplasm, small coils or rods of varying shapes from the pit of his stomach, to perform minor physical feats, and leave – after their disappearance – red marks like punctures behind on the medium's skin.

Weight gain measured during table levitation (Kathleen Goliger)

According to Nandor Fodor, in the *Encyclopedia of Psychic Science*, Dr William J. Crawford found that sitters as well as the medium vary in weight during a séance. During materialization phenomena, mediums have been recorded to lose half or more of their body weight, but the opposite seems to occur during table levitation.

Michael Tymn reports in his fifth article on Ectoplasm that in 1914, Dr William J. Crawford, a lecturer in mechanical engineering at Queen's University of Belfast, Ireland, began investigating the mediumship of 16-year-old Kathleen Goliger. The phenomena surrounding the young girl included communicating raps, trance voice, and table levitations. In all, Crawford had eighty-seven sittings over some two and a half years with the Goliger Circle. Crawford brought in a scale large enough to hold the medium while

,

she was sitting in her chair.

He discovered that when a table was being levitated, the weight of the table, usually around 16 poundswas transferred to the medium through what he called 'psychic rods' (ectoplasmic rods). Most of the time, the transfer of weight would be a few ounces short of the weight of the table. Further experimentation revealed that the extra weight was being transferred to the sitters in the room, who apparently furnished small amounts of the 'psychic force'.

Xenoglossy & Xenography

Xenoglossy and Xenograpy

*It would not be honest in me to disguise the fact that he who
meddles with mediumship does so at his peril. I do say that
the development of mediumship is sometimes
a very questionable benefit.*

William Stainton Moses

Coined by Professor Charles Richet, the term 'xenoglossy' is
speaking a real language that is entirely unknown to the speaker
through the phenomena of mediumship. The similar talent to write
in a foreign language is called 'xenography'. Xenoglossy is
sometimes termed xenoglossia or xenoglossis. There is some
confusion between the terms xenoglossy from glossolalia.
Glossolalia refers to speaking in an unknown or non-existent
language (i.e. 'speaking in tongues'). True cases of xenoglossy are
also distinguished from cryptomnesia which is the recollection of a
foreign language which the person learned or was exposed to in the
earlier years of that person's life.

Although anecdotal tales exist going back hundreds of years, one
of the first well-documented occurrences of this phenomenon took
place in 1862.

During a demonstration of 'mesmerizing' (hypnosis) that year, a
Prince Galtizin had a German woman who had no ability to speak
any language other than her native tongue suddenly conversing in
fluent French. Galtizin explained it as regression, claiming the
woman had mentally reverted to a past life in France. Another
confusing case of alleged xenoglossy is that of Swarnlata Mishra, a
young woman who had supposedly never been exposed to the
Bengali language, but could sing songs in the language and perform
native Bengali dances. However, this case was more consistent with
memories from a past life than a mediumistic experience.

Additionally, xenoglossy is a phenomenon of mediumship and is
thus differentiated from speaking a language which may have been
used in that person's past life. For all these reasons, actual
xenoglossy is rare and difficult to study. A typical case of claimed
xenoglossy is reported in Joe Fisher's *The Case for Reincarnation.*

Dr Morris Netherton reported a case of a blond, blue-eyed eleven year old boy who under hypnosis was taped for eleven minutes as he spoke in an ancient Chinese dialect. When the tape was taken to a professor at the Department of Oriental Studies at the University of California it turned out to be a recitation from a forbidden religion of Ancient China.

In 1970, a woman named Delores Jay was hypnotized. She claimed to be a reincarnation of a German woman from the 19th century and while hypnotized, she spoke German very well, despite never having studied the language. However, the evidence in these cases did not clearly demonstrate that the communication was from a spirit entity, so it was not conclusively mediumship. Mediumship requires an altered state of consciousness, but not specifically a state brought on by hypnosis. So, cases of presumed xenoglossy which are brought on via hypnosis in individuals with no other mediumistic phenomena are not strong cases for determining xenoglossy.

The first Xenoglossic medium in Modern Spiritualism (Laura Edmonds)

In the *Encyclopedia of Occultism and Parapsychology* we read that according to the testimony of Judge John Worth Edmonds of New York, his mediumistic daughter, Laura, could channel spirits who would then converse through her for long periods of time in various languages including Greek, Polish, Spanish and at least two Native American languages. Interestingly, Miss Edmonds claimed not to have any clue what she was saying during the trances. Visitors claimed that the spirits would converse with amazing fluency. Foreign sitters could converse through her with spirits in their native language, even if it was a country as remote as Greece or Poland.

Judge Edmonds wrote in a letter dated 27th October 1857:

> One evening when some twelve or fifteen persons were in my parlour, Mr E. D. Green, an artist of this city, was shown in, accompanied by a gentleman whom he introduced as Mr Evangelides, of Greece (now of New York). He spoke broken English, but Greek fluently. Before long, a spirit spoke to him through Laura, in English, and said so many things to him that

he identified him as a friend who had died at his house a few years before but of whom none of us had ever heard.

Occasionally through Laura, the spirit would speak a word or a sentence in Greek, until Mr E. inquired if he could be understood if he spoke in Greek. The residue of the conversation, for more than an hour, was, on his part, entirely in Greek, and on hers sometimes in Greek and sometimes in English.

At times Laura would not understand what was the idea conveyed, either by her or him. At other times she would understand him, though he spoke in Greek, and herself when uttering Greek words. One day my daughter and niece came into my library and began a conversation with me in Spanish, one speaking a part of a sentence and the other the residue. They were influenced, as I found, by a spirit of a person whom I had known when in Central America, and reference was made to many things which had occurred to me there, of which I knew they were as ignorant as they were of Spanish.

Laura has spoken to me in Indian, in the Chippewa and Menomonie tongues. I knew the language, because I had been two years in the Indian country.

Speaking and writing in a host of languages (Carlos Mirabelli)

A more authenticated case of true xenoglossy is reported in Richard Lazarus' *The Case against Death(121)*. The Brazilian medium Carlos Mirabelli spoke and wrote long technical documents in more than thirty languages including Syrian and Japanese in the presence of scientists and crowds up to 5,000. By 1926 Mirabelli had produced phenomena before a total of nearly 600 witnesses, most of whom had been recruited from the ranks of Brazil's leading scientists, medical doctors, administrators, and writers, with an occasional learned visitor from abroad.

As a trance-speaking medium, Mirabelli particularly excelled in xenoglossy. Not only did he speak in foreign tongues, but he gave spontaneous lectures on philosophy, astronomy, sociology, politics, medicine, history, and the natural sciences. These speeches were delivered alternately in German, French, Dutch, English,

Greek, Polish, Syrian, Albanian, Czech, four Italian dialects, Arabic, Turkish, Hebrew, Chinese, Japanese, and several African dialects, in addition to Latin, Ancient Greek, and his native tongue, Portuguese.

As an automatic-writing medium, he produced lengthy and erudite written dissertations in twenty-eight languages, at a speed impossible to achieve under normal writing conditions. While entranced, it is said that Mirabelli wrote treatises in the style of Lombroso, Kepler, Voltaire, and Galileo. These works included an essay on evil written in Hebrew and signed by Moses, a tract on the instability of empires by Alexander the Great, and an essay on the mysterious things between Heaven and Earth by Shakespeare. Although unable to verify such prestigious authorship, linguists were said to be amazed at the masterful control that the medium exercised over each of the languages employed in these treatises. Such accomplishments are made the more impressive by noting that Mirabelli's formal education ended with primary school.

Spirit doctors speak in languages unknown to healer (William Lilley)

In *The Gift of Healing*, Arthur Desmond, the biographer of spiritual healer William Lilley, wrote that through the influence of his spirit guide Dr Letari, William Lilley spoke in Hindu and Chinese and, under the influence of spirit guide Ramesoye, spoke in Latin, Greek, German and Russian even though Lilley had no previous knowledge of these languages.

Trance sitting done in French (Leonora Piper)

American medium Leonora Piper was continually tested over several decades by the American Society of Psychical Research. Most of her sittings were recorded and extensively analyzed.

Michael Tymn writes this in his biography of Dr Phinuit:

On 6th September 1888, J. Rogers Rich, an artist, had a sitting with Piper. He observed a remarkable change in Piper's voice as it became unmistakably male and rather husky. He was at once addressed in French and he responded in French. Piper's control, Dr

Phinuit, diagnosed Rich's physical ailments for him and prescribed various herbs, giving the manner of preparing them. Phinuit told him that his mother was beside him and accurately described her. In a second sitting, a month later, Phinuit told Rich that his deceased niece was at his side. To test him, Rich asked the niece, who had lived all her life in France, for his name in French, to which Phinuit accurately relayed 'Thames Rowghearce Reach' entirely in the French alphabet.

In another sitting, Phinuit's foreign accent gave way to a pure English accent and Rich was greeted by his old friend, Newell. Rich noted that the entranced Piper was twiddling her fingers as if twirling a moustache, a habit very characteristic of Newell. Rich was later told by Phinuit that his sister was often in his surroundings and had much influence over him. Rich replied that he had never had a sister. Phinuit corrected him, saying that he had a sister who died in infancy before he was born. Rich questioned an aunt about this and was informed that it was true.

Xenography from Patience Worth (Pearl Curran)

Although not a foreign language requiring translation, Victor Zammit records that Pearl Curran, a medium from Saint Louis who was barely literate, began to write in astonishingly accurate Middle English via the Ouija Board. Under the guidance of a spirit entity named Patience Worth, she produced sixty novels, plays and poems, including a 60,000 word epic poem.

Fodor enlarges on this telling us – Telka, Patience Worth's poem of around 70,000 words in Anglo-Saxon language, was dictated through Mrs Curran as rapidly as it could be written down by a secretary, and the medium was so independent of that which came through her that she was free to smoke a cigarette, to interrupt herself by taking part in the conversation of those present, or go into the next room to answer the telephone. The whole poem, a masterpiece, took a total of 35 hours. Another one of her works, set in 17th century England, was described by the Los Angeles Times as a 'masterpiece'.

Acknowledgements

The author has made a number of efforts to contact authors and publishers but if she has not been able to contact you she offers her thanks and appreciation for the material you have provided in her search for the phenomena of communication with a World Unseen.

For the permissions granted from those we have been able to contact, our deepest gratitude for enabling another generation to have access to the wonders that you and others have researched and recorded.

For all their books, articles and support our special thanks go to:

Ray Buckland

George Cranley at www.zerdinisworld.com

All those at Psypioneer (www.woodlandway.org)

Roy Stemman at Spiritual Truth Foundation for permission to quote from his own books and those of Maurice and Sylvia Barbanell now available from the website: www.Silver-Birch.net

Spiritualist National Union for excerpts from Arthur Findlay's books and Emma Harding Britten's Autobiography

Michael Tymn at White Crow Books

Steven Upton at SDU Publications for republishing the classics

Victor Zammit at www.victorzammit.com

Bibliography

Books referenced

Bailey, Dr W.G. (1923) *No, Not Dead: They live*, Huntzinger Co. - repub. 2013 by Literary Licensing, Whitefish MT.

Barbanell, M. (1933) *The Trumpet shall Sound*, Psychic Book Club: London.

Barbanell, M. (1938) *Parish the Healer*, Psychic Press: London

Barbanell, M. (1940) *Across the Gulf*, Psychic Book Club: London.

Barbanell, M. (1949) *Power of Spirit*, Psychic Book Club: London.

Barbanell, M. (1959) *This is Spiritualism*, Psychic Book Club: London.

Barbanell, M. (1969) *Spiritualism Today*, Psychic Book Club: London.

Barbanell, S. (1944) *Some Discern Spirits:The Mediumship of Estelle Roberts*, Psychic Press: London.

All books by the Barbanells & those about Silver Birch are available now at www.Silver-Birch.net

Baird, A.T. (1949) *The Life of Richard Hodgson*, Spiritual Truth Press: London.

Beard, P. (1980) *Living On: A study of altering consciousness after death*, Pilgrim Books: Norwich.

Beard, P. (1992) *Inner Eye, Listening Ear: An Exploration into Mediumship*, Pilgrim Books: Norwich.

Bird, J.M. (1925, 2007) '*Margery':The Medium*, SDU Publications: London.

Branch, R. (1982, 1991) *Harry Edwards: The Life Story of the Great Healer*, The Healer Publishing Company: London.

Brennan, J. (2013) *Whisperers: The Secret History of the Spirit World*, Overlook Press: New York.

Britten, E. (1869, 2006) *Modern American Spiritualism: A Twenty Years' Record of the Communion between Earth and the World of Spirits*, SNU Publications, Stansted, Essex

Britten, E. (1900, 1999) *Autobiography of Emma Hardinge Britten*, SNU Publications, Stansted, Essex.

Buckland, R. (2005) *The Spirit Book: The Encyclopedia of Clairvoyance, Channeling and Spirit Communication*, Visible Ink Press: Canton, MI.

Cattanach, R. (1998) *Best of Both Worlds: A Tribute to a Great Medium*, Pembridge Publishing: London.

Cook, C. (aka Ellen [Pennau] Cook) (1931) *The Voice Triumphant: The Revelations of a Medium*, Alfred Knopf Publishers: N.York.

Crookes, W. (1874) *Researches into the Phenomena of Spiritualism,*
i) Quarterly Journal of Science: London
(ii) The Two Worlds Publishing Co: Manchester (1926)

Cummins, G. (1946) *They Survive,* Rider and Co: London.

Cummins, G. (1932) *The Road to Immortality* (repub. 2012)

Desmond, A. (1949) *The Gift of Healing: The Story of William Henry Lilley the Healer,* Spiritualist Press: London.

Dixon-Smith, R, (1952) *New Light on Survival,* Rider & Co: London.

Doyle, Sir A. Conan (1921) *The Wanderings of a Spiritualist,* George Doran: London.

Doyle, Sir A. Conan (1926) *History of Spiritualism,* Cassell and Co: London. (&1989) in 2 vols, Spiritual Truth Foundation: London

Drayton Thomas, C. (1922) *Some Recent Evidence for Survival,* Lowfield Heath: London.

Edwards, H. (1941) *The Mediumship of Arnold Clare,* Psychic Press:London.

Edwards, H. (1967) *The Power of Healing,* Tandem Publishing: London.

Edwards, H. (c1970, 1998) A *Guide for the development of Mediumship,* Spiritual Truth Press: London.

Edwards, H. (1983) *The Healing Intelligence,* The Healer Publishing Co: Burrows Lea, England.

Edwards, H. (1974, 1992) *A Guide to the Understanding and Practice of Spiritual Healing,* The Healer Publisher Co:Burrows Lea, England.

Farmer, J.S. (1886) *Twixt two worlds* - available as e-book from www.forgottenbooks.com

Findlay, A. (1952) *Where Two Worlds Meet,* Psychic Press: London.

Findlay, A. (1961) *Looking Back: Autobiography of a Spiritualist,* Psychic Press: London.

Findlay, A. (1963 - orig 1931) *On the Edge of the Etheric or Survival After Death Scientifically Explained,* Psychic Press: London.

Fisher, J. (1986) *The Case for Reincarnation,* Grafton Books: London.

Fisher, J. (1991) *Hungry Ghosts,* McClelland & Stewart Inc. Toronto.

Flint, L. (1971) *Voices in the Dark: My Life as a Medium,* Macmillan:London.

Fodor, N. (1934, 1964) *Encyclopedia of Psychic Science,* Paperback Library: New York. (see www.spiritwritings.com)

Fodor, N. (1934) *These Mysterious People,* Rider &Co (see website www.survivalafterdeath.info)

Fontana, D. (2205) *Is There an Afterlife?,* O Books, Hants.

Fricker, E. (1977) *God is My Witness: The Story of the World-Famous Healer,* Arthur Baker: London.

Fuller, J. G. (1981) *The Airmen who would not die,* Corgi Books: London.

Funk, I. (1907) *The Psychic Riddle,* Funk and Wagnall: New York.

Geley, G.& de Brath, S. (1927) *Clairvoyance and Materialization: A Record of Experiments,* Kessinger Publishing: London.

Glenconner, P. (1921) *The Earthen Vessel: A Volume dealing with spirit communication received in the form of Book-tests,* John Lane: London.

Harris, L. (2009) *Alec Harris: the full story of his remarkable physical mediumship,* Saturday Night Press Publications: Beaconsfield, UK..

Harrison, T. (1989 & 2011) *Visits by Our Friends from the 'Other Side',* Saturday Night Press Publications(SNPP): Beaconsfield, UK.

Harrison, T. (2008) *Life After Death: Living Proof,* Saturday Night Press Publications (SNPP): Beaconsfield, UK.

Hegarty, N. Riley (2000) *The French Revelation,* Private publication USA

Houghton, G. (1882) *Evenings at home in Spiritual Séance,* Oxford University: Oxford, England.

Hutton, J.B. (1968) *Healing Hands,* Paperback Library: New York.

Jefts, Lena Barnes (Peggy Barnes), (circa 1957) *"Lo, I Am With You Always": Treatise on Physical Mediumship,* National Spiritualist Association of Churches: Cassadaga, FL.

Kase Col.S.F. *The Emancipation Proclamation, How, and By Whom It was given to President Lincoln in 1861,* (see website ref.)

Lazarus, R. (1993) *The Case Against Death,* Time/Warner Paperbacks: New York.

Leonard, G O. (1931) *My Life in two worlds,*

Lodge, O. (1916) *Raymond or Life and Death,* Methuen: London.

MacDonald, A. (1960, 2012) *A Path Prepared: The Story of Isa Northage,* Saturday Night Press Publications (SNPP): Beaconsfield, UK.

Marryat, F. (1891, 1917) *There is no Death,* Rider & Son: London.

Maynard, N. (1956) *Was Abraham Lincoln a Spiritualist?: Or, Curious Revelations from the Life of a Trance Medium,* Spiritualist Press: London. (now available in full edition as *Nettie Colburn, Trance Medium,* SDU Publications.)

Neech, W. F. (1957) *Death is her Life,* Spiritualist Press: London.

Northage, Ivy. (1994) *Mediumship made simple,* Woodfield Pubs: London.

Northage, Ivy. (1998) *While I remember,* Coll. of Psychic Studies: London

Perrimman, A. (1952) *Broadcasting from Beyond,* Spiritualist Press: London.

Playfair G.L. (2010) *Chico Xavier: Medium of the Century;* Roundtable Publishing: London.

Podmore, F. (1902) *Modern Spiritualism: A History and a Criticism,* Methuen: London.

Price, H. (1939) *Fifty Years of Psychical Research,* Longmans, Green & Co.: London. .

Richet, C. (1923) *Thirty Years of Psychical Research,* Translated from the French, Macmillan: New York.

Roberts, E. (1969, 2006) *Fifty Years a Medium,* SDU Publications: UK

Roberts, U. (1984, 1993) *Living in Two Worlds: The Autobiography of Ursula Roberts,* Regency Press: London.

Rose, A. (2006) *The Rainbow Never Ends: The Autobiography of Aubry Rose,* Lennard: London.

Smith, S. (1964) *The Mediumship of Mrs Leonard,* Award Books: N.York.

Smith, S.(1972) *She Speaks to the Dead - The Life of Gladys Osborne Leonard,* Award Books: New York.

Smith, S. (1974) *Life is Forever: Evidence for Survival after death,* Award Books: New York.

Stashower, D. (1999) *Teller of Tales: The Life of Arthur Conan Doyle,* Holt: New York.

Stead, W.T. (1908, 1952) *After Death or Letters from Julia,* Psychic Book Club: London

Stemman, R. (2005) *Spirit communication,* Piatkus: London.

Stemman, R. with Chapman, G. (1984) *Surgeon from another World,* Aquarian Press: London.

Swaffer, H. (1945) *My Greatest Story,* W.H.Allen: London

Trevor, G. (1950) *Death's Door Opens,* Psychic Book Club: London

Twigg, E. (1974). *Ena Twigg:Medium,* Star Books: London.

Tymn, M. (2008). *The Articulate Dead: They Brought the Spirit World Alive,* Galde Press: Lakeview, MN.

Tymn, M. (2011) *The Afterlife Revealed: What Happens After We Die,* White Crow Books

Tymn, M. (2011) *The Afterlife Explorers: The Pioneers of Psychical Research,* White Crow Books

Tymn, M. (2012) *Transcending the Titanic: Beyond Death's Door,* White Crow Books

Tymn, M. (2013) *Resurrecting Leonora Piper: How Science Discovered the Afterlife,* White Crow Books

Tymn, M. (2014) *Dead Men Talking: Afterlife Communication from World War I*, White Crow Books

Upton, B. (1946, 2006) *The Mediumship of Helen Hughes*, SDU Publ.UK.

Williamson, L. (1994). *Mediums and the Afterlife*, Robert Hale: London.

Wilson, C. (2000) *Afterlife: Survival of the Soul*, Llewellyn Publications: Woodbury MN.

Worrall, Ambrose, & Olga. (1985), *The Gift of Healing: A Personal Story of Spiritual Therapy*, Harper & Row: New York.

Zammit, Victor (2005) *A Lawyer Presents the Case for the Afterlife* (on line at http://victorzammit.com/book/4thedition)

Websites referenced

www.aeces.info/Legacy-Section/Bios (*M. Allen re R101 disaster*)

http://www.ascsi.org/ASCS/Library/EvidenceRoom

www.encyclopedia.com (*Encyclopedia of Occultism & Parapsychology*)

www.ghostcircle.com *(Patrick McNamara*)

www.Lightafterlife.freeforums.org *(Graham Jennings on Mrs Piper)*

www.longtonspiritualistchurch.com/fannyhigginson

www.montcabriol.com *(John Sloan re spirit light)*

http://parapsychologyinfo.com *(The Levitations of D. D. Home)*

www.prairieghosts.com *(Troy Taylor on Automatic writing)*

www.psychictruth.info/Medium_Ethel_Post_Parish.htm

www.seekeronline.info/journals/y2007 *(Kase re Lincoln Emancipation Dec)*

www.spiritcommunion/blogspot.com/2012/04 *(Howard: Automatic-writing)*

www.spiritwritings.com (*Fodor's Encylopedia of Psychic Science*)

www.spiritualismlink.com *(for Cartheuser & Best)*

www.survivalafterdeath.info *(Fodor 'These Mysterious People' & more)*

http://vermonthistory.org/journal/misc/ *(AchsaSpragueBiography.pdf.)*

http://victorzammit.com/book/4thedition *(Case for the Afterlife)*

www.victorzammit.com/evidence/writingmediums.htm

www.whitecrowbooks.com *(Mike Tymn 'Myst of Ectoplasm' part 5 & more)*

http://www.woodlandway.org/ *(for Psypioneer journals)*

www.zerdinisworld.com *(Cranley, G.- on various mediums with personal experiences.)*

Periodicals referenced

Evening Post

Hartford Times (August 8, 1852)

Guardian,The (1944 & 2001)

Journal of the Society for Psychical Research
Journal of the American Society for Psychical Research
Light (1918, 1919, 1931)
New York Tribune (1885)
Proceedings of the Society for Psychical Research
Psychic News (Feb. 14, 1948)
Psychic Observer (Oct 25, 1943)
Psychic Research (July 1930)
Psychic Science (July 1929)
Psychische Studien (Jan/Feb 1906)
Psypioneer Journal (Vol 7/7 & Vol 9/6, 2013) - (http://www.woodlandway.org)
Quarterly Journal of Science
Spiritual Magazine (July 1871)
Spiritualist (March 15, 1872 and October 26, 1877)
The Two Worlds (various)

Identity of mediums, researchers and spirits in the images on the front cover

Red Cloud (spirit)	Daniel Dunglas Home	Emily French	Nettie Colborn Maynard	Carlos Mirabelli	Mme Eliz. d'Esperance	Estelle Roberts at large demonstration
Richard Hodgson						Geraldine Cummins
Sir William Barrett	Gladys O. Leonard	Leonora Piper	Leslie Flint— ectoplasm	showing at shoulder	Kathleen Barkel	Helen Hughes
Harry Edwards	Isa Northage	Wm. Stainton Moses	Bertha Harris	Chico Xavier	Eileen Garrett	Ted Fricker
Minnie Harrison	Lilian Bailey	Franek Kluski	Emma Hardinge Britten	Ethel Post-Parish	Silver Belle (spirit)	'Margery' Crandon
F.W.H. Myers	Cora Scott Richmond	Mrs Agnes Abbott	W.T. Stead	Alec & Louie Harris	Ena Twigg	Andrew Jackson Davis
				Helen Duncan	John Sloan	Wm Eglington

Index

Mon. Mar 16, 2015
12:00 pm
DAKD "Just another
day in
paradise"

CPSIA information can be obtained at www.ICGtesting.com
Printed in the USA
BVOW04s1834210914

367602BV00020B/393/P